THE MOST VALUABLE PERSONAL LEGAL FORMS YOU'LL EVER NEED

THE MOST VALUABLE PERSONAL LEGAL FORMS YOU'LL EVER NEED

Mark Warda
James C. Ray
Attorneys at Law

SPHINX® PUBLISHING
A Division of Sourcebooks, Inc.®
Naperville, IL

First Edition, 2001
              Published by: Sphinx Publishing, a division of Sourcebooks, Inc.

Naperville Office
P.O. Box 4410
Naperville, Illinois 60567-4410
(630) 961-3900
FAX: 630-961-2168

This publication is designed to provide accurate and authoritative information in regard to the subject matter covered. It is sold with the understanding that the publisher is not engaged in rendering legal, accounting, or other professional service. If legal advice or other expert assistance is required, the services of a competent professional person should be sought.

*From a Declaration of Principles Jointly Adopted by a Committee of the
American Bar Association and a Committee of Publishers and Associations*

This product is not a substitute for legal advice.

Disclaimer required by Texas statutes.

Library of Congress Cataloging-in-Publication Data
Warda, Mark.
      The most valuable personal legal forms you'll ever need / Mark Warda, James C. Ray.
         p.   cm. -- (Legal survival guides)
      Includes index.
      ISBN 1-57248-130-7 (alk. paper)
      1. Forms (Law)--United States. 2. Law--United States--Popular works. I. Ray, James
C., 1945-II. Title. III. Series.

KF170.W37 2000
347.73'55--dc21

                                                                        00-066191

Printed and bound in the United States of America.

VHG Paperback — 10 9 8 7 6 5 4 3 2 1

CONTENTS

Using Self-Help Law Books

Before using a self-help law book, you should realize the advantages and disadvantages of doing your own legal work and understand the challenges and diligence that this requires.

THE GROWING TREND

Rest assured that you won't be the first or only person handling your own legal matter. For example, in some states, more than seventy-five percent of the people in divorces and other cases represent themselves. Because of the high cost of legal services, this is a major trend and many courts are struggling to make it easier for people to represent themselves. However, some courts are not happy with people who do not use attorneys and refuse to help them in any way. For some, the attitude is, "Go to the law library and figure it out for yourself."

We write and publish self-help law books to give people an alternative to the often complicated and confusing legal books found in most law libraries. We have made the explanations of the law as simple and easy to understand as possible. Of course, unlike an attorney advising an individual client, we cannot cover every conceivable possibility.

COST/VALUE ANALYSIS

Whenever you shop for a product or service, you are faced with various levels of quality and price. In deciding what product or service to buy, you make a cost/value analysis on the basis of your willingness to pay and the quality you desire.

When buying a car, you decide whether you want transportation, comfort, status, or sex appeal. Accordingly, you decide among such choices as a Neon, a Lincoln, a Rolls Royce, or a Porsche. Before making a decision, you usually weigh the merits of each option against the cost.

When you get a headache, you can take a pain reliever (such as aspirin) or visit a medical specialist for a neurological examination. Given this choice, most people, of course, take a pain reliever, since it costs only pennies; whereas a medical examination costs hundreds of dollars and takes a lot of time. This is usually a logical choice because it is rare to need anything more than a pain reliever for a headache. But in some cases, a headache may indicate a brain tumor and failing to see a specialist right away can result in complications. Should everyone with a headache go to a specialist? Of course not, but people treating their own illnesses must realize that they are betting on the basis of their cost/value analysis of the situation. They are taking the most logical option.

The same cost/value analysis must be made when deciding to do one's own legal work. Many legal situations are very straight forward, requiring a simple form and no complicated analysis. Anyone with a little intelligence and a book of instructions can handle the matter without outside help.

But there is always the chance that complications are involved that only an attorney would notice. To simplify the law into a book like this, several legal cases often must be condensed into a single sentence or paragraph. Otherwise, the book would be several hundred pages long and too complicated for most people. However, this simplification necessarily leaves out many details and nuances that would apply to special or unusual situations. Also, there are many ways to interpret most legal questions. Your case may come before a judge who disagrees with the analysis of our authors.

Therefore, in deciding to use a self-help law book and to do your own legal work, you must realize that you are making a cost/value analysis. You have decided that the money you will save in doing it yourself outweighs the chance that your case will not turn out to your satisfaction. Most people handling their own simple legal matters never have a problem, but occasionally people find that it ended up costing them more to have an attorney straighten out the situation than it would have if they had hired an attorney in the beginning. Keep this in mind while handling your case, and be sure to consult an attorney if you feel you might need further guidance.

LOCAL RULES   The next thing to remember is that a book which covers the law for the entire nation, or even for an entire state, cannot possibly include every procedural difference of every jurisdiction. Whenever possible, we provide the exact form needed; however, in some areas, each county, or even each judge, may require unique forms and procedures. In our state books, our forms usually cover the majority of counties in the state, or provide examples of the type of form which will be required. In our national books, our forms are sometimes even more general in nature but are designed to give a good idea of the type of form that will be needed in most locations. Nonetheless, keep in mind that your state, county, or judge may have a requirement, or use a form, that is not included in this book.

You should not necessarily expect to be able to get all of the information and resources you need solely from within the pages of this book. This book will serve as your guide, giving you specific information whenever possible and helping you to find out what else you will need to know. This is just like if you decided to build your own backyard deck. You might purchase a book on how to build decks. However, such a book would not include the building codes and permit requirements of every city, town, county, and township in the nation; nor would it include the lumber, nails, saws, hammers, and other materials and tools you would need to actually build the deck. You would use the book as your guide, and then do some work and research involving such matters as whether you need a permit of some kind, what type and grade of wood are available in your area, whether to use hand tools or power tools, and how to use those tools.

Before using the forms in a book like this, you should check with your court clerk to see if there are any local rules of which you should be aware, or local forms you will need to use. Often, such forms will require the same information as the forms in the book but are merely laid out differently or use slightly different language. They will sometimes require additional information.

CHANGES IN THE LAW

Besides being subject to local rules and practices, the law is subject to change at any time. The courts and the legislatures of all fifty states are constantly revising the laws. It is possible that while you are reading this book, some aspect of the law is being changed.

In most cases, the change will be of minimal significance. A form will be redesigned, additional information will be required, or a waiting period will be extended. As a result, you might need to revise a form, file an extra form, or wait out a longer time period; these types of changes will not usually affect the outcome of your case. On the other hand, sometimes a major part of the law is changed, the entire law in a particular area is rewritten, or a case that was the basis of a central legal point is overruled. In such instances, your entire ability to pursue your case may be impaired.

To help you with local requirements and changes in the law, be sure to read the section in chapter 2 on "Legal Research."

Again, you should weigh the value of your case against the cost of an attorney and make a decision as to what you believe is in your best interest.

Introduction

The Purpose of This Book

This book is similar to the book *The Most Valuable Business Legal Forms You'll Ever Need*, also published by Sourcebooks, Inc. While that book concentrates on the legal forms useful to businesses, this one covers those which are useful in personal relationships. While the basics of contracts, and some of the financial forms will be the same or similar, the this book covers such subjects as marriage and personal relationships, personal finance, and wills.

A book of this type, covering all of the most common legal situations a family faces, cannot possibly include or explain every possible legal situation. In most situations the forms are basic and simple, but occasionally legal relationships are more complicated. If, in using this book you find that your facts do not fit into the explanations or forms, you should seek further guidance. For most subjects, such as wills, trusts, real estate, hiring domestic help, and getting a divorce, Sphinx Publishing offers a detailed book on the subject. These books go into much deeper analysis and offer a wider variety of forms than this book. To receive a catalog of other books available from Sphinx, call 1-800-226-5291.

It is to be hoped that this book will make fewer the occasions on which you will need a lawyer. At a minimum it will help you be a wiser consumer of legal services and understand more of what a lawyer is doing for you. It will have served its purpose if it only helps you to recognize the occasions on which you do need a lawyer, and helps you to use your lawyer more efficiently.

Failing to hire a lawyer when you need one is not likely to be an economy. If, in reading this book, you discover that what you want to do is more complicated than you imagined or involves a large sum of money, then get a lawyer. If all goes well, you can complain about paying for something you didn't need after all. That's better than not hiring a lawyer and having something more serious to complain about.

Some clients believe that, having turned a matter over to the lawyers, they are released from all further responsibility. "After all," such a client thinks, "if I pay a large amount of money for my lawyer to draft a contract, why should I bore myself by reading it. It's the lawyer's job to make sure it's right."

But that makes the lawyer's job nearly impossible. You know your situation and what is important to you. The best lawyer's ideas about that may be completely wrong, and he or she may attach importance to the unimportant (because it was important to the last client) and gloss over a critical factor. Use this book to know what to expect from your lawyer and why. And then read and understand the work your lawyer does for you. Make sure it works for you.

The forms in this book have been limited to those which will be usable in the most common situations in most states. There are other forms books on the market which claim to be comprehensive, but include many forms which may not comply with state law.

The forms in this book will work in most situations, but you should check local requirements for certain documents like deeds which may need a certain portion left blank for recording information. Keep in mind that laws also change so you should check with the clerk of any office where a form will be filed to see if there are special requirements before bringing yours in for recording.

ORGANIZATION OF THIS BOOK

The first chapter of the book deals with some general principles of contract law and using legal forms, and following chapters apply those principles to specific situations. Before you use any of the contract forms in this book, pay careful attention to the first chapter, especially the information about the proper execution (signing) of contracts. Depending on the form you are using the who the parties are, you will need to insert the proper signature format to make sure the proper party executes the contract and does so correctly.

Chapters 2 through 7 cover specific situations, such as family relationships, financial mattersreal estate, personal property, hiring services, and wills. The final chapter has some miscelaneous forms which don't fint into the previous categories, but may be useful.

The sample forms in the main part of the book are presented with information filled in for fictional people. The forms may be abbreviated or otherwise slightly different from the forms in the appendix in order to save space. The forms in the appendix are designed to be used in most cases *as is*, although you may need to modify them to meet your specific needs. As stated above, those included in the appendix are the forms of most general use.

APPLICABLE LAWS

This book is intended to be used throughout the United States, and the laws of no specific jurisdiction are cited or relied on in this text. While the laws of the various states vary significantly, general principles of contract and agency apply in every state. However, it may be that your specific circumstances raise a legal issue unique to your jurisdiction. For that reason and others, competent legal advice is always desirable. Especially so in the areas where the need for a lawyer is explicitly mentioned in this book, but in other circumstances as well.

GENERAL LEGAL FORM ISSUES
1

TYPES OF LEGAL FORMS

There are several types of legal forms which people can execute. Some are contracts, which must be agreed to by two or more parties. Others are authorization forms and title transfer forms which only one person must sign. Some forms must have the signatures of witnesses or a notary in order to be legally effective. Others only need your signature.

Before using the forms in the back of this book you should be sure that you understand the legal ramifications of the form as explained in the text of the book and that you understand how to complete and execute it to be sure that it is legally enforceable.

This chapter explains the types of legal documents contained in this book and what the basics are to make them legal.

The following chapters of the book will explain how these types of legal forms are used in family, financial, wills and trusts, personal property, real estate, hired help and dispute resolution situations. The forms used in all of these kinds of situations will fall into the three categories discussed in the following sections.

CONTRACTS

A *contract* is an agreement between two or more people. One of the first things taught in law school is that to be legal, a contract must have three elements: an *offer*, an *acceptance* of that offer, and some *consideration*, a legal term that means something of value which is exchanged between the parties.

If you go over to your neighbor and say "Would you like to go fishing with me Saturday?" and he says "Sure," you have an offer and acceptance, but you do not have a legal contract because there is no legal consideration. But if you say to him, "I'll give you $25 to mow my yard" and he agrees and then does it, you do have a contract which the law would enforce (though it would not be worth getting a court involved for such a small amount).

There are many types of legal contracts with which you are involved in your daily life, though you probably don't realize that they are contracts. When you take your clothes to a dry cleaner; when you sell your lawnmower at a garage sale; when you hire someone to clean your carpets; when you move in with a friend to share expenses, you are usually creating legal contracts.

The important thing to know about these contracts which you are involved in on a daily basis is that unless you set the terms to them, the terms will be set for you, either by state law or by the forms provided by the party you are dealing with.

For example, in some states if you hire others to do work on your house, you may be liable if they injure themselves or are accidentally killed. However, you can avoid this risk by having a written agreement with them in which they agree to be responsible for their own safety. The benefit of knowing the rules of contracts and using your own forms is you can protect yourself from unexpected liability.

In some situations you may not be able to get the other party to go along with your terms. For example, if you store your property in a self-storage locker, the owner probably won't agree to be responsible for your property if the building burns down. Most likely the contract he uses protects him and makes it clear that you should obtain insurance to protect your property.

But sometimes, you can protect yourself even if the other party has his own forms and refuses to use yours. If you understand each clause of the contracts you are asked to sign, you can sometimes cross out something which would be risky to you.

Often business contracts are full of this standard "boilerplate" language to protect the company from anything that might happen. The contracts are usually prepared by the company's lawyer and the business owner doesn't always know why all the clauses are in there or what they mean. If a company is very eager to get your business, you may be able to cross out things in its contract and still have them accept it. For example, if you are paying a company to fix your roof, and their standard contract says the work is guaranteed for six months, you might be able to cross that off and put in "one year" and have them still do the job.

MUTUAL AGREEMENT

What happens in a situation where you change "six months" to "one year," sign the contract, and then they take it to their office, change it back to "six months," and they sign it? Contracts require two parties to agree to the same thing. If they do not, there is no legal contract. In the above example, the company would need to return the contract to you for you to sign or initial where they changed it back to "six months" before they had a binding contract.

What if they don't, and they do the job assuming that the six months applies while you assume that it is one year? That depends. If they called you and discussed it with you and you agreed to the change, it would probably be valid even if you didn't sign it. If they just did the job without telling you, then the terms of your agreement would be ambiguous and whether you had a six month or a one year guarantee

3

would have to be decided by a court, looking at all the facts of the case and using state law to determine who wins.

ORAL
CONTRACTS

Contrary to popular belief, contracts do not always have to be in writing to be legally enforceable. Verbal agreements can constitute legally binding contracts in many situations. The problem with verbal contracts is how to convince a court that they really existed and what the terms were. For this reason, you should try to always get your agreements in writing.

Statutes of Frauds. In some types of matters contracts are required by law to be in writing. Every state has what is called *statutes of frauds* that state which contracts must be in writing. For example, a typical statute of frauds might state that all sales of goods over $1,000, all leases over one year, and all sales of real estate must be in writing. This means that if your neighbor agrees to sell you his house but at the last minute changes his mind, the courts will not help you because the law clearly says that verbal agreements for sale of real estate are not enforceable.

Exceptions. There are many exceptions to the statutes of frauds, so if you get into a situation where they affect your rights, you should either check with a lawyer or do some legal research yourself.

For example, *partial performance* of a contract may make it enforceable, even if it violates the statute of frauds. If you agree to buy your neighbor's house and you move into it and pay him $1,000 a month for several months, a court might rule that the verbal agreement to sell it is enforceable. However, the court would have to be convinced that there really was an agreement to sell it to you. If the neighbor said you were only renting it and you had no proof otherwise, you would probably lose. But if he changed the insurance over to your name and gave you the tax bill, which you paid, then you would be more likely to win.

Another way a verbal agreement might be enforceable even if it violates the statute of frauds is if there is written proof of the agreement signed by the person trying to disclaim the agreement. For example, if someone verbally agrees to sell you their car for $5,000, it wouldn't be enforceable in a state where sales of that amount have to be in writing.

But if you gave them a deposit and they signed a receipt which said "deposit on Ford," then you might be able to go to court and force them to complete the sale.

Again, you have the problem of proving to a court what the terms were. What if the seller says the price was $6,000 but you remember it was $5,000? If there is no evidence, you might not win. The purpose of the statute of frauds is to avoid enforcing agreements where the terms are not known. What if the seller owns two Fords and you disagree about which one you were buying? Again, if there is no evidence you might lose.

As you can see, when coming to an agreement with someone, you should spell out as many details as possible so that there is no misunderstanding. (see form 1, p.105.) Below is a sample of a simple contract.

Sample of form 1. Simple Contract—

CONTRACT

THIS AGREEMENT is entered into by and between
_____Bob Jones_____ and _____Jon Dough_____.

In consideration of the mutual promises made in this agreement and other valuable consideration, the receipt and sufficiency of which is acknowledged, the parties agree as follows:

```
Bob Jones will mow Jon Dough's front and back
yards once a week during June, July, and August
2002, while Jon Dough is at Oxford studying
Sanskrit
```

The following addenda, dated the same date as this agreement, are incorporated in, and made a part of, this agreement:

☒ None.

This agreement shall be governed by the laws of
_____Georgia_____.

ADDENDUM TO
CONTRACT

An *addendum* to a contract is used to add lengthy details which would not easily fit into the contract form. (see form 2, p.106.) For example, if you were buying someone's collection of plants, you would probably want to list each one on an addendum as in the example below.

Sample of form 2. Addendum to a Contract—

ADDENDUM TO CONTRACT

The following terms are a part of the Contract dated <u>June 6, 2002</u>, between <u>Jon Dough</u> and <u>Marvin Gardene</u>:

```
1 Ficus, 5 feet high
2 Ficus, 3 feet high
1 African Violet
5 Bonzai trees
6 Venus Flytraps
1 Oak tree in 24" pot
3 ferns in hanging baskets
2 poison ivy in pots
2 Marigolds in pots
```

AMENDING A
CONTRACT

Sometimes the parties to a contract will come to the conclusion that the contract no longer reflects their agreement and needs to be modified or *amended*. Unless otherwise agreed to in the original contract, the modification of a contract is a contract in its own right and must contain all the elements described earlier in this chapter, including consideration. (see form 3, p.107.) A sample amendment to a contract follows.

Sample of form 3. Amendment to a Contract—

AMENDMENT TO CONTRACT

For valuable consideration, the receipt and sufficiency of which is acknowledged by each of the parties, this agreement amends a Contract dated <u>May 1, 2001</u>, between <u>Fred Farkle</u> and <u>Jon Dough</u>, relating to <u>1956 Chevrolet Belair ID #6J123456</u>. This contract amendment is hereby incorporated into the Contract.

Because the car needs a new clutch, the price will be lowered by $500 and the balance due will be $1,500.

ASSIGNING A
CONTRACT

The right to performance under a contract is a property right like any other and ordinarily can be bought and sold. Courts distinguish between the *assignment* of a right to receive performance from the other party and the delegation of your duty to perform. Because performance can vary from person to person, courts are less likely to allow an assignment of a duty to perform unless it is allowed in the contract. For example, if you hire a famous artist to paint a mural on your building, the artist could not assign the contract to an unknown painter. However, you could sell the building and assign the right to have the mural painted by the artist. (Unless, for some reason the artist only agreed to do it because you were the building's owner.)

The law of assignment of contracts varies by state. In some states, some contracts may be assigned unless they specifically state that they cannot be assigned. In other states, some contracts cannot be assigned unless they specifically state that they can. To be sure of your rights, you should be sure that the contracts you sign state whether or not you want them to be assignable. Even if a contract says that it may not be assigned, if all parties agree to an assignment, then the original contract is considered amended and the assignment is valid. If you wish to assign a contract and the other party won't agree to it, and if the contract does not spell out whether you have the right, you should check with an attorney to be sure you have the legal right to do so.

Many people use the term contract assignment to mean both the assignment of rights and the delegation of duties. However, if you intend to delegate a duty, it is better to be specific. If you wish to rid yourself of the possibility of ever having to perform the duty, you must be released from that duty by the person entitled to receive the performance.

Having assigned a contract, it is important to notify the person expecting to receive the performance that the assignment has been made. Suppose the assigned contract is an agreement to move 100 cases of wine from warehouse A to warehouse B. Quick Moving Company assigns the moving contract to Fast Movers, Inc. (the assignee), which promptly does the job but Quick Moving neglects to notify the owner of the wine that the contract has been assigned. The owner arrives at warehouse B, discovers the job complete, and sends a check for the moving job to Quick Moving Company Fast Movers then asks to be paid. Fast Movers cannot recover its fee from the owner, because the owner has performed his part of the contract - paying for the completed job - as required by the terms of the agreement. Fast Movers will have to hope it can recover the fee from Quick Moving. If Fast Movers had promptly notified the owner of the assignment, then the owner would have paid Fast Movers directly.

Following is an example of the type of letter that may be used to notify someone that the assignee of a contract has assumed the duty to perform some service for the person notified and that payment should therefore be sent to the assignee. Frequently, the contract being assigned is the right to receive payment for a debt. (see form 4, p.108.)

Sample Letter. Notice of Assignment of a Contract—

Jon Dough
8321 S. Main Street, Fort Worth, TX 76011
804-555-4441

June 8, 2001

Fred Jackson, President
Fred's Lawn Service
842 US Hwy. 81
Fort Worth, TX 76012

Dear Mr. Jackson:

    This letter is to inform you that we have sold our home at 1254 Purgatory Lane to William McClenaghan. The lawn service contract which we signed with your company has been assigned to him and he has agreed to be responsible for it. All further bills should be directed to him at the same address. If you have any questions, feel free to call

                Sincerely,

                Jon Dough

TERMINATING A CONTRACT

Contracts are *terminated* for different reasons and under different circumstances. One reason is that all the parties to a contract have completely performed the duties they had to perform according to its terms. But suppose that before the parties completely perform their duties, they decide to call it off. For example, suppose you hire a contractor to build a second story on your house and then both of you find out that the zoning prohibits second stories in your area. If you signed a contract with the contractor, the easiest way to indicate termination of it is to tear it up. If there were duplicate copies, be sure all copies are destroyed. Another way would be to sign an agreement of termination. This could be a simple letter of which a copy is signed by the recipient and returned.

The sample letter below is the basic language for an agreement between two parties to terminate a contract and release each other from all duties to be performed. (see form 5, p.109.)

Sample Letter. Agreement to Terminate–

Jon Dough
8321 S. Main Street, Fort Worth, TX 76011
804-555-4441

April 4, 2002

Bob Jones
Jones Construction
222 US Hwy. 20
Fort Worth, TX 76012

Dear Mr. Jones:

   This letter is to confirm our agreement to terminate our contract for you to build a second story on my home due to the fact that second stories are not permitted by law in this area.

   This will further confirm that the $1,000 deposit which we paid you on that contract will be used on our new contract to build a swimming pool in our back yard.

                    Sincerely,

                    Jon Dough

Agreed:
Jones Construction

By:_____

Termination for Breach. Another way to terminate a contract is for one or more parties to breach the agreement so completely that the other parties are relieved of their duties to perform. For example, if you contract to have your house painted and the painter completely fails to perform the job, then you are relieved of your promise to pay. However, this does not necessarily mean that the contract is terminated. If the contract required the job to be done by a certain day, but it has been raining all week, the painter could show up next week to do the job, and you will be required to pay under the contract. If, because the first painter didn't show up (due to rain) you then hired a second painter, you could end up having to pay both painters to paint your house!

For this reason, contracts should spell out as precisely as possible what is required of the parties. If something must be done by a certain date, the contract should say that if it is not done by that date the contract will terminate. A legal phrase which is used to signify that deadlines are important is, "Time is of the essence." Without wording such as this, the law will usually give a person a *reasonable* amount of time to perform under a contract. What is reasonable is always a grey area of law. It depends on what the situation is and who is making the determination.

If you have entered into a contract with someone and they have clearly violated the terms, you can terminate the contract. You should do so in writing. The following sample letter is a notice given by one party to another that the latter has violated a contract and it is being terminated.

Sample Letter. Notice of Breach—

Jon Dough

8321 S. Main Street, Fort Worth, TX 76011

804-555-4441

August 12, 2001

Fred Jackson, President
Fred's Lawn Service
842 US Hwy. 81
Fort Worth, TX 76012

Dear Mr. Jackson:

   This letter is to inform you that you have breached our contract to provide lawn service to my property by failing to show up since the middle of June despite numerous phone calls requesting you to.

   Because of your failure to perform as agreed, I consider our contract terminated and have hired another service to handle the mowing.

                              Sincerely,

                              Jon Dough

Most breaches are not so clear-cut of course. Usually if one party believes the other is not living up to its duties, the party in default will be notified of its shortcomings and a period of negotiation and compromise will follow.

Be very careful about terminating a contract without the other person's consent; especially if they have begun performance. If you have a legal contract and you attempt to terminate it without giving the other side a reasonable chance to perform, you may have to pay them even after you terminated it. If in doubt, ask an attorney what your rights are. But realize that because this is a grey area of law, even an attorney can be wrong when deciding whether a contract can be terminated.

Right of Rescission. One common misperception regarding contracts is that there is always a right of rescission (or cancellation) of, for example, three days or a week. This is the exception rather than the rule.

In some states, where there have been abuses in certain industries, such as with health club memberships, or door-to-door sales, laws have been passed allowing a right to cancel the contract. Also, in some consumer loan transactions there is a legal right to change your mind by signing a rescission notice within a certain number of days. But unless there is a law specifically giving a right of rescission, you are legally obligated the moment you sign.

Keep in mind you can add a right of rescission to any agreement. If you are considering leasing an apartment and the owner insists that you sign a lease before leaving so he can do a credit check, you can agree only if you have three days to rescind and he accepts this condition.

TITLE TRANSFER AND ACKNOWLEDGMENT

When transferring the ownership of property, such as with a deed, a bill of sale, or a will, the person receiving the property usually does not have to sign. Only the one doing the transferring signs.

In many cases these documents need to have one or two witnesses, and sometimes they need to be notarized.

The legal effect of a title transfer document usually does not take effect until it has been physically given to the recipient. For example, if you make a deed of your house to your children, it would be valid the moment you handed it to them. It would not be valid if it was found in your safe deposit box after your death.

Note: Although a deed kept in your safe deposit box might not be valid under the law, in many cases the issue would not come up. If there were no one contesting the validity of the deed, it might work fine. But, for example, if the deed was to one child and there was another who was unhappy about it, he or she could go to court and claim the deed was invalid since it was not delivered.

Title transfers and acknowledgements are a very broad area of legal documents. Specific examples of title transfers and acknowledgements are discussed in later chapters, such as wills (Chapter 3), bill of sale (Chapter 5), and deeds (Chapter 6).

AUTHORIZATION

Authorization forms usually only need to be signed by one party. For example, if you give a school permission to take your child on a trip, or if you give your neighbor permission to pick up your car from a mechanic, no one else has to sign. You are granting something (permission) without asking anything in return.

Suppose you want to receive something in return. For example, if you allow your child to go on a school trip only if the school promises to have six teachers accompany the group, then you usually need the other party to sign an acceptance of the terms. In such case you would have a contract and not merely an authorization.

Alternatively, if the school gave you an authorization form that said six teachers would accompany the group, it might be construed as a binding contract. But it could go either way. If your child was hurt and you sued the school saying they breached an agreement to have six teachers along, they could argue that six was a tentative number and that it wasn't a material part of your agreement. The only way to beat such an argument would be to write on the form something like "my child only has permission if six teachers accompany the group," and to get an agent of the school to sign it.

There are many different types of authorizations. For examples of specific authorizations, see child authorization (Chapter 2), authorization to check credit (Chapter 4), and authorization to release employment information (Chapter 7).

COMPONENTS OF LEGAL FORMS

Legal forms have various parts. Not all forms require the same parts, but each legal form has its own requirements that make that form binding. For example, while a contract requires signatures of the people who are contracting but not witnesses, a will requires witnesses. Form components are what make the documents legal in nature.

DUPLICATE COPIES

It is usually wise to make at least one duplicate copy of your legal forms in case the original is lost or destroyed. Contrary to popular belief, a contract does not need to have original signatures to be enforceable in court. A photocopy can be just as enforceable under the right circumstances.

DUPLICATE ORIGINALS

A *duplicate original* of a legal document is a copy with original signatures of the parties. For some types of legal forms, such as contracts, there should be two original copies that are signed by all parties. This way each party has a copy with everyone's original signature. The next best thing is for each party to have a copy with the other party's original signature. That way they can add their own. But in some cases you don't even need your own signature as long as you have the signature of the person against whom you wish to enforce the contract.

You should **not** make duplicate originals of documents that transfer title, such as deeds and wills, or of promissory notes. If you sign a duplicate of a promissory note, you may have to pay twice. And if you make a duplicate original of your will and later wish to revoke it by destroying it, your revocation may not be effective if someone else has the duplicate and files it after your death. For documents like these you can have photocopies of the signed originals, but do not sign them again.

SEALS

In ancient times, when few people could write, a *seal* was added to a legal document to make it valid. This was at times a wax seal, or later merely a hand-drawn one. Today seals are in most cases obsolete, but in some states they are necessary to make certain types of documents, such as deeds, valid. In some states they may give a party more legal rights, such as a longer time period in which to sue. In some cases, it is important to put the word "seal" next to the signature line. When you are unsure what your state law provides, it doesn't hurt to include it. Some of the forms in this book include the word seal for this reason.

SIGNATURES

In nearly all cases, a legal document must have a signature to be valid. Just as important, the signature must be done properly or the document might not be legal. For example, if both spouses don't sign a document, or if the wrong officer of a company signs a document, it might not be valid.

SPOUSES   For some types of legal documents it is necessary to have both spouse's signatures. For example, in some states, even if a home is owned by one spouse alone, a deed of the home is not valid unless the spouse signs it. Even if a spouse's signature is not required it can be a good idea. For example, if you loan money to someone and have them sign a promissory note, you may not be able to collect if all of their property is owned jointly with their spouse. Or, if you rent an apartment to a couple and only one signs the lease, you might not be able to hold the other spouse responsible for the rent.

For this reason, when you are getting someone to sign an obligation, you should usually get the spouse to sign as well. If *you* are signing an obligation, you should try to avoid having your spouse sign!

SOLE
PROPRIETORSHIPS

The signature of a sole proprietorship is really the same as an individual's signature, because the owner of the business operates it as an individual rather than as a separate entity. If the business is conducted under a trade name (or *fictitious* or *assumed* name), confusion may result. The following sample makes it clear that the signature is that of a sole proprietor rather than a corporation, or some other business organization. The letters "d/b/a" stand for "doing business as." In its place, you may sometimes see "t/a" for "transacting as."

Sample Signature of a Sole Proprietor Business—

_____ (Seal)
Henry Hardy, a sole proprietor
d/b/a Scrupulous Enterprises

CORPORATIONS

Like individuals, corporations can sign documents under seal or not. The corporate seal usually carries somewhat more meaning than an individual's. In addition to the effects of an individual's seal mentioned above, the corporate seal entitles other parties to the agreement to presume that the signer acted under the appropriate authorization of the corporation's board of directors. Corporate seals are usually rubber stamps or embossers, but anything the corporation's board of directors adopts by resolution as the corporate seal will do. The sample below shows the signature of a corporation not under seal. The next sample shows that of a corporation under seal. Note that the secretary of the corporation is the custodian of the seal and is responsible for "attesting" that the president or vice president's signature is affixed by the board's authority.

Sample Corporate Signature (one officer)—

Scrupulous Corporation

By: _____
Henry Hardy, President

Sample Corporate Signature (under seal)—

Scrupulous Corporation

By: _____
Henry Hardy, President

Attest:_____
Calvin Collier, Secretary

GENERAL
PARTNERSHIPS

It may be helpful to think of a *partnership* as a group of sole proprietors in business together, where each member of the group acts as the agent of all the others. It is fundamental to partnership law that each partner is bound by the acts of the others in furtherance of the business and that each partner is liable for the debts of the partnership. It used to be that the law refused to recognize the partnership as an entity separate from the partners. This meant, for example, that a real estate deed for partnership property had to be signed by all of the partners.

The modern rule, which is followed by the Uniform Partnership Act, the Revised Uniform Partnership Act (one of these has been enacted in all states except Louisiana), or the Louisiana Partnership Act, recognizes the separate existence of the partnership and holds that one partner, acting within his or her authority, can bind the rest of the partners on most contracts, including deeds. Many states do not require general partnerships to publish lists of partners or explanations of the limits of their authority. It's not always possible to tell who is a partner or what limits there may be on a signer's authority. For this reason, persons entering into agreements with general partners should take precautions to make sure that the person signing has adequate authority. Sometimes all the partners will be asked to sign a document even though it may not be strictly required by the law to make a contract enforceable.

You may see the initials *"LLP"* after the name of a partnership. It means that the partnership is a *limited liability partnership* which is not the same as a "limited partnership" described later. A partner in a LLP is not liable for certain damages caused by his or her partner. For example, a lawyer in a law firm organized as an LLP will not be liable for the legal malpractice committed by another partner in the firm unless the malpractice was committed under the supervision of the first lawyer.

The following sample shows the signature of a partnership, where one of the general partners has signed for the partnership.

General Partnership Signature—

Scrupulous Associates, a general partnership

By: _____ (Seal)
Henry Hardy, General Partner

LIMITED PARTNERSHIPS

A limited partnership is much like a general partnership except that, in addition to general partners, it has a special category of *limited partners* who do not participate in management of the business and are not liable for the debts and liabilities of the business beyond the amount of their investment or *contribution*. A limited partnership is created under a special state statute, usually the Uniform Limited Partnership Act, and will have the words "limited partnership" as part of its name.

Only a general partner (there may be one or more) will have authority to sign contracts. Limited partners usually have no authority to sign contracts for, or otherwise represent, the limited partnership. An example of a limited partnership signature follows.

Sample of a Limited Partnership Signature—

> Scrupulous Hardy Enterprises, a limited partnership
>
> By: _____ (Seal)
> Henry Hardy, General Partner

WITNESSES

For some types of legal documents, witnesses are required or the document has no legal validity. For example, in most states wills and deeds of real estate must have two witnesses. In some states, leases of longer than one year must have witnesses.

For other types of forms and agreements witnesses are usually superfluous. They are helpful in the occasional court case in which one party denies he or she signed a document. But even then a handwriting expert can usually substantiate the legitimacy of a signature enough to win in court.

NOTARIES AND ACKNOWLEDGMENTS

Some people think that having a document notarized makes it "legal." It does not. A contract signed by two people without a notary is in most cases perfectly legal.

A notary public is empowered by the state to administer various oaths and to testify to the genuineness of signatures. The term *acknowledgment* refers to a signer's statement that he or she truly is that person, intends to sign the document, and that (in the case of a corporate officer) he or she holds the corporate office claimed. The notary will verify the identity of the signer and affirm in writing that the person signing the document is who he or she claims to be. The next two samples are of what an acknowledgment by a notary looks like.

Sample of an Acknowledgment by an Individual—

STATE OF   TEXAS   )
COUNTY OF   HOCKLEY   )

    I certify that Mary Smith ,
who ❑ is personally known to me to be the person whose name is subscribed to the foregoing instrument ☒ produced a state driver's license as identification, personally appeared before me on March 5, 2001, and ☒ acknowledged the execution of the foregoing instrument ❑ ~~acknowledged that (s)he is (Assistant) Secretary of_____ and that by authority duly given and as the act of the corporation, the foregoing instrument was signed in its name by its (Vice) President, sealed with its corporate seal and attested by him/her as its (Assistant) Secretary.~~

Jon Dough
_____
Notary Public, State of

My commission expires: April 15, 2003

Sample of an Acknowledgment by a Corporation—

STATE OF   Texas   )
COUNTY OF Hockley   )

    I certify that Mary Smith ,who ❑ is personally known to me to be the person whose name is subscribed to the foregoing instrument ☒ produced passport as identification, personally appeared before me on March 5, 2001, and ❑ acknowledged the execution of the foregoing instrument ☒ acknowledged that (s)he is (Assistant) Secretary of Scrupulous, Inc, and that by authority duly given and as the act of the corporation, the foregoing instrument was signed in its name by its (Vice) President, sealed with its corporate seal and attested by him/her as its (Assistant) Secretary.

Jon Dough
_____
Notary Public, State of

My commission expires: April 15, 2003

FACSIMILE AND EMAIL ACCEPTANCE

Legally, there is no problem accepting an agreement by fax. Someone can fax you an agreement, you can sign it and fax it back. The only possible risk would be if a person tried to deny signing a document. For this reason, businesses such as banks do not like to accept documents by fax, though they may initially, if the original will be sent to them shortly.

Even some secretaries of state are accepting corporate filings by fax, so this type of signature is becoming more and more common.

As for signatures by email, that is something that is the subject of pending legislation as this book is being written. While the Internet has allowed instant transmission of data, it has been slower in finding an efficient way to transmit signatures. Some companies, like the United States Postal Service, are setting up systems which would offer signature guarantees for email.

For the present, you can't be sure that an agreement made solely by email is legally enforceable. To be sure, you can have the recipients print out the email and then mail or fax it back with a real signature on the copy.

FAMILY LEGAL FORMS 2

Although family living arrangements are rarely thought of as being legal agreements, they are. Most people don't realize that if they don't write up a legal agreement between themselves and their spouse or partner, the state and its judges will provide a legal agreement, based upon statutes and other cases.

Whether you are married, living together, or having a child on your own, your legal rights and those of others involved can either be decided by you in advance, or by the courts when a dispute comes up. If you wish to insure that your desires are met, you should come to an agreement with your partner and put it into writing.

To be sure that all issues are covered and that you have adequately protected yourself, you should either consult an attorney or a book which analyzes each issue in detail. (See references at the end of this book.) However, forms are included in this book to help you understand all of the issues and for your use in an emergency situation. For example, if your spouse announces that he or she is leaving for good, sitting down and filling out a property settlement agreement would be much better than trying to locate him or her through a divorce suit.

LIVING TOGETHER

Not many legal issues come up while a couple is happily living together. The trouble arises when one of them dies or they decide to split up. Usually the trouble involves who owns what property, and who is responsible for which debts. If they have had a child, custody and support become issues.

Often a person has conflicting desires in a situation like this. On the one hand you may want your partner to inherit the property you were using jointly if anything happens to you. On the other hand, if you split up, you don't want him or her claiming any interest in what you consider your property.

The best way to protect both of your interests is to have a *cohabitation* agreement stating which property is separate, and a will distributing your property as you wish. You may also want a trust or declaration of joint property. (Wills and trusts are discussed in Chapter 3.)

COHABITATION AGREEMENT

A cohabitation agreement usually lists which property each party claims as separate and which is joint. It can also spell out who will pay which expenses during the relationship and even list household duties if the parties think this will be an issue. A cohabitation agreement is included in the appendix. (see form 6, p.110.)

This agreement can also protect either of you from "palimony" claims. These are cases where one cohabitant claims that his or her partner agreed to support him or her forever. The cohabitation agreement could state that neither party promises to support the other in the event of separation and that any changes to this agreement must be in writing.

Note that two people who are merely sharing a house or apartment without a relationship or shared funds would be more likely to need a roommate agreement. (see Chapter 6.)

PREMARITAL AGREEMENTS

A *premarital agreement* (also called an *ante-nuptial agreement*) is an agreement which can spell out the legal rights of the parties during and after a marriage. It can cover how property will be divided in the event of divorce, and how property may be distributed in the event of death. In most states a spouse must give a certain percentage of property to a spouse at death or the spouse can claim it from heirs in the will. A premarital agreement can overrule those laws.

Some people even try to spell out in detail their rights during marriage, such as how often the parties will go out to dinner and have sex! However, not all things a couple agrees to are enforceable in court. Courts have been slow to accept premarital agreements. Such agreements were thought to encourage divorce by discussing the subject even before marriage, and so were held to be illegal. But that has changed in most states.

The legality of premarital agreements is determined by state law and what is acceptable varies from state to state. In some states such an agreement is not valid unless both parties make full disclosure of their assets. Some cases have held that such agreements are not enforceable if they were not fairly obtained. For example, where a premarital agreement was presented minutes before a wedding ceremony with the ultimatum, "sign it or the wedding's off," it was held by a judge to be void. There were similar results where one party was intoxicated, or unable to consult a lawyer.

Because premarital agreements often cover large amounts of property and affect important rights, it is best to consult a lawyer to be sure your agreement is legal in your state. At a minimum, you should do some research into your state's laws.

A premarital agreement form is included in the appendix. (see form 7, p.114.) In addition you will need to prepare the following exhibits:

Exhibit A: a financial statement for the husband.

Exhibit B: a financial statement for the wife.

Exhibit C: a list of the property which will be the separate property of the husband.

Exhibit D: a list of the property which will be the separate property of the wife.

If your assets are limited, you can make your own financial statement listing all of them and their estimated value. If your assets are substantial, you should have your accountant prepare a financial statement.

MARITAL AGREEMENTS

*Marital agreement*s are like premarital agreements, but they are signed by couples who are already married. The usual reason is that they are having some friction and want to spell out in detail their rights. The longer a marriage lasts, the more property the less wealthy spouse can usually get in a divorce. A marital agreement is sometimes offered as an alternative to a divorce. The wealthier spouse says " I want a divorce now, but if you sign this we can wait and see if things work out."

The big difference between a premarital and a marital agreement is that people who are married already have legal rights, while unmarried people do not. In the event of divorce the usual formula in most states is that each spouse gets one-half of all joint property and one-half of the property the other spouse accumulated during the marriage.

So, if one spouse built up a big pension plan, or accumulated a lot of wealth during a marriage, even if the marriage was short, the other spouse could be giving up half of that by signing a marital agreement that waives property rights.

For this reason, it is absolutely necessary that both spouses give complete financial disclosure before signing a marital agreement. If the disclosure is incomplete or false, the agreement can be held void.

A sample marital agreement is included in the appendix. (see form 8, p.118.) Because of the important legal rights that are involved, you should not sign such an agreement before you fully understand the legal consequences. (Some text references are included in the last section of this book.) You should also consider consulting an attorney if there is a considerable amount of property at stake.

Separation Agreements

A *separation agreement* is signed by parties who are married but wish to live apart. In some states you can't get a divorce until you have lived apart for a certain period, such as six months or a year.

Separation agreements usually cover such matters as who will be entitled to what marital property, who will pay each of the existing debts, whether there will be child support paid, and who will have custody of any minor children. (It is very similar to a divorce settlement agreement, discussed below.) Other things which may be covered are agreements that each party waives a right to the other's estate and agrees not to harass the other.

A sample Separation Agreement is included in the appendix. (see form 9, p.122.) Again, these forms determine important legal rights, so they should not be signed until you understand all your legal rights.

DIVORCE SETTLEMENTS

When a couple gets a divorce, it is usually necessary to come to an agreement regarding who will get the joint property and who will be responsible for the joint debts. This is usually called a *divorce settlement agreement*. (see form 10, p.125.) The only time it wouldn't be necessary is if the parties had no property, no debts, and no children.

A couple divorcing has two choices. They can decide between themselves how they will divide their property and handle issues such as child custody and support. Or, they can hire two separate lawyers to argue to a judge what is best, and let the judge decide.

If you can work these matters out with your spouse, you will come out ahead both financially and emotionally. Marital property is usually split 50/50 and child support is determined by income. There is not much advantage to fighting over the issue unless one spouse is being dishonest and hiding income and assets.

There are a lot of legal issues involved in a divorce. For example, alimony is tax deductible to the payer and taxable to the recipient, while child support and property settlements are not. And rights to each other's pension plans can be complicated. Therefore, if you and your spouse have any more than just minimal property you should either do some research or consult an attorney. Some good research references are in the last section of this book. Some attorneys will give you a consultation for a fixed fee of say, $75 or $150 and answer all of your questions of whether you have any rights to be concerned with or if your divorce can be simple.

CARE OF CHILDREN

Because you are not always present with your children, you may need to delegate your parental responsibility to someone in whose care you have entrusted them. This will allow that person to authorize necessary medical care and to have the right to discipline them when needed. For this purpose, a delegation of parental responsibility is included in the appendix. (see form 11, p.129.)

When your child is in an activity with a school or other organization, you will usually be asked to sign an authorization. Less formal groups may not have a form and the form used by your group may not cover all of the conditions you wish to impose upon the activity. For these instances, a child authorization form is included in the appendix. (see form 12, p.130.)

CARE OF PETS

If you leave your pet with a professional border they will most likely have their own contract. But if you hire someone who is not a professional to care for your pet, you should have your own agreement to cover their duties and obligations. (see form 13, p.131.)

ADDRESS CHANGE

To be sure that you do not miss any of your mail when you move, you should be sure to notify both the post office and your important contacts. The post office does not forward certain types of mail (catalogs, some publications) and it only forwards other mail for a limited time. After that it is returned to sender. The appendix includes one form to notify the post office and another to notify your contacts, such as doctors and other professionals, magazines and newspapers, friends, banks and credit card companies, and anyone else with whom you have an ongoing relationship. (see form 14, p.132.)

A separate form is included for notifying the IRS of your change of address. (see form 15, p.133.)

BIRTH AND DEATH CERTIFICATES

To obtain copies of birth and death certificates, you will need to contact the department which keeps vital statistics for your state. Sometimes you can get their number in your local phone book. If not, you can get the address, phone number and fees from the following web site:

http://www.cdc.gov/nchs/howto/w2w/w2welcom.htm

If you don't have access to a computer you can obtain it from:

U.S. DEPARTMENT OF HEALTH AND HUMAN SERVICES
Centers for Disease Control and Prevention
National Center for Health Statistics
Division of Data Services
Hyattsville, MD 20782-2003
(301) 458-4636

Form 16 in the appendix can be used to obtain a birth or death certificate. (see form 16, p.135.)

ANATOMICAL GIFTS

Lives can now be saved by using organs of people who have died. For example, a person who has died of head injuries in a motorcycle crash can donate a heart, two kidneys, a liver and several organs to people who would otherwise die without them. Permission can be given by the family of a deceased, but often family members are squeamish about giving away the organs of a loved one. For this reason, the law allows us to sign a card giving permission for organ donation. In some states this is included on the back of the drivers' license. If not, you can use the organ donor card in the appendix. (see form 35, p.167.)

PASSPORT APPLICATION

While you can visit a few countries (like Canada and Mexico) with just your driver's license, you must have a passport before visiting most countries of the world. If you have never had a passport you must apply in person at a Passport Agency. They are usually located in federal buildings or courthouses. Look in the government pages of your phone book. They could be under the federal, state or county listings. Call first to see if you need an appointment. If you need to renew a passport this can be done by mail. Forms for new and renewal passports are in the appendix. (see form 17, p.136.) (see form 18, p.138.)

SOCIAL SECURITY NUMBER

When you give birth to or adopt a child, you will need to obtain a social security number for that child if you want to take advantage of the tax deduction. To obtain one, you should use form SS-5 included in the appendix. (see form 19, p.140.)

FORMS FOR SETTLING AN ESTATE 3

This chapter explains the basics of wills and estate planning, and the forms that may be used for both. An estate is everything that a person owns (and owes). It includes property, bank accounts, jewelry, stocks, etc. A will, which is discussed below, is a way to gather your estate and distribute it after death. The will goes through a process called *probate*, which is 1) the determination by a court that a will is valid and 2) the estate should be distributed according to that will.

For simple estates, or if you already have done some estate planning and merely wanted to make changes, this may be enough information for you. However, if you have a large estate, or want to make any complicated arrangements such as disinheriting someone or avoiding taxes, you should consult a specialized book or an attorney.

WILL

A *will* is a document you can use to control who gets your property, who will be guardian of your children and their property, and who will manage your estate upon your death. Upon a person's death, a will is presented to a probate court and the court appoints a person (*executor*, *personal representative* or *administrator*) to manage the estate.

If you do not have a will, then the intestacy laws of your state decide who gets your property. In most states this is your spouse and children. But in some states, the intestacy law might not divide your property the way you want. For example, some states give half your property to your spouse and half to your children, whereas you might want it all to go to your spouse until he or she passes away.

Four different will forms are included in the appendix which will cover simple situations. If your situation is more complicated you should check one of the resources listed in the back of the book.

The wills in this book cover the following situations:

Simple Will—Spouse and Minor Children—One Guardian. Use this will if you have minor children and want all your property to go to your spouse, but if your spouse dies previously, then to your minor children. It provides for one person to be guardian over your children and their estates. (see form 20, p.146.)

Simple Will—Spouse and No Children. Use this will if you want your property to go to your spouse but if your spouse predeceases you, to others or to the descendants of the others. (see form 21, p.148.)

Simple Will—No Spouse—Minor Children—One Guardian. Use this will if you do not have a spouse and want all your property to go to your children, at least one of whom is a minor. It provides for one person to be guardian over your children and their estates. (see form 22, p.150.)

Simple Will—No Spouse and No Children. Use this will if you have no spouse or children and want your property to go to the survivor of the people you name. (see form 23, p.152.)

In some states a will can be valid if it is completely handwritten. However, in most states a will must be witnessed by two persons (three in Vermont). In some states the witnesses can be interested parties (people who will inherit), but this is not a good idea, especially if there is someone who might contest the will. When signing a will the witnesses don't have to read or know exactly what is in the will. The person making a will must tell the witnesses that it is a will and that it is being signed voluntarily.

The disadvantage of using a will to pass your property to people is that it requires a probate proceeding in court, which takes time and costs money. In many states the law allows attorneys to charge a percentage of the assets in an estate, no matter how little work there is. Sometimes this fee can be negotiated down, but a better alternative is to avoid probate altogether as explained in the next section.

SELF-PROVING
STATEMENT

A will does not need to be notarized to be valid. However if a notarized *self-proving statement* is attached to a will, this will usually allow it to be accepted by a probate court much quicker.

CODICIL

A *codicil* is a document which changes something in a will. Since a codicil should be signed with the same formality and number of witnesses as a will, it is often just as easy to prepare a new will than to prepare a codicil. A form for a codicil is included in the appendix. (see form 24, p.154.)

AVOIDING PROBATE

Everyone who knows what probate is wants to avoid it. As stated earlier, probate is the determination that a will is valid, and that the estate should be settled by the will's terms. It is often a long, arduous procedure. Luckily, the laws are changing to allow many different ways to avoid probate. This section explains the easiest ones. (For more detailed information, see one of the references at the end of this book.)

JOINT PROPERTY

The easiest way to avoid probate is to own all property in *joint tenancy with right of survivorship*. When property is owned this way, it automatically passes to the survivor when the other owner dies. Three disadvantages of this are: either owner can secretly take the property at any time; either party's creditor's can take it; and, if both parties die in the same accident, there still has to be a probate.

To set up property in joint ownership, it must be titled with the names of both parties and the words "as joint tenants with full rights of survivorship." Merely putting two names on an account without this language does not mean the survivor gets it. This language can be on deeds or real estate, stock certificates, brokerage accounts and bank accounts.

Most married couples who jointly own all their property do not need a will when the first one of them dies. The main reason they *should* have one is in the event of an accident which kills both of them.

One solution to this problem is for a couple to put their property in joint ownership with their children. The danger of this is that the children can take all of the property at any time and the creditors of a child might be able to seize it. The next subsections (Totten Trusts and Formal Trusts) describe solutions for this.

You should review how your bank accounts, stocks, mutual funds, motor vehicles, recreation vehicles, and other property are titled. If you want them to go to your relatives or through your will, they should be in your name alone. If you want them to go to your joint owner, you should be sure they are properly set up as a joint account with right of survivorship.

TOTTEN TRUSTS

Even better than joint ownership is a *Totten Trust*. This is a method of setting up the title to property so that it automatically passes at death without the beneficiary having any rights to it until the first owner's life. It was named after the court case in which a court held that it was legal to do.

A Totten Trust is when the property is set up *in trust for*, or I/T/F, with a named beneficiary. Some institutions may use the letters POD for *pay on death* or TOD for *transfer on death*. Either way the result is the same. No one except you can get the money until your death. Upon death, it immediately goes directly to the person you name, without a will or probate proceeding.

Totten Trusts have been valid for a long time for bank accounts. During the last decade, more than half the states have passed laws allowing them to be used for securities such as stocks, bonds and mutual funds. They are not yet used for real estate, though in some states the law seems Check with a lawyer before attempting to use it for real estate.

If your mutual fund or brokerage will not or cannot set up your account to pay on death, check with some others. One may be located in a state where the law has passed while the other may not.

FORMAL TRUSTS

Another way to avoid needing a will (and to avoid probate) is to set up a formal trust. A *trust* is an agreement that someone holds property that really belongs to someone else and is used for that person's benefit. For example, a person might transfer all their stocks to a bank to hold in trust. The trust would provide that during that person's life he or she gets all the dividends from the stock, and after his or her death the income goes to the children.

If the trust is revocable, the person setting up the trust (the settlor) can change the trust or even dissolve it. If it is irrevocable, it cannot be changed. The benefit of a revocable trust is that no one else can get to it, meaning if you or your children later have a large liability (medical bills or liability for an accident), the creditors can't touch the money in the trust (if it is set up correctly).

A *living trust*, often called a revocable living trust, is usually a trust which a person or couple sets up in which they become their own trustees. The main benefit of this is that their property then avoids probate. (see form 30, p.160.)

There are many other benefits of trusts, and the laws differ from state to state as to the legal requirements, such as whether a person can be his own trustee. A thorough discussion is beyond the scope of this book. If you think a living trust could benefit you, you should consult one of the references at the end of this book.

One of the biggest problems with setting up a living trust is that people forget to put their property into it! After the trust agreement is signed, all of the person's property must be transferred to the trust. Usually, all of the assets are listed on a "Schedule of Assets" which goes with the trust. A form for this is included in the appendix. (see form 27, p.157.) But for some types of property, such as real estate and motor vehicles, the title must be reregistered. This means getting a new deed or title certificate. Also, bank and brokerage accounts must be retitled, rather than just listed on the schedule of assets.

If a living trust needs to be changed (such as when one beneficiary dies), this is done with an *amendment*. A blank amendment is contained in the appendix. (see form 28, p.158.) A termination form to end the trust is also included. (see form 29, p.159.)

Personal property ownership is not registered or documented by a title certificate. As a result, ownership of such items can be questionable. For example, what if you own a valuable coin collection and after your death your spouse claims ownership as joint property, while your child claims inheritance as personal property under your will?

To avoid problems like this, you can specifically list personal items you wish to give people in your will, and you can sign a declaration with your spouse or partner as to how your personal property is titled. A Declaration of Joint Property is included in the appendix.(see form 25, p.155.) Below is an example of such a form.

Sample of form 25. Declaration of Joint Property—

DECLARATION OF JOINT PROPERTY

The undersigned, in consideration of the mutual agreement herein contained, agree that all property owned by them and located in their place of residence, shall be owned in joint tenancy with full rights of survivorship, except the following items which shall remain separate property for all purposes:

```
Except John Smith's coin collection which will be
willed to his son.
Except Mildred Smith's family photo album which
will be willed to her sister's children.
```

In addition to the property located at the residence, the following property shall also be owned in joint tenancy with full rights of survivorship:

```
John Smith's canoe which is usually kept by the
river.
```

In witness whereof, the parties affix their signatures and seals this 29 day of January , 20 02

In some cases you might be more concerned that the title to your property is separate. For example, in California and many other western states, all property acquired during marriage is considered community property and each spouse has 50% interest in it. If you and your spouse want to keep your property separate (for example to leave it to your separate children) you could execute a Declaration of Separate Property, a form for which is included in the appendix. (see form 26, p.156.)

POWER OF ATTORNEY

A *power of attorney* is a document which gives someone the right to take some legal action in your name. For example you might give someone a power of attorney to sign a deed selling your house if you are going to be out of the country. Or you could give someone power of attorney to handle all of your legal affairs in case you were medically disabled.

A person holding a power of attorney to act for someone is called an *attorney in fact*. (This has no relationship to an *attorney at law*.) The person giving someone a power of attorney is called the *grantor*. While an attorney in fact should only take action which his grantor wishes, legally he has the power to do anything that the power of attorney grants him. For example, he can withdraw money from an account and spend it on himself. Of course, this would be criminal.

For this reason, a power of attorney should only be given to a trusted person, and it should be limited to the necessary acts. For example, if you need someone to sign a real estate deed, it is not necessary to give them a general power of attorney, which allows them to do anything regarding all of your property. (see form 31, p.162.) Instead you would give them a specific power of attorney for the specific act of signing the deed. (see form 32, p.163.) A sample of a specific power of attorney is shown on the following page.

Sample of form 32. Power of Attorney - Specific—

POWER OF ATTORNEY - SPECIFIC

<u>   Jon Dough   </u> (the "Grantor")
hereby   grants   to
<u>   Noah Dough   </u> (the
"Agent") a limited power of attorney. As the Grantor's attorney in fact, the Agent shall have full power and authority to undertake and perform the following on behalf of the Grantor:

To sign a sales contract on my house if an offer of over $100,000 comes in while I am travelling in India.

By accepting this grant, the Agent agrees to act in a fiduciary capacity consistent with the reasonable best interests of the Grantor. This power of attorney may be revoked by the Grantor at any time; however, any person dealing with the Agent as attorney in fact may rely on this appointment until receipt of actual notice of termination.

IN WITNESS WHEREOF, the undersigned grantor has executed this power of attorney under seal as of the date stated above.

There may be times when you have given someone a power of attorney and then later decide to cancel it. This is done with a form called a Revocation of Power of Attorney. You should deliver it to the person with the power of attorney as well as anyone whom you think has or will see the original power of attorney. A revocation of power of attorney is included in the appendix. (see form 33, p.164.)

LIVING WILL

A *living will* is a document which allows you to state that if you become so ill that you will never recover, you do not wish unusual medical techniques to be used to prolong your life. Today medical science can keep a body alive long after it is able to fully function, and doctors often feel they should do everything possible to keep a body alive (or else get sued!) In some cases people have been in comas or in pain for years with no hope for recovery. This prolonged the agony of both the patient and the family, and often cost a fortune.

For this reason, laws were passed to allow people to sign a document (living will) stating that they wish to be allowed to die naturally. One is included in the appendix. (see form 34, p.165.)

FINANCIAL LEGAL FORMS 4

RECEIPT

A *receipt* is a written confirmation that you have received something, usually cash. Whenever you pay cash for anything it is important to get a receipt, otherwise the recipient can deny that the cash was ever received.

However, receipts have another use. They can prove and give the terms of a contract. If you buy something, a car for example, and do not have a written contract, the receipt for the transaction can be used to prove the terms of the sale. If you put the make, model, mileage and other description on the receipt, and the car doesn't comply, you have a better legal case than if you didn't write it on the receipt.

Courts have ruled that a document such as a receipt can help a person win a case even if they have no written contract; whether or not the law says they must have one. As explained earlier, statutes of frauds require that certain contracts be in writing. Many court cases have held that if a receipt, or other documentation such as letters between the parties, contain enough details of the intended transaction, then those documents can constitute the contract.

Whenever you complete a transaction with someone, and don't have a written contract spelling out the terms, you should be sure that you have a receipt with as much detail as possible. (see form 36, p.168.)

Sample of form 36. Receipt–

RECEIPT

The undersigned hereby acknowledges receipt of the sum of
___one thousand_____($__1,000__)

in for form of

☒ cash

❑ a check numbered _____, dated _____,
20_____

as payment for: _1956 Chevrolet Belair, Blue and white,_
ID # 6J503021, 89,651 miles and all spare parts
_in trunk_____
_____
_____

Balance due: ___five hundred_____($ 500.00____)

Date __May 10,_____, 20_02___

PROMISSORY NOTE

A *promissory note* is a promise to pay (or repay) money. It is the legal term for an "I O U." The variety of terms of how a note can be repaid are unlimited. A lump sum can be due on a certain day. (see form 37, p.169.) Smaller payments can be due each week or month. (see form 38, p.170.) Or, the note can be payable *on demand*, meaning whenever the lender needs the money. (see form 39, p.171.)

AMORTIZATION   When a note is paid in regular payments (such as monthly) the amount is usually calculated to allow the entire loan to be paid off by a certain date. For example, if you borrow $1,000 at 12% interest and want to pay it off within a year, you need to make payments of $93.33 each month for 12 months. Prior to the Great Depression, people usually only paid the interest on the loan each month and then had to come up with the entire principal amount at the end of the loan. That's why most people defaulted.

How do you know the amount of payment for any sum? In the past there were little books called *amortization tables*, or *mortgage payment tables*. Now, the Internet has several sites that provide free amortization calculators, such as http://ray.met.fsu.edu/~bret/amortize.html. Some electronic calculators also calculate amortizations of loans. Using these tables or calculators, you can be sure that the principal and correct interest is paid.

INTEREST   There is nearly an infinite number of ways to calculate interest on a loan. When not using an amortization calculation the most common way is simple interest, or the percentage per year times the balance. To get more interest from the same percentage rate, you can calculate it by the month. For example, 12% of $1,000 is $120 for one year. But, if it is calculated by the month, it is $126.84. Not much of a difference on a small loan, but for large amounts it adds up.

One thing to be careful of when setting the interest rate is your state's *usury* law. This is the law which sets a limit on the amount of interest that can be charged on loans. The purpose is to eliminate loan sharking, but the laws usually apply to all loans. The penalties can be severe. If you charge too much interest, you may lose the right to collect interest, or have to pay double interest to the borrower, or be charged with criminal usury! Some people have tried to be clever and raise the price to include hidden interest. For a single transaction this would be hard to prove. Where multiple items are usually sold at one price, but the price is raised when selling on credit, usury could be found by a court.

NEGOTIABILITY   Sometimes a person holding a promissory note needs the money before the loan is due. One way to get it is to sell the note. A note can be sold if it is *negotiable*. A note is negotiable if: 1) the promise to pay the money is not subject to any conditions, 2) it is written and signed, 3) it is payable to a named person, a person to whom the note has been *negotiated* (sold), or to the *bearer* or *holder* of the note, and 4) if it is to be paid either on a specified date or on the demand of the person the debt is to be paid to.

These requirements account for some of the odd language that notes and other negotiable instruments, such as checks, use. For example, the words "pay to the order of" mean that the person who owes the money has to pay it to the person named or to whomever that person orders it to be paid. That is, to whomever it has been negotiated. There are other kinds of contracts that create an obligation to repay money, but promissory notes are the most reliable and readily enforceable.

Before agreeing to accept a promissory note from someone, it is common to check out their credit history to be sure that they pay their bills. To obtain a person's credit report you need to have them sign an authorization. A form for this purpose is included in the appendix. (See form 40, p.172.)

GUARANTEE   When a person does not have either good credit history or any assets, lenders often look for another person to guarantee the loan. For young people this is often a parent. For others it may be a successful relative.

If you sell something to someone whose credit looks questionable, consider asking if they have someone who could guarantee the amount owed. This is done either by having the guarantor sign the note, or a separate guaranty.

> **Warning:** Do not sign duplicate copies of a promissory note! Each signed note is an enforceable promise to pay the money referred to in the note. So if you sign three copies of the same note, you have promised to pay the same amount of money three times. Even machine copies of a note should be made before the note is signed (and the copy should not be signed) so there won't be any mistakes.

As mentioned before, there are three blank promissory note forms included in the appendix - a lump payment note, an amortized note, and an on demand note. The amortized note has a paragraph for a guaranty by another party. The note can be used without a guaranty, and the guaranty clause can be added to any of the other notes.

SECURITY   Except for small loan amounts, a loan represented by a promissory note is often *secured*, meaning the person owing the money pledges some property to guaranty payment of the loan. If it is not paid on time, the lender can take the property and sell it to recover the amount owed.

The forms for securing a loan with real estate are explained in Chapter 6 and those for personal property are explained in Chapter 5.

FORMS FOR CREDIT MATTERS

CREDIT REPORT   A good credit profile is important in that it allows you to borrow the money necessary to buy a home, car, business and other large items. It allows the purchase of large assets with payments spread over a long period. Imagine having to save up the cash to buy a house, rather than borrowing the money and paying each month!

Whether or not you are given credit will be determined by your *credit report*. It is important to you that it contain accurate information. Often the wrong information gets into these reports.

Every few years you should review your report, especially if you expect to apply for loan. If you are denied a loan, you have a right to a free copy of the report which the lender used to deny you th loan. They should give you the name, address and phone number of the agency they used at the time they inform you that credit is denied. If you have not been denied a loan, you can get a copy of your report for a fee. There are a few consumer reporting agencies, so you should check with any lenders you plan to use to see which ones you need to check. You can use the form in the appendix to request a copy of your report. (see form 41, p.173.)

If you find an error on your report, you should explain to the agency what the error is and ask them to remove it from your report. A form for this is also in the appendix. (see form 42, p.174.) A sample of how to fill in this form follows.

Sample of form 42. Request for Correction of Credit Report–

REQUEST FOR CORRECTION OF CREDIT REPORT

To: Acme Credit Bureau
     125 Side Street
     Anytown, USA 12345

From: Jon Dough
Address: 9 Leisure Lane
          Midville, USA 12345

Social Security No 123-45-6789

Your report on my credit history contains the following error(s):

1. You show that I owe $45,000 to Midville Bank. This loan was paid in full when I wold my house on May 6, 1999.

2. You show a Visa card with MajorBanc. I never had a credit card with MajorBanc, so this account must belong to another Jon Dough.

Kindly correct these errors and provide me with a corrected copy of my report.

DEALING WITH DEBTS

Most state's laws provide that if you do not deny owing a debt you can be held legally responsible for it. The legal theory is called *account stated*. If a merchant sends you a statement and it is wrong (it includes billing for something you never ordered or received), you need to contest it to avoid being liable for it.

This is not likely to happen if you have never done business with someone. If you have done regular business with them, and you accept statements without complaint, you could become liable for the amounts in dispute. (see form 43, p.175.)

Under the federal law (Fair Debt Collection Practices Act), collection agencies are not allowed to harass you over a debt once you request that they stop. (see form 44, p.176.)

JUDGMENTS

If someone gets a judgment against you and you eventually pay it off, they are required to satisfy or release the judgment on the records where it was originally filed. This is their legal responsibility. However, if they do not know what to do and you want to speed the process along, you can provide them with the Satisfaction of Judgment form included in the appendix. (see form 45, p.177.) Be sure to first check with the clerk where the judgment is filed to see if there are any special requirements. (They may even have their own form.)

CREDIT CARDS

If you lose your credit cards, you should immediately inform the issuers or you may be liable for any amounts charged on them. Usually, they have a toll-free number which can be used for this purpose, and you should make the call immediately. But, you should also confirm this in writing using the form in the appendix. (see form 46, p.178.)

Sometimes, just having credit cards, even if you do not use them, will keep you from getting new credit. The creditors feel that if you took your other cards to their limits you would be overextended. Therefore, it is sometimes necessary to close old accounts before qualifying for new ones. If you wish to close a credit card account you should send written notice to the issuer. (see form 47, p.179.) Some companies request that you cut in half your card and return it to them. However, they will usually accept your word that you destroyed the card.

LOANS

If you get to a point where you find it hard to meet your bills, you may be able to get a creditor to give you an extension of time in which to pay. Interest will still accrue on your loan, but you may be able to skip a payment or two and extend the life of the loan while you get caught up on your finances. Call your lender to discuss this.

For student loans, however, there are federal guidelines as to under what circumstances you may be granted a *forbearance*. A forbearance is a tactic used to put off payments, while still accruing interest, without defaulting. A *default* in a loan is a mark against your credit stating non-payment when payment was due. You can get more information about this from:

U.S. Department of Education
400 Maryland Avenue, SW
Washington, DC 20202

1-800-USA-LEARN

Their web site is:

http://sfahelp.ed.gov/

For a general request for forbearance of a student loan you can use the form in the appendix. (see form 48, p.180.)

If you have several loans at high interest rates (like credit cards) you may be able to get one new loan at a lower rate in which to pay off the others. This way, your monthly payment would be lower. Most lenders have a formal application for this, but you can start the ball rolling with a Request for Consolidation of Loans. (see form 49, p.182.)

When a person dies, it is no longer required that their family pay their bills. If they owned property, the creditors can make claims against the estate. If not, then the creditors are out of luck. To inform a creditor that a person is deceased, you can use a Notice of Death of Debtor. (see form 50, p.183.)

When a person who receives social security dies, their payments stop as of the last one received prior to death. If he or she has a surviving spouse, then the spouse's payment may be increased due to the death. To inform the Social Security Administration of a death you should phone them at 1-800-772-1213. For more information you can access the Social Security Administration web site at:

http://www.ssa.gov

Personal Property Forms

This chapter explains legal forms you could use for transactions relating to personal property. Examples are buying a car from a private party, loaning a valuable tool to a neighbor, or selling a collection of baseball cards. While such transactions are usually done without legal forms, these simple pieces of paper, signed in a few seconds, can save you months of aggravation and thousands of dollars in legal fees if the transaction goes wrong.

For example, what if you buy a car you believe has 35,000 miles on it, but later discover it has 135,000, and all you have is a cancelled check? Or, you let your neighbor borrow a farm implement and then he dies, after which his heirs claim it was his. Or, you sell your valuable baseball card collection to a neighbor, and two months later, he wants to rescind the deal, but the cards are no longer in the condition they were in when you sold them. The forms in this chapter will help you avoid most legal problems that could come up in these types of situations.

Placing an Order

When you purchase something from a catalog or "off the rack" you usually know exactly what you are getting. When you need something made to your specifications, such as a driveway, or a cabinet, you may get something completely different from what you expected because you and the seller were assuming different specifications. Don't assume anything! To be sure you will get what you want, you should put in writing all of the specifications you are expecting.

The best form for this is a Request for Quotation. (see form 51, p.184.) While many companies have their own specification form, this form will help you remember and organize all of the specifications you are looking for.

Sample of form 51. Request for Quotation—

REQUEST FOR QUOTATION

To: Acme Supply
        321 Fleet St.
        Mytown, USA

We are considering the purchase of the following:

```
12 cubic yards of clean top soil
25 pounds of Bahai grass seed
12 pressure-treated 4 x 4 inch posts 8 feet long
```

All to be delivered to 100 Easy Street, Mytown, USA on or before May 12, 2002

If you are able to provide this as specified, kindly provide us with a quotation of total price and completion or delivery date.

BUYING AND SELLING

While a sale of real estate usually involves a contract, a simple cash purchase will usually just involve a bill of sale. A bill of sale is like the deed used for real estate, but it is used for personal property. For some types of property, such as motor vehicles and boats, you can transfer title by signing over the state registration (the title). However, it is always a good idea to have a bill of sale as well because this can include the important terms of the transaction. The price can be used for tax reasons and the description and/or mileage can be used as evidence that the property was misrepresented (if it was).

A bill of sale can be with warranty or without warranty. The most basic warranty is that the seller actually owns the property being sold. Since stolen property nearly always must be returned to its original owner, even if an innocent person buys it, a seller's warranty of ownership will help you collect from him in the event you lose the item because it was originally stolen. (see form 54, p.187.)

A bill of sale can also include warranties as to condition, age or other aspects of the property. As a buyer of property, you want as many warranties as possible. As a seller you want to give as few warranties as possible, because then there will be less things you can be accountable for.

For both parties, it is best to describe the property as accurately as possible. If the item has a serial number, that should be included. If not, the make, model, style, color, and other identifying aspects should be included.

In the appendix are bills of sale with and without warranty. A bill of sale needs only be signed by the person selling the property. Below is a sample of a Bill of Sale with no warranty. (see form 53, p.186.)

Sample of form 53. Bill of Sale—

BILL OF SALE

For $ 50.00 , the receipt of which is hereby acknowledged, the undersigned hereby sells and transfers to Jon Dough all of the undersigned's rights in the following property:

Toro 21" lawnmower model Go5, serial no. CV123456 with grass catcher and instruction book

Executed under seal on August 9, , 20 03 .

INSTALLMENT SALES

When a person cannot afford to pay cash for an item, two ways to purchase it are to borrow the money, or to buy it on an installment purchase agreement. If you are buying something from a private party, they will probably want cash. If you can convince them to take payments, you might be able to get a better deal than borrowing from a bank or your credit cards.

If you are selling something, you would rather get cash. In some cases you might get a higher price if you agree to sell on an installment agreement. Keep in mind that this is risky. The buyer might disappear with the property and never pay you. Or, if the buyer fails to pay and gives the property back, it might be in such bad condition you cannot resell it at the balance due. Then again, if the buyer puts a big enough down payment, you might be able to sell the property again and make a double profit. You will need to weigh the benefits of selling on an installment agreement against the risks.

When selling on an installment agreement, the most important thing to do is to place a *lien* on the property so that it cannot be resold without you being paid off. Like a *mortgage*, which is a lien on real estate, a *chattel mortgage* is a lien on personal property. (see form 55, p.188.) In addition to a chattel mortgage you should file a *financing statement* in the public records. This protects you by giving notice to the world of your interest in the property. A financing statement is usually called a UCC-1 because it is covered by the Uniform Commercial Code.

FORMS   While the Uniform Commercial Code is supposed to be uniform, each state has made it's own changes to it. One unfortunate situation is that most states prefer that you use their own form. They don't supply the form, and they instruct you to purchase it from a private company. Some of those states charge a few dollars extra if the form you use does not exactly match theirs. Because the official forms can be hard to get ahold of, we have included generic UCC-1 and UCC-3 forms in the appendix. You may find it preferable to pay a couple dollars extra than to take the effort and delay to track down the right one.

The UCC-1 form is usually filed both with the secretary of state and a county recoding office. (see form 56, p.189.) After the debt has been paid the UCC-1 is released by filing a UCC-3 form. (see form 57, p.191.)

In addition to the chattel mortgage, you should have a *promissory note* that the buyer signs promising to pay the balance due. See Chapter 3 for promissory notes. These notes can be used here to purchase goods as well as under loans in Chapter 3. You can also have a formal *sales agreement*, but for a simple transaction it is not necessary.

For motor vehicles, some boats, and other property which has a registration with a government agency, there is an easier system. Usually the agency that registers the titles has a form that you can use to register a financial interest in the vehicle or property. Check with your state or county registration office as to what forms are available to place a lien on property which will be sold.

LOANING PROPERTY

If your neighbor needs to borrow your manual post hole digger you don't need to use a legal form. If you loan something valuable to someone and want to be sure of getting it back, and not being liable for its use, you should use a written *receipt for personal property*. (see form 52, p.185.)

For example, if your neighbor will be borrowing one of your farm implements and storing it on his property, or if someone will be borrowing something valuable on a long term basis, you should get something in writing. Besides insuring that you get it back, this can protect you from potential liability.

When using the receipt for personal property you should be sure to describe the property carefully so that it cannot be mistaken for other property.

Again, you don't want to be pulling out legal forms whenever someone borrows something, but keep in mind that if you loan someone a dangerous tool, like a chain saw, and they are injured, you can be liable. This would be especially likely if they injured someone else, or if you had somehow modified the tool making it more dangerous. Other than not loaning dangerous tools, one thing you can do is tell the borrower that you will only loan it on the condition that you will not be held responsible for any injuries. While a verbal agreement like this is harder to prove than a written one, it could still work in court, if it came to that. If a disinterested third party heard the agreement, that would be even better.

REAL ESTATE FORMS 6

BUYING AND SELLING REAL ESTATE

The purchase or sale of real estate is a major financial transaction. If you have not done it before you should be represented by an attorney or broker. Keep in mind that a real estate agent or broker works on commission.

While traditionally a real estate broker has been paid by and responsible to the seller, a *buyer's broker* is a real estate broker who represents the buyer. This can offer more protection to a new buyer, and one who comes recommended by other happy buyers will probably be good to work with.

Some people think that if they are getting a loan, the bank will make sure that the real estate papers are right. You must keep in mind that the bank is looking out for its own interest, and that is not always the same as yours.

There are many types of problems which only an experienced investor or attorney would notice. For example, beach front property might have a strip of land owned by someone else blocking access to the beach; a utility easement might run through the middle of the house; the house you looked at might not actually be on the lot you are buying; deed restrictions might prevent you from building what you want on the property; the deed might not include all the property you expected. All of these are actual examples of what happened at a real estate closing. Some of them are things that a broker or bank would not notice or care about. Until you are able to notice problems like this in the closing papers, you should have a real estate attorney review the papers when you are buying property.

If you find property you really want, you should tell an attorney that you want it. If there are problems with it, tell the attorney you would prefer to solve them than to walk away.

The seller in a real estate transaction has less concerns than the buyer. If the buyer fails to pay, then he wants to be protected so that he gets the property back in good condition.

Another concern for the seller is that he not have any responsibilities after the sale. He usually doesn't want to guarantee anything because he doesn't want to get sued if the buyer is not happy about something with the property. The ancient principle *caveat emptor*, "buyer beware," has been changed in most states in recent years to "seller beware." Today sellers are often expected to disclose to the buyer every conceivable problem with the property, even if not asked. Real estate agents often demand disclosures from sellers before listing a property to protect themselves from lawsuits by buyers. Legally, real estate agents are not liable if a seller lies on the disclosure. Only the seller is liable.

REAL ESTATE
CONTRACT

Most buyers of real estate do not realize the importance of the initial contract. They sign a contract with no legal advice, and then hire an attorney for the closing. But if the contract is not prepared right, there is little the attorney can do. One way to protect yourself is to add a clause to the contract such as "subject to approval of buyer's attorney."

Unless you understand every clause of a real estate contract, you should not sign it without some guidance. Once you have done a few transactions, you may be comfortable enough to handle most of the legal issues yourself. A sample real estate contract is included in the appendix. (see form 58, p.192.) Keep in mind that real estate transactions are covered by state law and your state might have some local requirements. The best way to learn the local requirements is to get a sample contract from an attorney or real estate broker. Keep in mind that both of these may include clauses which are not required by law. Usually, an office supply store is not a good place to get a contract because most of them stock only bare bones national forms which do not include any state requirements. A sample of how a real estate contract is filled-in is included below.

Sample of form 58. Real Estate Contract—

REAL ESTATE CONTRACT

Date: June 6, 2003

PARTIES: Jon Dough

as "Buyer" of_____ Phone: (123) 456-7890

and_____ Mary Smith _____ as

"Seller" of _____ Phone: (987) 654-3210

hereby agree that the Buyer shall buy and the Seller shall sell real property described below under the following terms and conditions:

Street
Address: 6 Hilltop Lane, Mytown, USA

Legal Description:

Lot 1, Shady Oaks Subdivision according to the plat recorded in Plat Book 6, Page 12, Public Records of Harrison County

1. PURCHASE PRICE: The full purchase price shall be
$_____ 100,000 _____ payable as follows:

a) Deposit held in escrow by __Acme Title Co.__ $2,000.00

b) New mortgage* to be obtained by Buyer _____

_____ $80,000.00

c) Subject to [ ] , or assumption of [ ] mortgage* to _____

_____ with interest rate of _____%, payable $_____

per month, having an approximate balance of $_____

d) Mortgage* and Note to be held by seller at ___% interest payable _____ for _____ years in the amount of $_____

e) Other _____

_____ $_____

f) Balance to close (U.S. cash, certified or cashier's check) subject to adjustments and prorations, plus closing costs

$18,000.00

Total . . . .$ 100,000

*or deed of trust

---

1. FINANCING: Contingent upon Buyer obtaining a firm commitment for a mortgage loan for a minimum of $ __80,000__ at a maximum interest rate of __8__% for a term of at least __30__ years. Buyer agrees to make application for and use reasonable diligence to obtain said loan.

2. EXISTING MORTGAGES: Seller represents to Buyer that the existing mortgage on the property is held by _____ and bears interest at _____% per annum with monthly payments of $_____ principal and interest plus $_____ for escrow. Said loan is fully assumable under the following terms:

_____.

3. CLOSING DATE & PLACE: Closing shall be on __August 1__, __2003__ at the office of the attorney or title agent selected by Seller.

4. ACCEPTANCE: If this contract is not executed by both parties on or before __June 7__, __2003__ it shall be void and Buyer's deposit returned.

5. PERSONAL PROPERTY: This sale includes all personal property listed on Schedule A. The parties agree that the portion of the purchase price attributable to these items is $ __2,000.00__ to provide access for inspection upon reasonable notice.

Federal law requires that a lead paint disclosure form be completed by the buyer and seller of property built before 1978. This form is also included in the appendix. (see form 59, p.196.)

REAL ESTATE
DEED

A *deed* is a document which formally transfers title, or ownership, of property. There are several types of deeds in regular use. In most cases, you probably need a *warranty deed* in which the seller guarantees, among other things, that the seller has good title to the property, and that, after selling it, the buyer will have good title. (see form 60, p.197.) What makes a warranty deed special is language such as the following:

> To have and to hold such property together with all rights and appurtenances thereto belonging. The grantor is seized of the premises in fee simple and has the right to convey the same in

fee simple clear of all encumbrances, and the grantor hereby covenants to warrant and forever defend title to the property against the lawful claims of all persons whomsoever except for the exceptions above stated.

An alternative deed, and the type you would prefer to use if you are the seller, is the *quitclaim deed* which merely says that the seller sells to the buyer whatever the seller owns, if anything, with no guarantees. (see form 61, p.198.) Quitclaim deeds have their uses, but you shouldn't buy property relying on a quitclaim deed alone, and it is unlikely that a knowledgeable person would accept one from you. These days most deeds are fill-in-the-blank forms. Each state has its own preferred form. The forms in this book should suffice in most states, but check with your recorder of deeds for any special local requirements.

Transfers of real property are usually made under seal and acknowledged. They are "within the Statute of Frauds" and must be in writing. (see Chapter 1.) Since real property can't be literally handed over to the buyer, recording of deeds is critical. It is the way you prove your ownership, and the way you prevent someone else from purporting to sell the property that belongs to you.

As always, the signatures on options, contracts for purchase and sale, and deeds must be appropriate for the situation, depending upon whether the property owner is an individual, married couple, partnership, corporation, etc. (See the section on signatures in Chapter 1.)

FINANCING
REAL ESTATE

Since few people pay cash for real estate, the transfer usually includes a loan transaction. The buyer borrows money, usually from a bank or the seller, and signs papers pledging the real estate as a guaranty of payment of the loan. This is usually done with a *mortgage*, although some states use a document called a *deed of trust*. A mortgage or deed of trust will describe the real estate, refer to the promissory note it secures, and have numerous provisions relating to what happens if the promissory note goes into default.

If your property is being mortgaged, the lender on the promissory note will probably prepare the mortgage documents. If you are going to take a mortgage to secure money someone owes to you, you will need to prepare the documents. Since the form for a mortgage, and the requirements for its execution and recording, vary from state to state, no useful form can be provided in a book like this. Mortgage forms or Deed of Trust forms can usually be obtained from an office supply store, or possibly from a real estate agent, bank, or mortgage company.

If you hold a mortgage, you may want to sell it to another party. To do so, you will need to execute an Assignment of Mortgage. (see form 62, p.199). If you hold the mortgage until it is paid off, you will need to execute a Satisfaction of Mortgage. (see form 63, p.200.)

REAL ESTATE OPTIONS

An *option* is a kind of contract within a contract. It is an agreement to keep an offer "open" for a period of time in exchange for some consideration, such as money. As always in a contract, the consideration part is important. It must be real and not just a formal recital. Otherwise, you might find that you don't have an option at all. Options may be recorded just as deeds. Recording will protect the party with the option from subsequent claims, but it may also trigger a "due on sale" clause in some mortgages.

The *optionor* is the person granting the option to someone and the *optionee* is the person getting the option to buy the property. One common mistake with options is for the optionee to neglect to follow the terms of the option. If the seller is eager to sell the property this might not matter. If the seller would rather keep the property and the option money, forgetting to follow the terms of the option (such as giving notice prior to the end) could cause the optionee to lose all rights.

An option agreement form is included in the appendix. (see form 64, p.201.) A form for exercising the option is included as well. (see form 65, p.202.)

LEASING AND RENTING REAL ESTATE

AS A
LANDLORD

Leasing real property is somewhat like buying it. In fact you are buying it for a period of time, so the process is in some ways similar. A lease or rental agreement is the document that grants the right to temporary possession of real estate. Although it transfers an interest in real estate, as does a deed, a lease is a very different animal. Deeds are usually quite short. Leases are usually quite long. Deeds look very much alike, while leases vary tremendously depending upon the type and function of the property being leased.

If you go into the rental business by investing in real estate, you should get a good lease form to use with your tenants and be sure that you understand every clause of it. In the beginning, you may wish to get the advice of an attorney. The best way to find one who is both knowledgeable about real estate and charges reasonable fees is to join a local landlords' association. Many of these clubs are mostly small-time landlords who can give you valuable advice about the business and legalities of renting real estate.

If you don't plan to get so deeply into rentals, and only occasionally need to do so, such as when you are transferred out of town and need to rent out your home, you should still consider getting legal advice. Your home is probably the most valuable piece of property you own, and by renting it to someone you risk them doing damage.

The first thing you should do when renting is screen the tenants carefully. Get permission to get a copy of their credit report, and check their references. Don't just check with their current landlord; he may be eager to get rid of them. Ask one or two past landlords if they took care of the property. A rental application is included in the appendix. (see form 66, p.203.)

Forms are included in the appendix for leasing property. Two house leases are included, one which can be used for renting a single family home for a set term(see form 67, p.204.) and one on a month-to-month basis (see form 68, p.206.) Two Apartment Rental Agreements are included, one which can be used to rent a room or apartment for a flexible period of time, (see form 70, p.210.) and one for renting on a set term. (see form 69, p.208.)

Under federal law, if the property was built before 1978 you must attach a lead paint rider. This is the same rider attached to the real estate contract. (see form 59, p.196.) so you can use that one. Your state might require other clauses or riders relating to such matters as security deposits, lead-based paints, and radon testing. The failure to include one of these required clauses could render the lease unenforceable or create some kind of penalty for the landlord. Check with a knowledgeable real estate agent or attorney. You can add them to the lease by using the addendum.

AS A TENANT

As a tenant, you will usually be offered a lease on a "take it or leave it" basis by a landlord. If the landlord is desperate to get a tenant, you may be able to negotiate more favorable terms. If you do so, these should always be in writing. Verbal agreements are usually not enforceable when you have a written agreement to the contrary.

If there is no way to fit all of your changes onto the landlord's lease form, you can use an *amendment to lease*. (see form 71, p.212.) A sample is below.

Sample of form 71. Amendment to Lease—

AMENDMENT TO LEASE AGREEMENT

For valuable consideration, the receipt and sufficiency of which is hereby acknowledged by each of the parties, this agreement amends a lease agreement (the "Lease") between _____ _____ Jon Dough _____ (the "Landlord") and _____ Jane Rowe _____ (the "Tenant") dated _____, relating to property located at _____ 9 Shady Lane, Mytown, USA _____ _____. This agreement is hereby incorporated into the Lease.

```
     1. Paragraph 5 of the Lease is hereby amended
to read in its entirety as follows:

     5. Assignment. The Tenant shall not
     assign this Agreement or sublet the
     Premises in whole or in part without
     the written consent of the Landlord.
     2. Paragraph 20.3 of the Lease is hereby
deleted in its entirety.

     3. There is hereby added to the Lease a new
paragraph number 9.4 which shall read in its
entirety as follows:

     9.4. Provide the Tenant with 10 des-
     ignated and sign-posted parking
     spaces in the center parking lot.
```

Except as changed by this amendment, the Lease shall continue in effect according to its terms. The amendments herein shall be effective on the date this document is executed by both parties.

Executed on ___May 1, 2002_____.

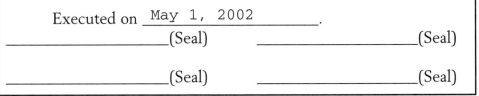

_____(Seal)   _____(Seal)

_____(Seal)   _____(Seal)

Lease assignments and subleases. Chapter 1 discussed the assignment of contracts. From the tenant's point of view, assigning a lease means moving out and finding a new tenant. When a landlord assigns a lease, it is usually when the building is sold.

Assignments and sublets are different. In an *assignment* by a tenant, the new tenant steps into the shoes of the old tenant and deals with the landlord directly. If all goes well, the old tenant is out of the picture. Remember that, while a tenant can assign his or her right to use the property, he or she can only delegate the duty to pay rent. This means that, absent an agreement by the landlord, the old tenant always remains ultimately responsible for payment of the rent if the lease assignee fails to do so. (see form 72, p.213.) (The sample assignment form below provides an optional provision in which the landlord discharges the old tenant from further obligations under the lease. In the example, the partnership tenant has incorporated, and the lease is being assigned to the corporation.)

In a *sublease*, the old tenant stands between the landlord and the subtenant. In essence, the tenant becomes the landlord to the subtenant. The subtenant will pay rent to the old tenant, who will then pay rent to the landlord. The subtenant may pay more rent to the tenant than the tenant will pay to landlord, leaving the tenant a profit. A sublease is actually a special type of lease, and is just as complex as a lease. The failure to include certain provisions required by a state or local law can invalidate a sublease, therefore you should consult an attorney or a book specifically about leases before preparing or signing one. Because of the variety of state and local leasing laws, it is not practical to provide a sublease form in this book.

Almost every written lease agreement will require the landlord's permission before the tenant can validly assign the lease or sublet the premises. (see form 73, p.214.) Examples of a lease assignment and a consent to sublease follow. Sample of form makes the landlord a party giving consent to an assignment. As stated earlier, an assignment may or may not release the original tenant from further liability to the landlord, so be sure to note the optional language for paragraph 4 in the example.

Sample of form 72. Lease Assignment—

LEASE ASSIGNMENT

This Lease Assignment is entered into by and among _____Jane Rowe_____(the "Assignor"), ___Freddie Foe_____ (the "Assignee"), and _____Jon Dough_____ (the "Landlord"). For valuable consideration, it is agreed by the parties as follows:

1. The Landlord and the Assignor have entered into a lease agreement (the "Lease") dated _May 1, 2002_____ concerning the premises described as:

1264 Main Street, #24, Decatur, Georgia.

---

2. The Assignor hereby assigns, transfers and delivers to the Assignee all of Assignor's rights and delegates all of Assignor's duties under the Lease effective on __Sept. 1, 2002__ (the "Effective Date").

3. The Assignee hereby accepts such assignment of rights and delegation of duties and agrees to pay all rents promptly when due and perform all of Assignor's obligations under the Lease accruing on and after the Effective Date. The Assignee further agrees to indemnify and hold the Assignor harmless from any breach of Assignee's duties hereunder.

4. ❑   The Assignor agrees to transfer possession of the leased premises to the Assignee on the Effective Date. All rents and obligations of the Assignor under the Lease accruing before the Effective Date shall have been paid or discharged as of the Effective Date.

❑   The Landlord hereby assents to the assignment of the Lease hereunder and as of the Effective Date hereby releases and discharges the Assignor from all duties and obligations under the Lease accruing after the Effective Date.

❑   The Landlord hereby assents to the assignment of the Lease hereunder provided that Landlord's assent hereunder shall not discharge the Assignor of its obligations under the Lease in the event of breach by the Assignee. The Landlord will give notice to the Assignor of any such breach by the Assignee, and, provided the Assignor pays all accrued rents and cures any other default of the Assignee, the Assignor may enforce the terms of the Lease and this Assignment against the Assignee, in the name of the Landlord, if necessary.

5. There shall be no further assignment of the Lease without the written consent of the Landlord.

6. This agreement shall be binding upon and inure to the benefit of the parties, their successors, assigns and personal representatives.

This assignment was executed under seal on __May 1, 2002__.

Sample of form 73. Landlord's Consent to Sublease—

LANDLORD'S CONSENT TO SUBLEASE

FOR VALUABLE CONSIDERATION, the undersigned (the "Landlord") hereby consents to the sublease of all or part of the premises located at ___9 Shady Lane, Mytown, USA___ _____, which is the subject of a lease agreement between Landlord and ___Jane Rowe_____ (the "Tenant"), pursuant to an Agreement to Sublease dated ___May 1, 2002_____, between the Tenant and ___Freddie Foe_____ as Subtenant dated ___Sept. 1, 2002_____.

This consent was signed by the Landlord on ___May 1, 2002_____.

ROOMMATES

Getting a roommate or two can be a great way to afford a much better place to live. Usually a $1,000 place is more than twice as big as two $500 places because you don't have to duplicate the kitchen and bath facilities.

When searching for a roommate, be sure to check them out as thoroughly as possible. If you can visit them where they are presently living, you can see how they live, and if you can talk with the current landlord or neighbors, you can find out if they are good tenants.

One thing to keep in mind when renting a place with other roommates, is that the lease you sign will probably make each of you liable for the full rent. That means that if your roommates stop paying the rent after the first month, you can be sued for the full amount of rent for the full term.

One way to protect yourself is to have an agreement with your roommates that they can be evicted for not paying rent, and that you can sue them in small claims court for it. Such an agreement will not stop the landlord from suing you, but it may give you leverage against your roommates. A roommate agreement is included in the appendix. (see form 74, p.215.) A sample of how to fill it out follows.

Sample of form 74. Roommate Agreement—

ROOMMATE AGREEMENT

The undersigned, intending to share a dwelling unit located at
446 Main St. Mayberry, USA,
in consideration of the mutual promises contained in this agreement,
agree as follows:

1. They shall share the unit as follows: _Mary Cunningham_
gets north bedroom, Joan Peterson gets south bed-
room

2. Rent shall be paid as follows: _$400 each_

3. Each party shall be responsible for his/her own long distance and toll charges on the telephone bill(s) regardless of whose name the bill is in.

4. The other utilities and fees shall be paid as follows:
water, electricity, gas, trash - 50% each.
cable tv - $10 by Mary $30 by Joan.

5. No party is obligated to pay another party's share of the rent or other bills, but in the event one party finds it necessary to pay a bill for another party to stop eviction or termination of service, the party paying shall have the right to reimbursement in full plus a $_20_ charge. In the event the nonpaying party fails to reimburse such amounts, the paying party shall be entitled to interest at the highest legal rate, attorneys' fees, and court costs if legal action is necessary.

6. The parties also agree:
Smoking _only outside_
Overnight guests _only on weekends (Fri. & Sat.)_

7. The parties agree to respect each other's privacy, to keep the shared areas reasonably clean, not to make unreasonable noise during normal sleeping hours, not to leave food where it would invite infestation, and to be courteous and considerate of the other's needs. They agree that if their guests do not follow these rules, such guests shall not be permitted in the unit. They further agree not to do anything which violates the lease and could cause eviction.

One way to avoid the risk of being liable for your roommates' share of the rent is to have a lease that only makes you responsible for your share. For example, it would state that you are to pay $400 per month, and roommate A is to pay $400 per month, and roommate B is to pay $400 per month. Unless there is another clause in the lease that states that you are liable for the other's rent, this would protect you. Unfortunately, most landlords won't go for such an arrangement because they don't want to just evict one roommate.

Another way to protect yourself is to rent the place in your own name and then sublease rooms to roommates. That way you could evict them and replace them if they violated the terms of the sublease with you. To do this, you would need your lease with the landlord to allow you to have subtenants. In this arrangement you would still be liable for the full rent, but you would have control over your roommates' stay.

TENANT MAINTENANCE PROBLEMS

Occasionally a tenant of a home or apartment will have a maintenance problem that is not repaired promptly. Depending upon the type and severity of the problem, the tenant may be allowed to fix the problem and deduct the cost from rent, decrease the rent paid, or move out.

The tenant's rights are determined by state laws, which are usually specific as to how and when the tenant can take these actions. It is important to follow state law precisely before taking any action. Therefore you should obtain a copy of your state's landlord/tenant act. You can usually get it from your state legislator, or a local housing official, or you can photocopy it at your local library.

In all cases a tenant should give written notice to the landlord of the problem at the earliest possible time. A form, Notice to Landlord to Make Repairs, can be used for this purpose. (see form 75, p.216.) However, be sure to check your state statute to be sure you include everything necessary. In most cases, it must be sent by certified mail.

WAIVER AND ASSUMPTION OF RISK

One way to make money is to sue someone. Many juries feel this way as well and award large sums of money to people claiming injuries. If you own or lease property, you could be the target of one of these lawsuits if someone is injured on your property.

The first way to protect yourself is to have insurance. Many awards, however, are well in excess of insurance limits.

One step you can take to protect yourself is to require anyone who does something risky on your property to sign a *waiver and assumption of risk*. This is a document in which a person agrees that in exchange for the right to use your property, they agree not to sue you if they are injured. Such an agreement would probably not work if you did something negligent, or if there was some hidden danger on your property. If the person was just injured or killed doing some normal activity on your property, you might be protected. Sometimes, you might use such a form if you have rural property and you allow people to hunt, fish or swim on it. You might also use such a form if you let neighbors use your swimming pool, trampoline or other dangerous property. If it is a child using it, you must get the signature of the parent or guardian.

It might seem difficult or tacky to make neighbors sign such a document, but if you present it right, it might go over well. You could say something like "I'd love to invite you over to swim in our lake but I'm told I'd be liable if anything happened. If you'd sign something that I'm not responsible, I'd be glad to have you over.

While these do not always hold up in court, they may dissuade some people from suing. A waiver and assumption of risk form is included in the appendix. (see form 76, p.217.)

DECLARATION OF HOMESTEAD

When a person uses property as his or her home, in many states he or she obtains special legal benefits. These may include lower taxes and immunity from having the property taken by creditors. Also, when a person makes a state his personal residence, he may obtain benefits, such as lower tuition at state schools.

Usually these benefits can be obtained by filing a Declaration of Homestead at the county courthouse. Some states and counties have their own form for this, but if one is not available we have included one in the appendix. (see form 77, p.218.)

EMPLOYMENT FORMS 7

There are many instances when you may need to hire people to help you get things accomplished. You might need a caretaker for your children or house. You may need some major work done on your house. If you hire professionals, they will usually have their own forms and agreements. But if your neighbor offers to work for you for a fee, or if you hire someone who does not have a business set up, you may need your own forms to protect yourself legally.

EMPLOYEES

The hiring of an employee, whether for a household or a business, is a risky endeavor. If the person you hire kills someone while driving, or molests a neighborhood child, or injures a visitor to your home, you could be sued for millions of dollars in damages. There is also the risk of damage or injury to your home and family.

There are numerous governmental laws and regulations which cover hiring, and failure to comply can result in financial penalties. For example, if someone does not have the legal right to work in this country, you can be fined for hiring them.

For these reasons, you should thoroughly check the background of anyone you hire. An Employment Application can be used to get references and other information. (see form 78, p.219.) While former employers may be afraid to say anything negative about a person, a glowing review can work well in the applicant's favor.

APPLICANT'S
BACKGROUND

To check an applicant's background you can use an Authorization to Release Employment Information, Verification of Education and Verification of Licensure. These forms are signed by the applicant and grant you permission to obtain the information you need. The Authorization to Release Employment Information can be used to check on employees for any type of job. (see form 79, p.221.) The other two forms would only be necessary if the applicant's education or license was important to the job. (see form 80, p.222.) (see form 81, p.223.) However, you might check these things just to see if the employee was honest on the application.

To confirm an employee's legal status, you should use Form I-9. (see form 82, p.224.) This shows you which documentation is adequate to check eligibility to work. If the applicant uses fake identification, you are not liable for hiring them, as long as you made an honest effort to be sure they produced the documentation required by law. This form should not be used until you have decided to hire a person.

TAXES

If you hire someone for more than a few hours work, you are required to register with the state and federal government to withhold taxes. If you are tempted to ignore these requirements, keep in mind that more than one person lost a Supreme Court justiceship for failure to comply with these laws.

Before you hire someone, you must obtain an employer identification number using IRS form SS-4 which is included in the appendix. (see form 83, p.227.) Once you hire someone you must have them complete IRS form W-4 in order to calculate their withholding of income taxes. (see form 84, p.231.)

Most states have their own registration and reporting requirements. You should contact your state department of revenue for forms and applications.

EMPLOYMENT
AGREEMENT

Whenever you hire an employee for household help you should have a written agreement with them. This is useful for spelling out their rights and responsibilities and protecting you from misunderstandings and liability. (see form 85, p.233.) This is a basic form, but you can add additional terms under paragraph 15, such as additional duties or benefits that were promised.

INDEPENDENT CONTRACTORS

Independent contractor is a legal term for a person who works for you but is not your employee. You pay them to do a job, but they are an independent business that takes care of it's own taxes and insurance.

You can't just avoid all employment laws by calling your workers independent contractors. There are rules and regulations detailing when a person can and cannot be an independent contractor. The most important rule is that a person cannot be an independent contractor if you control how and when they do their work. If you just hire them to do a job, and let them do it in their way at their time, then they can be considered independent contractors. But if you supervise, give them the tools to use, and tell them when to show up, most likely you will have to treat them as employees.

There is a list of factors to be considered. A "yes" answer to all or most of the following questions will likely mean that the person hired is an independent contractor rather than an employee. For more certainty, use IRS Form SS-8 (see form 86, p.235):

1. Does the person hired exercise independent control over the details of the work, such as the methods used to complete the job?

2. Is the person hired in a business different from that of the person hiring? (For example, a plumber is hired by a lawyer.)

3. Does the person hired work as a specialist without supervision by the person hiring?

4. Does the person hired supply his or her own tools?

5. Is the person hired for only a short period of time rather than consistently over a relatively long period?

6. Does the job require a relatively high degree of skill?

7. Is the person paid "by the job" rather than "by the hour"?

CONTRACTOR AGREEMENT

Contracts with independent contractors don't have to be in writing, but it's often even more important that they are writing than having an employment agreement in writing. For one thing, the writing is an opportunity to state clearly that you intend it to be an independent contractor arrangement. Also, since by definition you have relatively little control over the way an independent contractor does the work, the writing may be your last chance to influence important matters, like exactly what the job is and when it must be completed. It's often tempting to use the word "employer" in these contracts, however, it is not appropriate since the independent contractor is not "employed" (and you don't want the IRS thinking otherwise).

An independent contractor agreement is included in the appendix. (see form 87, p.239.) A sample of how to complete the form follows.

Sample of Form 87. Independent Contractor Agreement—

INDEPENDENT CONTRACTOR AGREEMENT

This agreement is entered into by and between
Jon Dough
(the "Company") and ___ Bill Morton ___
_____ (the "Contractor"). It is agreed by the parties as follows:

1. The Contractor shall supply all of the labor and materials to perform the following work for the Company as an independent contractor:

Painting all exterior painted surfaces of home at 123 Elm Street, Anytown, U.S.A. with Everlast Exterior paint, white for walls, and Beige 304 for trim.

❏ The attached plans and specifications are to be followed and are hereby made a part of this Agreement.

2. The Contractor agrees to the following completion dates for portions of the work and final completion of the work:

<u>Description of Work</u>   <u>Completion Date</u>

Complete entire job by June 25, 2002.

3. The Contractor shall perform the work in a workman-like manner, according to standard industry practices, unless other standards or requirements are set forth in any attached plans and specifications.

CHANGES TO CONTRACT

Occasionally it becomes necessary to change the terms of your agreement with an independent contractor, or to terminate it altogether. For example, for the sample contract, if it rained the whole two weeks in which the party was to paint your house, it would have been impossible to complete the job. Therefore you would probably want to modify the contract to change the completion date. (see form 88, p.241.) Or, if the independent contractor broke his leg before completion, you would want to terminate the agreement unless he could get someone to complete it for him. (see form 89, p.242.)

Miscellaneous Forms 8

This chapter explains several useful forms that do not fit into the categories of the previous chapters, or can be used in matters covered by several chapters.

Affidavit

An *affidavit* is a form in which a person swears something is true or that certain facts occurred. There are limitations on how an affidavit can be used. Because a person in court has a right to confront witnesses, an affidavit cannot be used in court in place of a live witness. However, it can be used outside of court in negotiations. For example, if you get three people to sign an affidavit that your neighbor was constantly teasing your dog, this may convince your neighbor's attorney not to file a dog bite case against you. An affidavit form is included in the appendix and a sample is shown below. (see form 90, p.243.)

Sample of form 90. Affidavit—

AFFIDAVIT

The undersigned, being first duly sworn, deposes and says:

```
I live at 125 Elm Street, Anytown, Iowa across the
street from Jon Dough and I have observed on many
occasions Billy Williams throwing rocks at and
taunting Jon Dough's dog Fifi.I have never seen
Fifi attack Billy Williams without provocation.
```

```
    This    affidavit    was    executed    by    me    on
May 1, 2001
_____.
```

[Notary omitted to save space.]

DISPUTE RESOLUTION

Going to court is expensive, slow, and chancy. In recent years, various means of *alternative dispute resolution* have become popular. Used correctly, the alternative dispute resolution procedures of *arbitration* and *mediation* can be much more efficient than litigation at settling disputes between parties who cannot come to an agreement on their own. These days there are trained arbitrators, mediators, and arbitration and mediation organizations in most areas. You can locate them through your lawyer or by calling your local or state bar association.

ARBITRATION

An *arbitrator* is a person who, like an umpire or judge, has the power to decide. The disputants, either by themselves or with the assistance of lawyers, present their arguments to the arbitrator, agreeing in advance to abide by his or her decision. It is a kind of private court system in which the parties get to choose the judge and make their own rules about procedure and evidence.

The samples below are clauses to be inserted in a contract by which the parties agree that any disputes to arise will be arbitrated. The first provides for arbitration under the rules of an organization that provides arbitration services. There are many such organizations, the most prominent one being the American Arbitration Association providing such services around the country. The second sample provides for arbitrators to be appointed by the parties without being overseen by such an organization.

Sample of a Contract Clause. Arbitration of disputes; organization rules—

> The parties agree that any controversy, claim
> or dispute arising out of or related to this
> agreement or any breach of this agreement
> shall be submitted to arbitration by and
> according to the applicable rules of the
> American Arbitration Association and that
> judgment upon an award rendered by the arbi-
> trator may be entered in any court having

Sample of a Contract Clause. Arbitration of disputes (arbitrator selected by parties)—

> The parties agree that any controversy, claim
> or dispute arising out of or related to this
> agreement or any breach of this agreement
> shall be submitted to arbitration. Such arbi-
> tration shall take place in ___Denver,
> Colorado___ or at such other place as may be
> agreed upon by the parties. The parties shall
> attempt to agree on one arbitrator. If they
> are unable to so agree, then each party shall
> appoint one arbitrator and those appointed
> shall appoint a third arbitrator. The
> expenses of arbitration shall be divided
> equally by the parties. The prevailing party
> shall be entitled to reasonable attorneys'
> fees. The arbitrators shall conclusively
> decide all issues of law and fact related to
> the arbitrated dispute. Judgment upon an
> award rendered by the arbitrator may be

After a dispute has arisen, there is an agreement to submit to arbitration. (see form 94, p.247.)

Sample of form 94. Arbitration Agreement—

ARBITRATION AGREEMENT

This Arbitration Agreement is made this ___12th___ day of
__October_____, ___2001_____, by and between
__Western Distributors, Inc.,_____
and _____Mountain Packaging_____,
who agree as follows:

1. The parties agree that any controversy, claim or dispute arising out of or related to:
   the contract executed by and between the parties
   on March 3, 2001.
shall be submitted to arbitration. Such arbitration shall take place at
_____7635 Red Rocks Hwy.,
__Denver, CO_____ or at such other place as may be agreed upon by the parties.

2. The parties shall attempt to agree on one arbitrator. If they are unable to so agree, then each party shall appoint one arbitrator and those appointed shall appoint a third arbitrator.

3. The expenses of arbitration shall be divided equally by the parties.

4. The arbitrators shall conclusively decide all issues of law and fact related to the arbitrated dispute. Judgment upon an award rendered by the arbitrator may be entered in any court having jurisdiction.

5. The prevailing party ☒ shall ☐ shall not be entitled to reasonable attorneys' fees.

MEDIATION

A *mediator* has no power to decide disputes. A mediator is a neutral party who acts as a "go between" to help the parties reach their own compromises and agreements. You might think that a mediator would be useless. If the parties can't agree by themselves, why would they suddenly be able to do so with the help of a mediator who has no power to make decisions? Nevertheless, it frequently works. And it has an advantage over both litigation and arbitration. In court or arbitration, you put the results in the hands of outsiders. The judge or arbitrator gets to fill in the terms any way he or she wants. In mediation, the only people who can decide are the parties themselves. They keep complete control over the process. (see form 95, p. 248.)

The sample below presumes that the parties can agree on a mediator, which is usually easy to do since the mediator has no decision making power. Besides, if you can't even agree on a mediator, mediation probably won't be successful.

Sample of form 95. Mediation Agreement—

MEDIATION AGREEMENT

The undersigned parties are engaged in a dispute regarding <u>the contract between the parties dated February 12, 2001</u>. We hereby agree to submit such dispute to mediation by <u>Neighborhood Mediation Services</u> and that all matters resolved in mediation shall be reduced to a binding written agreement signed by the parties. The costs of mediation shall be borne equally by the parties.

Dated: <u>August 8, 2001</u>.

COVENANT NOT TO SUE

There is a difference between (a) agreeing that one person has no further claim of liability against another and (b) promising that, although there may be a claim, the person will not bring a law suit based on it. The former is a release, and the latter is a covenant not to sue. Once a claim has been released, it no longer exists and (unless there has been fraud involved) can't be revived. But if you promise not to sue on a claim, the claim doesn't go away. You have just promised not to try to enforce it. If the promise not to sue goes away, the claim is still there, ready to be enforced.

If a claimant receives cash in an agreed settlement of the claim, it is appropriate to give a release. There will never be any need to enforce a debt that has been fully paid. If you only have a promise to pay something in the future, such as a promissory note, then maybe a "covenant not to sue" is appropriate. The claimant promises not to bring a law suit on the claim as long as the note is not in default. (see form 96, p.249.)

Sample of form 96. Covenant Not to Sue—

COVENANT NOT TO SUE

This agreement is made by and between _____ Jon Dough _____ (the "Covenantor"), for [itself/himself/herself] and for its heirs, legal representatives and assigns, and _____ Mary Smith _____ (the "Covenantee").

1. In exchange for the Covenantor's covenant herein, the Covenantee _promises and agrees to pay all of the Covenantor's medical bills and $50 per day for lost wages arising out of injuries Covenantor received on July 4, 1998 at the Covenantee's premises_ .

2. In exchange for the consideration stated in paragraph 1 above, the receipt and sufficiency of which is hereby acknowledged by the Covenantor, the Covenantor covenants with the Covenantee never to institute any suit or action at law or in equity against the Covenantee by reason of any claim the Covenantor now has or may hereafter acquire related to: _injuries Covenantor received on July 4, 1998 at the Covenantee's premises_ .

DISCHARGING LIABILITY AFTER IT ARISES

A *liability* is a debt owed. Like other debts, liabilities of tort (personal injury) or contract can be discharged in various ways, including the payment of money or promise to pay money. The first sample below is a release from all liabilities that the person released may owe to the signer. (see form 91, p.244.) The second sample below is limited to matters related to a specific event or contract. (see form 92, p.245.) In the third sample below, the parties release each other from liabilities. (see form 93, p.246.)

Sample of form 91. General Release of Liability—

GENERAL RELEASE

In exchange for the sum of $10.00 and other valuable consideration, the receipt and sufficiency of which is hereby acknowledged, the undersigned hereby forever releases, discharges and acquits Jon Dough_____, and [its/his/her] successors, assigns, heirs and personal representatives, from any and all claims, actions, suits, agreements or liabilities in favor of or owed to the undersigned, existing at any time up to the date of this release.

IN WITNESS WHEREOF, the undersigned has executed this release under seal on May 8, 2002.

Sample of form 92. Specific Release of Liability—

SPECIFIC RELEASE

In exchange for the sum of $10.00 and other valuable consideration, the receipt and sufficiency of which is hereby acknowledged, the undersigned hereby forever releases, discharges and acquits   Scrupulous Corporation , and [its/his/her] successors, assigns, heirs and personal representatives, from any and all claims, actions, suits, agreements or liabilities arising out of or related to:

any and all injuries and damages sustained by the undersigned, pursuant to the undersigned slipping and falling at the premises of Scrupulous Corporation on July 4, 1998.

IN WITNESS WHEREOF, the undersigned has executed this release under seal on August 28, 2003.

Sample of form 93. Mutual Release of Liability—

MUTUAL RELEASE

In exchange for the sum of $10.00 and other valuable consideration, the receipt and sufficiency of which is hereby acknowledged, the undersigned hereby forever release, discharge and acquit each other, and their successors, assigns, heirs and personal representatives, from any and all claims, actions, suits, agreements or liabilities arising out of or related to: the contract executed by and between the parties on March 3, 1998.

IN WITNESS WHEREOF, the undersigned have executed this release under seal and by authority of their respective boards of directors as of October 27, 2001.

FREEDOM OF INFORMATION ACT REQUEST

The laws of the federal government and most states give you a right to obtain information held by government agencies. While a few matters are exempt for purposes of national security, most other information is available. To obtain information, you must usually make a written request. In some cases there is a small fee for copies of the information. This should not exceed the actual cost of producing these forms.

A form in the appendix can be used to request information under the federal Freedom of Information Act. (see form 97, p.250.) For obtaining state information you can adapt the form using the law for your state listed below.

State Freedom of Information/Open Records Laws

Alabama	Open Records Statute	Ala. Code § 36-12-40
Alaska	Public Records Act	Alaska Stat. §§09.25.120, -.220
Arizona	Public Records Law	Ariz. Rev, Stat. § 39-121
Arkansas	Ark. Freedom of Infrmtn Act	Ark. Code Ann. § 25-19-103
California	Public Records Act	Cal. Gov't Code § 6252
Colorado	Open Records Act	Colo. Rev. Stat. § 24-72-202(6)

Connecticut	Freedom of Information Act	Conn. Gen. Stat. § 1-18a(d)
Delaware	Freedom of Information Act	Del. Code Ann. tit. 29, § 10002(d)
D. C.	Freedom of Information Act	D.C. Dode Ann. §§ 1-1502, 1-1529
Florida	Florida Constitution	Fl. Const. of 1885, art. I, § 24
	Sunshine Law	Fla. Stat. ch. 119.011(1)
Georgia	Open Records Act	Ga. Code Ann. § 50-18-70(a)
Hawaii	Uniform Info. Practices Act	Haw. Rev. Stat. § 92F-3
Idaho	Open Records Act	Idaho Code § 9-337
Illinois	Freedom of Information Act	Ill. Ann. Stat. ch.5, para. 140/2(c)-(d)
Indiana	Access to Public Records Act	Ind. Code § 5-14-3-2
Iowa	open records act	Iowa Code 22.1
Kansas	Open Records Act	Kan. Stat.Ann. § 45-217(f)(1)
Kentucky	Open Records Act	Ky.Rev.Stat.Ann. § 61.870(2)
Louisiana	Public Records Act	La. Rev. Stat. Ann.§ 44:1
Maine	Freedom of Access Act	Me.Rev.Stat.Ann.tit. 1, § 402(3)
Maryland	Public Information Act	Md.Code Ann., State Gov't § 10-611
Massachusetts	Public Records Law	Mass.Gen. Laws Ann. ch.4, § 7, cl. 26
		Mass.Admin.Code tit. 950, § 32.03
Michigan	Freedom of Information Act	Mich.Comp.Laws Ann. § 15.232(2)(e)
Minnesota	Gov't Data Practices Act	Minn.Stat. § 13.01, Subd. 7
Mississippi	Public Records Act	Miss.Code Ann. § 25-61-3(b)
Missouri	Sunshine Law	Mo.Rev.Stat. § 610.010(6)
Montana	Public Records Act	Mont. Code Ann. § 2-6-110(1)
Nebraska	open records Law	Neb.Rev.Stat. § 84-712.01(1)
Nevada	Open Records Law	Nev. Rev .Stat. § 239.010
New Hampshire	Right to Know Law	N.H. Rev.Stat.Ann. § 91-A:4, para. V
New Jersey	Right to Know Law	N.J. Stat.Ann. § 47:1A-2
New Mexico	Public Records Act	N.M. Stat. Ann. § 14-2-6
New York	Freedom of Information Law	N.Y.Pub.Off.Law § 86(4)
North Carolina	Public Records Law	N.C. Gen. Stat. § 132-1
North Dakota	Open Records Statute	N.D. Cent. Code § 44-04-18

Ohio	State laws	Ohio Rev. Code § 149.011(G)
Oklahoma	Open Records Act	Okla. Stat. tit. 51, § 24A.3(1)
Oregon	Public Records Law	Ore. Rev. Stat. § 192.410
Pennsylvania	Open Records Law	Pa. Cons. Stat. Ann. tit. 65,§ 66.1(2)
Rhode Island	Access to Public Records Act	R.I. Gen. Laws § 38-2-2(d)
South Carolina	Freedom of Information Act	S.C. Code Ann. § 30-4-20(c)
South Dakota	open records statute	S.D. Codified Laws Ann. § 1-27-1
Tennessee	Public Records Act	Tenn. Code Ann. § 10-7-503(a)
Texas	Open Records Act	Tex. Gov't Code Ann. § 552.002
Utah	Gov't Records Access and Management Act	Utah Code Ann. § 63-2-103(18)(a)
Vermont	Access to Public Records Law	Vt.Stat.Ann.tit.1, § 317(b)
Virginia	Freedom of Information Act	Va. Code Ann. § 2.1-341
Washington	public records law	Wash.Rev. Code § 40.14.010
West Virginia	Freedom of Information Act	W.Va. Code § 29B-1-2
Wisconsin	open records statute	Wis.Stat. § 19.32(2)
Wyoming	Public Records Act	Wyo. Stat. § 16-4-201ß

GLOSSARY

A

acceptance   an agreement to the terms of an offer.

account stated   the legal theory that if you do not deny owing a debt, you can be held legally responsible for it.

acknowledgement   refers to a signer's statement that he or she truly is that person, intends to sign the document, and that (in the case of a corporate officer) he or she holds the corporate office claimed.

addendum   a document adding terms to a contract, usually which would be too lengthy to include in the contract itself.

administrator   a person appointed by a court, or named in a will, to manage a person's state (if female, sometimes called administratrix).

affidavit   a document in which a person swears to some statements under oath.

amendment   an agreement to change the terms of a contract.

amortization   dividing the payments on a loan equally over a set period of time.

anatomical gifts   the donation of one's organs for medical or scientific purposes after one's death.

ante-nuptial agreement (see *pre-marital agreement*.)

arbitration a proceeding in which parties ask an arbitrator to settle their dispute.

assignment the transfer of rights in a contract to another party.

assumption of risk an agreement that a person will take responsibility for his or her own safety and will not hold another liable.

attorney in fact a person holding a power of attorney to act for someone.

B

beneficiary a person who is left property in a will.

bequeath to leave someone personal property in a will.

bequest a gift of personal property in a will.

bill of sale a document which transfers ownership of personal property.

"boiler plate" language added to a contract to cover any possible legal contingency when one act is predicated upon the happening of another act.

breach failing to comply with the terms of a contract.

buyer's broker a real estate broker who represents the buyer.

C

chattel mortgage a lien on personal property.

codicil an amendment to a will.

cohabitation living with someone in a familial arrangement.

consideration something of value which is exchanged between parties.

consolidation the process of combining debt loans from different lenders under one lender.

contract an agreement between two or more parties.

covenant not to sue an agreement between parties not to sue each other in the event a dispute arises or has arisen.

credit report a document used to determine whether or not you are given credit by itemizing your bill paying, and potential for debt history.

D

decedent a person who has died.

deed a document which transfers ownership of real property.

deed of trust a document describing real estate, the promissory note it secures, and numerous provisions relating to what happens if the promissory note goes into default.

default failure to pay a lender on time and in the proper amount.

descendant a child, grandchild, great-grandchild, etc.

devise a gift of real property in a will; also to leave real property in a will.

divorce settlement agreement following a divorce, an agreement regarding who will get the joint property and who will be responsible for the joint debts.

duplicate original a replica of the original document that, when signed, holds the signor liable for that document *in addition* to holding the signor liable for the original, signed document.

E

elective share the amount of property a spouse can claim even if nothing was left to them in the will.

executor   (see ***administrator***.)

exempt property   with regard to creditors, it is money and/or property that a creditor cannot take from the debtor.

F

family allowance   an amount allowed by law to the spouse and children of a decedent.

forbearance   agreeing not to enforce the terms of a contract (usually a monetary contract such as a promissory note.)

forced share   (see ***elective share***.)

G

grantor   the person giving someone a power of attorney, or any rights and property under the law.

H

heir   a person who inherits property from a person without a will.

homestead   in some states, the residence of a person who is married or has minor children.

I

independent contractor   a person who works for another not as an employee but as a business paid to do a job.

interested parties   people who have a stake in the outcome of an event.

intestate/intestacy   the state of dying without a valid will.

intestate share the amount of property an heir receives from the estate of a person who died without a will.

J

joint tenancy/joint tenancy with right of survivorship ownership of property in which, upon death, an owner's share goes to the other joint owner.

L

lease a contract to rent living space or property for a certain period of time.

legacy (see *bequest*.)

liability a debt or responsibility owed.

lien a claim against a piece of property which has priority over future claims.

LLP (limited liability partnership) a structure for a business in which none of the parties is liable for the debts of the business.

living trust trust agreement which one sets up while alive so that one's property passes at death without probate.

living will document in which the signer states that he or she does not want extraordinary measures taken to prolong life if he or she becomes terminally ill, or after certain life functions have ceased.

M

marital agreements agreements signed by couples who are already married, sometimes as an alternative to a divorce, to spell out each other's legal marital obligations.

mediation proceeding in which parties ask a mediator to help them come to a settlement of their dispute.

mortgage a document that describes the real estate, the promissory note it secures, and numerous provisions relating to what happens if the promissory note goes into default.

N

negotiable freely transferable.

notarized when a document is signed before a notary public and authenticated with the signature and seal of the notary.

notary an officer who administers oaths and verifies identification of a person signing a document.

O

offer to present a proposal for acceptance or rejection.

option a right to do something at a future time under certain conditions.

P

partial performance doing part of what is required under a contract.

partnership a group of sole proprietors in business together, where each member of the group acts as the agent of all the others.

performance doing what is required under a contract.

personal representative (see *administrator*.)

POD (pay on death) Usually used on bank accounts, and in some states on securities. (also P/O/D)

power of attorney document which gives another person the right to take legal action on one's behalf.

premarital agreement   an agreement which can spell out the legal rights of the parties during and after a marriage.

probate   the court procedure of gathering a decedent's assets and distributing them to the heirs or beneficiaries according to a valid will.

promissory note   document promising to pay a sum of money.

Q

quit claim deed   document which gives any interest the seller has in property to a buyer without guaranteeing that interest.

R

receipt   a written confirmation that you have received something, usually cash.

release   freeing someone from a legal duty or obligation.

remainder   the balance of an estate after all specific gifts have been distributed.

rescission   when a contract is undone and the parties returned to their former positions.

residue   (see *remainder*.)

S

security   property which is given as collateral for money owed.

seal   part of the signature necessary in some states to make certain types of documents, such as deeds, valid.

self-proving statement   document added to a will where the testator and witnesses signatures are notarized so that the will can be admitted to probate without delay.

separation agreement   a document signed by parties who are married but wish to live apart, spelling out their legal rights and obligations.

specific bequest   the gift of a specific item of personal property to a specific person in a will.

specific devise   the gift of a specific parcel of real property to a specific person in a will.

statute of frauds   law which requires certain agreements to be in writing.

sublease   contract for living space where the first tenant leases to and collects rent from the second tenant. (the first tenant is still liable to the landlord for rent and condition of living space.)

survivorship account   account set up so that upon the death of one owner the title immediately transfers to the surviving owner(s).

T

tenancy by the entireties   in some states, the ownership of property by a husband and wife as one entity. When one dies the other still owns the entire property.

tenancy in common   ownership of property in which, upon death, each owner's share goes to his or her heirs or beneficiaries.

terminate/termination   the ending of a contract.

testate   to be with a valid will, as in "a testate estate."

testator   a person who dies with a valid will.

title transfer   changing the ownership of property which is evidenced by a document called a title.

TOD   transfer on death. Usually used on bank accounts and in some states on securities. (also T/O/D)

tort   a wrongful act.

Totten Trust 1) a method of setting up the ownership of property so that upon death it passes to another person automatically. 2) property which is owned "in trust for" another person, but which can be changed at any time before death.

trust an agreement in which one person holds property for the benefit of another person.

U

usury an interest rate that is higher than allowed by law.

W

waiver the giving up of some legal right.

warranty deed a document which gives an interest in property and includes a guarantee that the seller actually owns the property he is selling.

will a document in which a person divides his or her property upon death and makes other arrangements such as for a guardian for children.

APPENDIX
FORMS

The forms in this appendix are blank forms for you to use. However, it is suggested that you photocopy the blank forms before use, in case you make a mistake. These forms can also be modified by retyping them to fit your specific needs. However, this should not be done unless you are sure of what you are doing. In some states some changes could make the forms invalid. Consult an attorney or detailed legal reference if you are unsure. The forms in the appendix are in order by chapter.

Lines are provided for signatures. There may be more lines than you need on the forms. If so, just ignore the extra lines.

The requirements for notary public acknowledgments varies from state to state. Some states just require a simple statement that the person signed before the notary, some require the notary to see some form of identification and to keep a record, and others require the document itself to state what form of identification was produced. For the forms in this book, a more detailed format was used. It may exceed what is required in your state, or something may need to be changed or added. The notary in your state should know the requirements, and can modify the form if necessary to comply with legal requirements.

TABLE OF FORMS

CONTRACT

THIS AGREEMENT is entered into by and between _____ and _____. In consideration of the mutual promises made in this agreement and other valuable consideration, the receipt and sufficiency of which is acknowledged, the parties agree as follows:

The following addenda, dated the same date as this agreement, are incorporated in, and made a part of, this agreement:

❏ None.

This agreement shall be governed by the laws of _____.

If any part of this agreement is adjudged invalid, illegal, or unenforceable, the remaining parts shall not be affected and shall remain in full force and effect.

This agreement shall be binding upon the parties, and upon their heirs, executors, personal representatives, administrators, and assigns. No person shall have a right or cause of action arising out of or resulting from this agreement except those who are parties to it and their successors in interest.

This instrument, including any attached exhibits and addenda, constitutes the entire agreement of the parties. No representations or promises have been made except those that are set out in this agreement. This agreement may not be modified except in writing signed by all the parties.

IN WITNESS WHEREOF the parties have signed this agreement under seal on _____, 20____.

_____   _____

_____   _____

ADDENDUM TO CONTRACT

Addendum No. _____

    The following terms are a part of the Contract, dated _____, 20____, by and between _____ and _____ :

_____   _____

_____   _____

AMENDMENT TO CONTRACT

For valuable consideration, the receipt and sufficiency of which is acknowledged by each of the parties, this agreement amends a Contract dated _____, 20_____, between _____ and _____, relating to _____.
This contract amendment is hereby incorporated into the Contract.

Except as changed by this amendment, the Contract shall continue in effect according to its terms. The amendments herein shall be effective on the date this document is executed by all parties.

IN WITNESS WHEREOF the parties have signed this agreement under seal on _____, 20_____.

_____   _____

_____   _____

form 4

ASSIGNMENT OF CONTRACT

FOR VALUE RECEIVED the undersigned (the "Assignor") hereby assigns, transfers, and conveys to _____ (the "Assignee") all the Assignor's rights, title and interests in and to a contract (the "Contract") dated _____, 20____, between _____ and _____.

The Assignor hereby warrants and represents that the Contract is in full force and effect and is fully assignable.

The Assignee hereby assumes the duties and obligations of the Assignor under the Contract and agrees to hold the Assignor harmless from any claim or demand thereunder.

The date of this assignment is _____, 20_____.

IN WITNESS WHEREOF the parties have signed this agreement under seal on _____, 20____.

Assignor: Assignee:

_____   _____

_____   _____

TERMINATION OF CONTRACT

For valuable consideration, the receipt and sufficiency of which is acknowledged by each of the parties to that certain Contract dated _____, 20____, between
_____ and
_____ , relating to
_____

hereby agree that said contract shall be terminated by mutual agreement and that each party releases the other from any and all claims thereunder.

IN WITNESS WHEREOF the parties have signed this termination of contract under seal on _____, 20____.

_____   _____

_____   _____

COHABITATION AGREEMENT

This agreement is entered into on _____, 20____ by and between _____ and _____, as follows:

1. PURPOSE. The parties to this agreement wish to live together in an unmarried state. The parties intend to provide in this agreement for their property and other rights that may arise because of their living together. Both parties currently own assets, and anticipate acquiring additional assets, which they wish to continue to control and they are entering into this agreement to determine their respective rights and duties while living together.

2. DISCLOSURE. The parties have fully revealed to each other full financial information regarding their net worth, assets, holdings, income, and liabilities; not only by their discussions with each other, but also through copies of their current financial statements, copies of which are attached hereto as Exhibits A and B. Both parties acknowledge that they have had sufficient time to review the other's financial statement, are familiar with and understand the other's financial statement, have had any questions satisfactorily answered, and are satisfied that full and complete financial disclosure has been made by the other.

3. LEGAL ADVICE. Each party has had legal and financial advice, or has the opportunity to consult independent legal and financial counsel, prior to executing this agreement. Either party's failure to so consult legal and financial counsel constitutes a waiver of such right. By signing this agreement, each party acknowledges that he or she understands the facts of this agreement, and is aware of his or her legal rights and obligations under this agreement or arising because of their living together in an unmarried state.

4. CONSIDERATION. The parties acknowledge that each of them would not continue living together in an unmarried state except for the execution of this agreement in its present form.

5. EFFECTIVE DATE. This Agreement shall become effective and binding as of _____, 20____ , and shall continue until they no longer live together or until the death of either party.

6. DEFINITIONS. As used in this agreement, the following terms shall have the following meanings:

(a) "Joint Property" means property held and owned by the parties together. Such ownership shall be as tenants by the entirety in jurisdictions where such a tenancy is permitted. If such jurisdiction does not recognize or permit a tenancy by the entirety, then ownership shall be as joint tenants with rights of survivorship. The intention of the parties is to hold joint property as tenants by the entirety whenever possible.

(b) "Joint Tenancy" means tenancy by the entirety in jurisdictions where such a tenancy is permitted, and joint tenancy with rights of survivorship if tenancy by the entirety is not recognized or permitted. The intention of the parties is to hold joint property as tenants by the entirety whenever possible.

7. SEPARATE PROPERTY. _____ is the owner of certain property, which is listed in Exhibit A attached hereto and made a part hereof, which he intends to keep as his nonmarital, separate, sole, and individual property. All income, rents, profits, interest, dividends, stock splits, gains, and appreciation in value, relating to any such separate property shall also be deemed separate property.

_____ is the owner of certain property, which is listed in Exhibit B attached hereto and made a part hereof, which she intends to keep as her nonmarital, separate, sole, and individual property. All income, rents, profits, interest, dividends, stock splits, gains, and appreciation in value, relating to any such separate property shall also be deemed separate property.

8. JOINT PROPERTY. The parties intend that certain property shall, from the effective date of this agreement, be joint property with full rights of survivorship, which property is listed and described in Exhibit C attached hereto and made a part hereof.

9. PROPERTY ACQUIRED WHILE LIVING TOGETHER. The parties recognize that either or both of them may acquire property during the time they are living together. The parties agree that the the the ownership of such property shall be determined by the source of the funds used to acquire it. If joint funds are used, it shall be jointly owned property with full rights of survivorship. If separate funds are used, it shall be separately owned property unless it is added to Exhibit C by the purchaser.

10. BANK ACCOUNTS. Any funds deposited in either party's separate bank accounts shall be deemed that party's separate property. Any funds deposited in a bank account held by the parties jointly shall be deemed joint property.

11. PAYMENT OF EXPENSES. The parties agree that their expenses shall be paid as follows:

_____
_____
_____
_____

12. DISPOSITION OF PROPERTY. Each party retains the management and control of the property belonging to that party and may encumber, sell, or dispose of the property without the consent of the other party. Each party shall execute any instrument necessary to effectuate this paragraph on the request of the other party. If a party does not join in or execute an instrument required by this paragraph, the other party may sue for specific performance or for damages and the defaulting party shall be responsible for the other party's costs, expenses and attorney's fees. This paragraph shall not require a party to execute a promissory note or other evidence of debt for the other party. If a party executes a promissory note or other evidence of debt for the other party, that other party shall indemnify the party executing the note or other evidence of debt from any claims or demands arising from the execution of the instrument. Execution of an instrument shall not give the executing party any right or interest in the property or the party requesting execution.

13. PROPERTY DIVISION UPON SEPARATION. In the event of separation of the parties, they agree that the terms and provisions of this agreement shall govern all of their rights as to property, property settlement, rights of community property, and equitable distribution against the other. Each

party releases and waives any claims for special equity in the other party's separate property or in jointly owned property.

14. EFFECT OF SEPARATION OR DEATH. Each of the parties waives the right to be supported by the other after their separation or after the death of either party.

15. DEBTS. Neither party shall assume or become responsible for the payment of any pre-existing debts or obligations of the other party because of the marriage. Neither party shall do anything that would cause the debt or obligation of one of them to be a claim, demand, lien, or encumbrance against the property of the other party without the other party's written consent. If a debt or obligation of one party is asserted as a claim or demand against the property of the other without such written consent, the party who is responsible for the debt or obligation shall indemnify the other from the claim or demand, including the indemnified party's costs, expenses, and attorneys' fees.

16. FREE AND VOLUNTARY ACT. The parties acknowledge that executing this agreement is a free and voluntary act, and has not been entered into for any reason other than the desire for the furtherance of their relationship in living together. Each party acknowledges that he or she has had adequate time to fully consider the consequences of signing this agreement, and has not been pressured, threatened, coerced, or unduly influenced to sign this agreement.

17. SEVERABILITY. If any part of this agreement is adjudged invalid, illegal, or unenforceable, the remaining parts shall not be affected and shall remain in full force and effect.

18. FURTHER ASSURANCE. Each party shall execute any instruments or documents at any time requested by the other party that are necessary or proper to effectuate this agreement.

19. BINDING EFFECT. This agreement shall be binding upon the parties, and upon their heirs, executors, personal representatives, administrators, successors and assigns.

20. NO OTHER BENEFICIARY. No person shall have a right or cause of action arising out of or resulting from this agreement except those who are parties to it and their successors in interest.

21. RELEASE. Except as otherwise provided in this agreement, each party releases all claims or demands to the property or estate of the other, however and whenever acquired, including acquisitions in the future.

22. ENTIRE AGREEMENT. This instrument, including any attached exhibits, constitutes the entire agreement of the parties. No representations or promises have been made except those that are set out in this agreement. This agreement may not be modified or terminated except in writing signed by the parties.

23. PARAGRAPH HEADINGS. The headings of the paragraphs contained in this agreement are for convenience only, and are not to be considered a part of this agreement or used in determining its content or context.

24. ATTORNEYS' FEES IN ENFORCEMENT. A party who fails to comply with any provision or obligation contained in this agreement shall pay the other party's attorneys' fees, costs, and other expenses reasonably incurred in enforcing this agreement and resulting from the noncompliance.

25. SIGNATURES AND INITIALS OF PARTIES. The signatures of the parties on this document, and their initials on each page, indicate that each party has read, and agrees with, this entire Premarital Agreement, including any and all exhibits attached hereto.

26. __ OTHER PROVISIONS. Additional provisions are contained in the Addendum to Premarital Agreement attached hereto and made a part hereof.

_____   _____
(Signature of male)   (Signature of female)

STATE OF   )
COUNTY OF   )

    The foregoing Agreement, consisting of _____ pages and Exhibits _____ through _____, was acknowledged before me this _____ day of _____, 20____, by _____, who are personally known to me or who have produced _____ _____ as identification.

_____
Signature

_____
(Typed Name of Acknowledger)
NOTARY PUBLIC
Commission Number:_____
My Commission Expires:

PREMARITAL AGREEMENT

This Agreement is entered into on _____, 20____, by and between _____ (hereafter referred to as the Husband), and _____ (hereafter referred to as the Wife), who agree that:

1. MARRIAGE. The parties plan to marry each other, and intend to provide in this agreement for their property and other rights that may arise because of their contemplated marriage.

2. PURPOSE OF AGREEMENT. Both parties currently own assets, and anticipate acquiring additional assets, which they wish to continue to control and they are executing this Agreement to fix and determine their respective rights and duties during the marriage, in the event of a divorce or dissolution of the marriage, or on the death of one of the parties.

3. FINANCIAL DISCLOSURE. The parties have fully revealed to each other full financial information regarding their net worth, assets, holdings, income, and liabilities; not only by their discussions with each other, but also through copies of their current financial statements, copies of which are attached hereto as Exhibits A and Exhibit B. Both parties acknowledge that they have had sufficient time to review the other's financial statement, are familiar with and understand the other's financial statement, have had any questions satisfactorily answered, and are satisfied that full and complete financial disclosure has been made by the other.

4. ADVICE OF COUNSEL. Each party has had legal and financial advice, or has the opportunity to consult independent legal and financial counsel, prior to executing this agreement. Either party's failure to so consult legal and financial counsel constitutes a waiver of such right. By signing this agreement, each party acknowledges that he or she understands the facts of this agreement, and is aware of his or her legal rights and obligations under this agreement or arising because of their contemplated marriage.

5. CONSIDERATION. The parties acknowledge that each of them would not enter into the contemplated marriage except for the execution of this agreement in its present form.

6. EFFECTIVE DATE. This Agreement shall become effective and binding upon the marriage of the parties. In the event the marriage does not take place, this agreement shall be null and void.

7. DEFINITIONS. As used in this agreement, the following terms shall have the following meanings:
    (a) "Joint Property" means property held and owned by the parties together. Such ownership shall be as tenants by the entirety in jurisdictions where such a tenancy is permitted. If such jurisdiction does not recognize or permit a tenancy by the entirety, then ownership shall be as joint tenants with rights of survivorship. The intention of the parties is to hold joint property as tenants by the entirety whenever possible.
    (b) "Joint Tenancy" means tenancy by the entirety in jurisdictions where such a tenancy is permitted, and joint tenancy with rights of survivorship if tenancy by the entirety is not recognized or permitted. The intention of the parties is to hold joint property as tenants by the entirety whenever possible.

8. HUSBAND'S SEPARATE PROPERTY. The Husband is the owner of certain property, which is set forth and described in Exhibit C attached hereto and made a part hereof, which he intends to keep as his nonmarital, separate, sole, and individual property. All income, rents, profits, interest, div-

114

idends, stock splits, gains, and appreciation in value, relating to any such separate property shall also be deemed separate property.

9. WIFE'S SEPARATE PROPERTY. The Wife is the owner of certain property, which is set forth and described in Exhibit D attached hereto and made a part hereof, which she intends to keep as her nonmarital, separate, sole, and individual property. All income, rents, profits, interest, dividends, stock splits, gains, and appreciation in value, relating to any such separate property shall also be deemed separate property.

10. JOINT OR COMMUNITY PROPERTY. The parties intend that certain property shall, from the beginning of the marriage, be marital, joint, or community property, which is set forth and described in Exhibit E attached hereto and made a part hereof.

11. PROPERTY ACQUIRED DURING MARRIAGE. The parties recognize that either or both of them may acquire property during the marriage. The parties agree that the manner in which such property is titled during the marriage shall control such property's ownership and distribution in the event of any divorce, dissolution of marriage, separation, or death of either party. Such property shall be held as provided in the instrument conveying or evidencing title to such property. If the instrument does not specify or if there is no instrument, the property shall be held as a tenancy by the entirety, or as a joint tenancy with rights of survivorship in the event tenancy by the entirety is not recognized by the court having jurisdiction over the distribution of such property. Any property acquired that does not normally have a title or ownership certificate shall be considered as joint property unless otherwise specified by the parties in writing. All wedding gifts shall be deemed joint property, unless specified as separate property in either Exhibit C or D.

12. BANK ACCOUNTS. Any funds deposited in either party's separate bank accounts shall be deemed that party's separate property. Any funds deposited in a bank account held by the parties jointly shall be deemed joint property.

13. PAYMENT OF EXPENSES. The parties agree that their expenses shall be paid as set forth in Exhibit F attached hereto and made a part hereof.

14. DISPOSITION OF PROPERTY. Each party retains the management and control of the property belonging to that party and may encumber, sell, or dispose of the property without the consent of the other party. Each party shall execute any instrument necessary to effectuate this paragraph on the request of the other party. If a party does not join in or execute an instrument required by this paragraph, the other party may sue for specific performance or for damages, regardless of the doctrine of spousal immunity, and the defaulting party shall be responsible for the other party's costs, expenses and attorney's fees. This paragraph shall not require a party to execute a promissory note or other evidence of debt for the other party. If a party executes a promissory note or other evidence of debt for the other party, that other party shall indemnify the party executing the note or other evidence of debt from any claims or demands arising from the execution of the instrument. Execution of an instrument shall not give the executing party any right or interest in the property or the party requesting execution.

15. PROPERTY DIVISION UPON DIVORCE, DISSOLUTION OF MARRIAGE, OR SEPARATION. In the event of divorce, dissolution of marriage, or separation proceedings being filed and pursued by either party, the parties agree that the terms and provisions of this agreement shall govern all of their rights as to property, alimony including permanent periodic, rehabilitative, and lump sum, property settlement, rights of community property, and equitable distribution against the other. Each party releases and waives any claims for special equity in the other party's separate property or in

jointly owned property. If either party files for divorce, dissolution, alimony, or spousal support unconnected with divorce, separation, or separate maintenance, the parties agree that either shall, in the filing of said proceedings, ask the court to follow the provisions and terms of this premarital agreement and be bound by the terms of this agreement.

16. ALIMONY. In the event of divorce or dissolution of marriage proceedings being filed by either party in any state or country, each party forever waives any right to claim or seek any form of alimony or spousal support, attorneys' fees and costs from the other. Any rights concerning distribution of property are otherwise covered by this agreement, and any rights to community property or claims of special equity are waived and released. In the event that a final judgment or decree of divorce or dissolution of marriage is entered for whatever reason, the parties agree that the provisions of this agreement are in complete settlement of all rights to claim or seek any form of financial support, except child support for any living minor children of the parties, from the other.

17. DISPOSITION UPON DEATH. Each party consents that his or her estate, or the estate of the other, may be disposed of by will, codicil, or trust, or in the absence of any such instrument, according to the laws of descent and distribution and intestate succession as if the marriage of the parties had not taken place. In either event, the estate shall be free of any claim or demand of inheritance, dower, curtesy, elective share, family allowance, homestead election, right to serve as executor, administrator, or personal representative, or any spousal or other claim given by law, irrespective of the marriage and any law to the contrary. Neither party intends by this agreement to limit or restrict the right to give to, or receive from, the other an inter vivos or testamentary gift. Neither party intends by this agreement to release, waive, or relinquish any devise or bequest left to either by specific provision in the will or codicil of the other, any property voluntarily transferred by the other, any joint tenancy created by the other, or any right to serve as executor or personal representative of the other's estate if specifically nominated in the other's will or codicil.

18. DEBTS. Neither party shall assume or become responsible for the payment of any pre-existing debts or obligations of the other party because of the marriage. Neither party shall do anything that would cause the debt or obligation of one of them to be a claim, demand, lien, or encumbrance against the property of the other party without the other party's written consent. If a debt or obligation of one party is asserted as a claim or demand against the property of the other without such written consent, the party who is responsible for the debt or obligation shall indemnify the other from the claim or demand, including the indemnified party's costs, expenses, and attorneys' fees.

19. HOMESTEAD. Each party releases any claim, demand, right, or interest that the party may acquire because of the marriage in any real property of the other because of the homestead property provisions of the laws of any state concerning the descent of the property as homestead.

20. FREE AND VOLUNTARY ACT. The parties acknowledge that executing this agreement is a free and voluntary act, and has not been entered into for any reason other than the desire for the furtherance of their relationship in marriage. Each party acknowledges that he or she has had adequate time to fully consider the consequences of signing this agreement, and has not been pressured, threatened, coerced, or unduly influenced to sign this agreement.

21. GOVERNING LAW. This agreement shall be governed by the laws of

_____.

22. SEVERABILITY. If any part of this agreement is adjudged invalid, illegal, or unenforceable, the remaining parts shall not be affected and shall remain in full force and effect.

23. FURTHER ASSURANCE. Each party shall execute any instruments or documents at any time requested by the other party that are necessary or proper to effectuate this agreement.

24. BINDING EFFECT. This agreement shall be binding upon the parties, and upon their heirs, executors, personal representatives, administrators, successors and assigns.

25. NO OTHER BENEFICIARY. No person shall have a right or cause of action arising out of or resulting from this agreement except those who are parties to it and their successors in interest.

26. RELEASE. Except as otherwise provided in this agreement, each party releases all claims or demands to the property or estate of the other, however and whenever acquired, including acquisitions in the future.

27. ENTIRE AGREEMENT. This instrument, including any attached exhibits, constitutes the entire agreement of the parties. No representations or promises have been made except those that are set out in this agreement. This agreement may not be modified or terminated except in writing signed by the parties.

28. PARAGRAPH HEADINGS. The headings of the paragraphs contained in this agreement are for convenience only, and are not to be considered a part of this agreement or used in determining its content or context.

29. ATTORNEYS' FEES IN ENFORCEMENT. A party who fails to comply with any provision or obligation contained in this agreement shall pay the other party's attorneys' fees, costs, and other expenses reasonably incurred in enforcing this agreement and resulting from the noncompliance.

30. SIGNATURES AND INITIALS OF PARTIES. The signatures of the parties on this document, and their initials on each page, indicate that each party has read, and agrees with, this entire Premarital Agreement, including any and all exhibits attached hereto.

31. __ OTHER PROVISIONS. Additional provisions are contained in the Addendum to Premarital Agreement attached hereto and made a part hereof.

_____   _____
Husband   Wife

Executed in the presence of:

_____   _____

Name:_____   Name:_____

Address:_____   Address:_____

_____   _____

STATE OF   )
COUNTY OF   )

MARITAL AGREEMENT

This Agreement is entered into on _____, 20____, by and between _____ (hereafter referred to as the Husband), and _____ (hereafter referred to as the Wife), who agree that:

1. MARRIAGE. The parties were married on _____ .

2. PURPOSE OF AGREEMENT. Both parties currently own assets, and anticipate acquiring additional assets, which they wish to continue to control and they are executing this Agreement to fix and determine their respective rights and duties during the marriage, in the event of a divorce or dissolution of the marriage, or on the death of one of the parties.

3. FINANCIAL DISCLOSURE. The parties have fully revealed to each other full financial information regarding their net worth, assets, holdings, income, and liabilities; not only by their discussions with each other, but also through copies of their current financial statements, copies of which are attached hereto as Exhibits A and Exhibit B. Both parties acknowledge that they have had sufficient time to review the other's financial statement, are familiar with and understand the other's financial statement, have had any questions satisfactorily answered, and are satisfied that full and complete financial disclosure has been made by the other.

4. ADVICE OF COUNSEL. Each party has had legal and financial advice, or has the opportunity to consult independent legal and financial counsel, prior to executing this agreement. Either party's failure to so consult legal and financial counsel constitutes a waiver of such right. By signing this agreement, each party acknowledges that he or she understands the facts of this agreement, and is aware of his or her legal rights and obligations under this agreement or arising because of their contemplated marriage.

5. CONSIDERATION. The parties acknowledge that the mutual promises and covenants of this agreement are the consideration for their acceptance.

6. EFFECTIVE DATE. This Agreement shall become effective and binding upon execution.

7. DEFINITIONS. As used in this agreement, the following terms shall have the following meanings:
　　(a) "Joint Property" means property held and owned by the parties together. Such ownership shall be as tenants by the entirety in jurisdictions where such a tenancy is permitted. If such jurisdiction does not recognize or permit a tenancy by the entirety, then ownership shall be as joint tenants with rights of survivorship. The intention of the parties is to hold joint property as tenants by the entirety whenever possible.
　　(b) "Joint Tenancy" means tenancy by the entirety in jurisdictions where such a tenancy is permitted, and joint tenancy with rights of survivorship if tenancy by the entirety is not recognized or permitted. The intention of the parties is to hold joint property as tenants by the entirety whenever possible.

8. HUSBAND'S SEPARATE PROPERTY. The Husband is the owner of certain property, which is set forth and described in Exhibit A attached hereto and made a part hereof, which he intends to keep as his nonmarital, separate, sole, and individual property. All income, rents, profits, interest, dividends, stock splits, gains, and appreciation in value, relating to any such separate property shall also be deemed separate property.

9. WIFE'S SEPARATE PROPERTY. The Wife is the owner of certain property, which is set forth and described in Exhibit B attached hereto and made a part hereof, which she intends to keep as her nonmarital, separate, sole, and individual property. All income, rents, profits, interest, dividends, stock splits, gains, and appreciation in value, relating to any such separate property shall also be deemed separate property.

10. JOINT OR COMMUNITY PROPERTY. The parties intend that certain property shall, from the beginning of the marriage, be marital, joint, or community property, which is set forth and described in Exhibit C attached hereto and made a part hereof.

11. PROPERTY ACQUIRED DURING MARRIAGE. The parties recognize that either or both of them may acquire property during the marriage. The parties agree that the manner in which such property is titled during the marriage shall control such property's ownership and distribution in the event of any divorce, dissolution of marriage, separation, or death of either party. Such property shall be held as provided in the instrument conveying or evidencing title to such property. If the instrument does not specify or if there is no instrument, the property shall be held as a tenancy by the entirety, or as a joint tenancy with rights of survivorship in the event tenancy by the entirety is not recognized by the court having jurisdiction over the distribution of such property. Any property acquired that does not normally have a title or ownership certificate shall be considered as joint property unless otherwise specified by the parties in writing. All wedding gifts shall be deemed joint property, unless specified as separate property in either Exhibit A or B.

12. BANK ACCOUNTS. Any funds deposited in either party's separate bank accounts shall be deemed that party's separate property. Any funds deposited in a bank account held by the parties jointly shall be deemed joint property.

13. PAYMENT OF EXPENSES. The parties agree that their expenses shall be paid as set forth in Exhibit F attached hereto and made a part hereof.

14. DISPOSITION OF PROPERTY. Each party retains the management and control of the property belonging to that party and may encumber, sell, or dispose of the property without the consent of the other party. Each party shall execute any instrument necessary to effectuate this paragraph on the request of the other party. If a party does not join in or execute an instrument required by this paragraph, the other party may sue for specific performance or for damages, regardless of the doctrine of spousal immunity, and the defaulting party shall be responsible for the other party's costs, expenses and attorney's fees. This paragraph shall not require a party to execute a promissory note or other evidence of debt for the other party. If a party executes a promissory note or other evidence of debt for the other party, that other party shall indemnify the party executing the note or other evidence of debt from any claims or demands arising from the execution of the instrument. Execution of an instrument shall not give the executing party any right or interest in the property or the party requesting execution.

15. PROPERTY DIVISION UPON DIVORCE, DISSOLUTION OF MARRIAGE, OR SEPARATION. In the event of divorce, dissolution of marriage, or separation proceedings being filed and pursued by either party, the parties agree that the terms and provisions of this agreement shall govern all of their rights as to property, alimony including permanent periodic, rehabilitative, and lump sum, property settlement, rights of community property, and equitable distribution against the other. Each party releases and waives any claims for special equity in the other party's separate property or in jointly owned property. If either party files for divorce, dissolution, alimony, or spousal support unconnected with divorce, separation, or separate maintenance, the parties agree that either shall, in

the filing of said proceedings, ask the court to follow the provisions and terms of this premarital agreement and be bound by the terms of this agreement.

16. ALIMONY. In the event of divorce or dissolution of marriage proceedings being filed by either party in any state or country, each party forever waives any right to claim or seek any form of alimony or spousal support, attorneys' fees and costs from the other. Any rights concerning distribution of property are otherwise covered by this agreement, and any rights to community property or claims of special equity are waived and released. In the event that a final judgment or decree of divorce or dissolution of marriage is entered for whatever reason, the parties agree that the provisions of this agreement are in complete settlement of all rights to claim or seek any form of financial support, except child support for any living minor children of the parties, from the other.

17. DISPOSITION UPON DEATH. Each party consents that his or her estate, or the estate of the other, may be disposed of by will, codicil, or trust, or in the absence of any such instrument, according to the laws of descent and distribution and intestate succession as if the marriage of the parties had not taken place. In either event, the estate shall be free of any claim or demand of inheritance, dower, curtesy, elective share, family allowance, homestead election, right to serve as executor, administrator, or personal representative, or any spousal or other claim given by law, irrespective of the marriage and any law to the contrary. Neither party intends by this agreement to limit or restrict the right to give to, or receive from, the other an inter vivos or testamentary gift. Neither party intends by this agreement to release, waive, or relinquish any devise or bequest left to either by specific provision in the will or codicil of the other, any property voluntarily transferred by the other, any joint tenancy created by the other, or any right to serve as executor or personal representative of the other's estate if specifically nominated in the other's will or codicil.

18. DEBTS. Neither party shall assume or become responsible for the payment of any pre-existing debts or obligations of the other party because of the marriage. Neither party shall do anything that would cause the debt or obligation of one of them to be a claim, demand, lien, or encumbrance against the property of the other party without the other party's written consent. If a debt or obligation of one party is asserted as a claim or demand against the property of the other without such written consent, the party who is responsible for the debt or obligation shall indemnify the other from the claim or demand, including the indemnified party's costs, expenses, and attorneys' fees.

19. HOMESTEAD. Each party releases any claim, demand, right, or interest that the party may acquire because of the marriage in any real property of the other because of the homestead property provisions of the laws of any state concerning the descent of the property as homestead.

20. FREE AND VOLUNTARY ACT. The parties acknowledge that executing this agreement is a free and voluntary act, and has not been entered into for any reason other than the desire for the furtherance of their relationship in marriage. Each party acknowledges that he or she has had adequate time to fully consider the consequences of signing this agreement, and has not been pressured, threatened, coerced, or unduly influenced to sign this agreement.

21. GOVERNING LAW. This agreement shall be governed by the laws of _____.

22. SEVERABILITY. If any part of this agreement is adjudged invalid, illegal, or unenforceable, the remaining parts shall not be affected and shall remain in full force and effect.

23. FURTHER ASSURANCE. Each party shall execute any instruments or documents at any time requested by the other party that are necessary or proper to effectuate this agreement.

24. BINDING EFFECT. This agreement shall be binding upon the parties, and upon their heirs, executors, personal representatives, administrators, successors and assigns.

25. NO OTHER BENEFICIARY. No person shall have a right or cause of action arising out of or resulting from this agreement except those who are parties to it and their successors in interest.

26. RELEASE. Except as otherwise provided in this agreement, each party releases all claims or demands to the property or estate of the other, however and whenever acquired, including acquisitions in the future.

27. ENTIRE AGREEMENT. This instrument, including any attached exhibits, constitutes the entire agreement of the parties. No representations or promises have been made except those that are set out in this agreement. This agreement may not be modified or terminated except in writing signed by the parties.

28. PARAGRAPH HEADINGS. The headings of the paragraphs contained in this agreement are for convenience only, and are not to be considered a part of this agreement or used in determining its content or context.

29. ATTORNEYS' FEES IN ENFORCEMENT. A party who fails to comply with any provision or obligation contained in this agreement shall pay the other party's attorneys' fees, costs, and other expenses reasonably incurred in enforcing this agreement and resulting from the noncompliance.

30. SIGNATURES AND INITIALS OF PARTIES. The signatures of the parties on this document, and their initials on each page, indicate that each party has read, and agrees with, this entire Marital Agreement, including any and all exhibits attached hereto.

31. OTHER PROVISIONS. Additional provisions are contained in the Addendum to Marital Agreement attached hereto and made a part hereof.

_____   _____
Husband   Wife

Executed in the presence of:

_____   _____

Name:_____   Name:_____

Address:_____   Address:_____

_____   _____

STATE OF   )
COUNTY OF   )
    The foregoing Premarital Agreement, consisting of _____ pages and Exhibits _____ through _____, was acknowledged before me this _____ day of _____, 20___, by the above-named Husband, Wife and Witnesses respectively, who are personally known to me or who have produced _____ as identification.

SEPARATION AGREEMENT

This Agreement is entered into on _____, 20___, by and between
_____ and _____

The parties were married on _____,_____.

As a result of disputes and serious differences, they have separated and are now living separate and apart and wish to continue living apart. They intend to settle by this agreement their marital matters, including child custody, child support, division of property and debts and their rights to alimony.

For these reasons and in consideration of the mutual promises contained in this agreement, Husband and Wife agree as follows:

1. LIVING SEPARATE. Husband and Wife will live separate and apart from each other, as if they were single and unmarried.

2. NO HARASSMENT OR INTERFERENCE. Neither party will in any manner harass, annoy or interfere with the other.

3. CHILD CUSTODY
__   There are no minor children.
__   The parties will share in parenting responsibilities; however, physical custody of the minor child(ren), _____
shall be awarded to the _____ and the _____ shall have reasonable and liberal visitation rights.
__   Other:

4. CHILD SUPPORT
__   There are no minor children.
The _____ shall pay the sum of $ _____ per _____ as support and maintenance for the minor child(ren)   in the physical custody of the other parent.

__   The _____ shall maintain health insurance coverage for the minor child(ren) as long as such insurance is available at a reasonable group rate.
__   Other:

5. DIVISION OF PROPERTY
The Husband transfers to the Wife as her sole and separate property:

_____
_____
_____
_____
_____

____ Continued on Additional Sheet.

The Wife transfers to the Husband as his sole and separate property:

_____

_____

_____

_____

_____

___ Continued on Additional Sheet.

6. DIVISION OF DEBTS
The Husband shall pay and will not at any time hold the Wife responsible for the following debts:

_____

_____

_____

_____

_____

___ Continued on Additional Sheet.

The Wife shall pay and will not at any time hold the Husband responsible for the following debts:

_____

_____

_____

_____

_____

___ Continued on Additional Sheet.

7. ALIMONY
The   __Husband __Wife shall pay alimony in the sum of $ _____ per _____, for a period of _____; or until the __Husband__Wife dies or remarries, whichever occurs first.
__ Other:

8. EFFECT OF DIVORCE OR DISSOLUTION OF MARRIAGE.
In the event of a divorce or dissolution of marriage this Separation Agreement shall, if the court approves, be merged with, incorporated into and become a part of any subsequent decree or judgment for divorce or dissolution of marriage.

9. FINANCIAL DISCLOSURE.
The parties have fully revealed to each other full financial information regarding their net worth, assets, holdings, income, and liabilities; not only by their discussions with each other, but also through copies of their current financial statements, copies of which are attached hereto as Exhibits A and B. Both parties acknowledge that they have had sufficient time to review the other's financial statement, are familiar with and understand the other's financial statement, have had any questions

satisfactorily answered, and are satisfied that full and complete financial disclosure has been made by the other.

10. WAIVER OF ESTATE. Both parties to this agreement agree to waive any and all right to the estate of the other, including dower, curtesy, elective share, community property rights, or rights of intestacy. Each party shall be allowed to pass his or her property freely by will.

11. INDEPENDENT REPRESENTATION BY COUNSEL. Each party has the right to representation by independent counsel. Each party fully understands his or her rights and considers the terms of this agreement to be fair and reasonable.

12. EXECUTION OF NECESSARY INSTRUMENTS. The parties will execute and deliver any other instruments and documents that may be necessary and convenient to carry out all of the terms of this agreement.

13. ENTIRE AGREEMENT. This instrument, including any attached exhibits, constitutes the entire agreement of the parties. No representations or promises have been made except those that are set out in this agreement. This agreement may not be modified or terminated except in writing signed by the parties.

14. GOVERNING LAW. This agreement shall be governed by the laws of _____.

15. BINDING EFFECT. This agreement shall be binding upon the parties, and upon their heirs, executors, personal representatives, administrators, successors and assigns.

_____   _____
(Husband's signature)   (Wife's signature)

    Sworn to and subscribed before me on _____,20____, by _____ and _____, who __ are personally known to me __ produced _____ as identification.

_____
Notary signature

_____
(Typed Name of Acknowledger)
NOTARY PUBLIC
Commission Number:_____
My Commission Expires:

DIVORCE SETTLEMENT AGREEMENT

This Agreement is entered into on _____, 20____, by and between
_____ and _____
herein referred to as the Husband   herein referred to as the Wife

_____   _____
(Address)   (Address)

_____   _____
(City)   (City)

_____   _____
(County)   (County)

_____   _____
(State)   (State)

The parties were married on _____, _____.

As a result of disputes and serious differences, they have separated and are now living separate and apart and wish to continue living permanently apart. They intend to settle by this agreement their marital matters, including child custody, child support, division of property and debts and their rights to alimony.

For these reasons and in consideration of the mutual promises contained in this agreement, Husband and Wife agree as follows:

1. LIVING SEPARATE. Husband and Wife will live separate and apart from each other, as if they were single and unmarried.

2. NO HARASSMENT OR INTERFERENCE. Neither party will in any manner harass, annoy or interfere with the other.

3. CHILD CUSTODY

___ The parties will share in parenting responsibilities; however, physical custody of the minor child(ren), _____
_____ shall be awarded to the Wife and the Husband shall have reasonable and liberal visitation rights.

__ The parties will share in parenting responsibilities; however, physical custody of the minor child(ren), _____ shall be awarded to the Husband and the Wife shall have reasonable and liberal visitation rights.
__ Other:

4. CHILD SUPPORT

__ The __ Husband __ Wife shall pay the sum of $ _____ per _____ as support and maintenance for the minor child(ren) in the physical custody of the other parent.

__ The __ Husband __ Wife shall maintain health insurance coverage for the minor child(ren) as long as such insurance is available at a reasonable group rate.

__ Other:

5. DIVISION OF PROPERTY

The Husband transfers to the Wife as her sole and separate property:

_____
_____
_____
_____
_____

__ Continued on Additional Sheet.

The Wife transfers to the Husband as his sole and separate property:

_____
_____
_____
_____
_____

__ Continued on Additional Sheet.

6. DIVISION OF DEBTS

The Husband shall pay and will not at any time hold the Wife responsible for the following debts:

_____
_____
_____
_____
_____
_____

__ Continued on Additional Sheet.

The Wife shall pay and will not at any time hold the Husband responsible for the following debts:

_____
_____
_____
_____
_____
_____

__ Continued on Additional Sheet.

7. ALIMONY

__ The __ Husband __ Wife shall pay alimony in the sum of $ _____ per _____, for a period of _____;
    or until the __ Husband __ Wife dies or remarries, whichever occurs first.

__ Other:

8. EFFECT OF DIVORCE OR DISSOLUTION OF MARRIAGE. In the event of a divorce or dissolution of marriage this Marital Settlement Agreement shall, if the court approves, be merged with , incorporated into and become a part of any subsequent decree or judgment for divorce or dissolution of marriage.

9. FINANCIAL DISCLOSURE. The parties have fully revealed to each other full financial information regarding their net worth, assets, holdings, income, and liabilities; not only by their discussions with each other, but also through copies of their current financial statements, copies of which are attached hereto as Exhibits A and B. Both parties acknowledge that they have had sufficient time to review the other's financial statement, are familiar with and understand

the other's financial statement, have had any questions satisfactorily answered, and are satisfied that full and complete financial disclosure has been made by the other.

10. INDEPENDENT REPRESENTATION BY COUNSEL. Each party has the right to representation by independent counsel. Each party fully understands his or her rights and considers the terms of this agreement to be fair and reasonable.

11. EXECUTION OF NECESSARY INSTRUMENTS. The parties will execute and deliver any other instruments and documents that may be necessary and convenient to carry out all of the terms of this agreement.

12. ENTIRE AGREEMENT. This instrument, including any attached exhibits, constitutes the entire agreement of the parties. No representations or promises have been made except those that are set out in this agreement. This agreement may not be modified or terminated except in writing signed by the parties.

13. GOVERNING LAW. This agreement shall be governed by the laws of _____.

14. BINDING EFFECT. This agreement shall be binding upon the parties, and upon their heirs, executors, personal representatives, administrators, successors and assigns.

_____   _____
(Husband's signature)   (Wife's signature)

Sworn to and subscribed before me on _____, 20____, by _____ and _____, who are personally known to me or who have produced _____ as identification.

_____
Notary signature

_____
(Typed Name of Acknowledger)
NOTARY PUBLIC
Commission Number:_____
My Commission Expires:

DELEGATION OF PARENTAL AUTHORITY

The undersigned, being the natural parent of _____, a minor, hereby grants to _____ as Custodian, the following authority over said child:

1. To have custody of the child during the following periods:

2. To discipline said child in a reasonable manner as discussed previously.

3. To authorize any and all emergency medical treatment which is deemed necessary or advisable for any injury or illness while child is in his/her custody.

Custodian agrees to use all reasonable means to protect the child while in his/he custody and to make reasonable effort to reach the undersigned in the event of an emergency. Parent can be reached at the following:

        Cell phone:_____
        Beeper: _____
        Other phone:_____
        Other phone:_____

Parent:

_____

Child's Custodian:

_____

form 12

CHILD AUTHORIZATION

To:

This is to confirm that my child, _____ is authorized to participate in: _____
on _____, 20___ under the following conditions:

If these conditions will not be met, my child may not participate.

During participation, I can be reached at:
Cell phone:_____
Beeper: _____
Other phone:_____
Other phone:_____

If I cannot be reached in any of these ways, I authorize _____ to consent to any emergency medical care which may be necessary.

Parent:

_____

Accepted by:

_____

PET CARE AGREEMENT

This is agreement is made between _____ (Owner) as pet owner, and _____ (Care Giver) who has agreed to care for a pet known as _____ which is a _____

The parties agree that Care Giver shall care for Owner's pet from _____ until _____.

Pet shall be cared for at Owner's house Care Giver's house

Pet shall be fed and given fresh water at least ___ times each day.

Care Giver shall be paid the sum of $_____ per _____ for said services.

If Owner cannot be reached Care Giver is authorized to consent to any emergency medical care which may be necessary.

Date: _____

Owner:

_____

Care Giver:

_____

ADDRESS CHANGE NOTICE TO POST OFFICE

OFFICIAL MAIL FORWARDING CHANGE OF ADDRESS FORM

| U.S. Postal Service **CHANGE OF ADDRESS ORDER** | Instructions: Complete Items 1 thru 10. You must SIGN Item 9. Please PRINT all other items including address on face of card. | OFFICIAL USE ONLY |

1. Change of Address for: (See instruction #1 above)
☐ Individual ☐ Entire Family ☐ Business

2. Start Date: Month Day Year

Zone/Route ID No.

3. Is This Move Temporary? *(Check one)*
☐ No ☐ Yes, Fill in ▶

4. If TEMPORARY move, print date to discontinue forwarding: Month Day Year

Date Entered on Form 3982
M M D D Y Y

5. Print Last Name *(include Jr., Sr., etc.)* or Name of Business *(If more than one, use separate form for each).*

Expiration Date
M M D D Y Y

6. Print First Name *(or Initial)* and Middle Name *(or Initial).* Leave blank if for a business.

Clerk/Carrier Endorsement

7a. For Puerto Rico Only: If OLD mailing address is in Puerto Rico, print urbanization name, if appropriate.

7b. Print **OLD** mailing address: House/Building Number and Street Name (include St., Ave., Rd., Ct., etc.).

Apt./Suite No. or PO Box No. or ☐RR/☐HCR *(Check one)* RR/HCR Box No.

City State ZIP Code ZIP+4

8a. For Puerto Rico Only: If NEW mailing address is in Puerto Rico, print urbanization name, if appropriate.

8b. Print **NEW** mailing address: House/Building Number and Street Name (include St., Ave., Rd., Ct., etc.).

Apt./Suite No. or ☐ PO Box No. / ☐ PMB No. *(Check one)* or ☐RR/☐HCR ☐PMB No./☐RR/HCR Box No.

City State ZIP Code ZIP+4

9. Sign and Print Name (see conditions on reverse)
Sign: _____
Print:

10. Date Signed: Month Day Year

OFFICIAL USE ONLY
Verification Endorsement

PS FORM 3575, September 2000   See http://www.usps.com/moversnet for more information.   0090

ADDRESS CHANGE NOTICE TO CONTACTS

Mail this postcard to businesses and people who send you mail.

Please send mail to new address beginning: Month Day Year

My Name (Last name, first name, middle)

OLD Address

OLD Complete Street Address or PO Box or Rural Route and RR Box Apt./Suite #

City or Post Office State ZIP or ZIP +4 Code

NEW Address

NEW Complete Street Address or PO Box or Rural Route and RR Box Apt./Suite #

City or Post Office State ZIP or ZIP +4 Code

NEW Telephone Number (Optional)

Account Number (If applicable)

Signature Today's Date: Month Day Year

PS FORM 3576, September 2000   See http://www.usps.com/moversnet for more information.

ADDRESS CHANGE NOTICE TO INTERNAL REVENUE SERVICE

Form **8822** (Rev. Oct. 2000) Department of the Treasury Internal Revenue Service	**Change of Address** ▶ Please type or print. ▶ See instructions on back. ▶ Do not attach this form to your return.	OMB No. 1545-1163

Part I	**Complete This Part To Change Your Home Mailing Address**

Check **all** boxes this change affects:

1 ☐ Individual income tax returns (Forms 1040, 1040A, 1040EZ, TeleFile, 1040NR, etc.)

▶ If your last return was a joint return and you are now establishing a residence separate
from the spouse with whom you filed that return, check here . . . . ▶ ☐

2 ☐ Gift, estate, or generation-skipping transfer tax returns (Forms 706, 709, etc.)

▶ For Forms 706 and 706-NA, enter the decedent's name and social security number below.

▶ Decedent's name   ▶ Social security number

3a Your name (first name, initial, and last name)	**3b** Your social security number
4a Spouse's name (first name, initial, and last name)	**4b** Spouse's social security number

5 Prior name(s). See instructions.

6a Old address (no., street, city or town, state, and ZIP code). If a P.O. box or foreign address, see instructions.	Apt. no.
6b Spouse's old address, if different from line 6a (no., street, city or town, state, and ZIP code). If a P.O. box or foreign address, see instructions.	Apt. no.
7 New address (no., street, city or town, state, and ZIP code). If a P.O. box or foreign address, see instructions.	Apt. no.

Part II	**Complete This Part To Change Your Business Mailing Address or Business Location**

Check **all** boxes this change affects:

8 ☐ Employment, excise, and other business returns (Forms 720, 940, 940-EZ, 941, 990, 1041, 1065, 1120, etc.)
9 ☐ Employee plan returns (Forms 5500 and 5500-EZ).
10 ☐ Business location

11a Business name	**11b** Employer identification number
12 Old mailing address (no., street, city or town, state, and ZIP code). If a P.O. box or foreign address, see instructions.	Room or suite no.
13 New mailing address (no., street, city or town, state, and ZIP code). If a P.O. box or foreign address, see instructions.	Room or suite no.
14 New business location (no., street, city or town, state, and ZIP code). If a foreign address, see instructions.	Room or suite no.

Part III	**Signature**

Daytime telephone number of person to contact (optional) ▶ (   )

Sign Here

Your signature	Date	If Part II completed, signature of owner, officer, or representative	Date
If joint return, spouse's signature	Date	Title	

For Privacy Act and Paperwork Reduction Act Notice, see back of form.   Cat. No. 12081V   Form **8822** (Rev. 10-2000)

Purpose of Form

You may use Form 8822 to notify the Internal Revenue Service if you changed your home or business mailing address or your business location. If this change also affects the mailing address for your children who filed income tax returns, complete and file a separate Form 8822 for each child. If you are a representative signing for the taxpayer, attach to Form 8822 a copy of your power of attorney.

Changing Both Home and Business Addresses? If you are, use a separate Form 8822 to show each change unless the service center under **Where To File** is the same for both home and business.

Prior Name(s)

If you or your spouse changed your name because of marriage, divorce, etc., complete line 5. Also, be sure to notify the **Social Security Administration** of your new name so that it has the same name in its records that you have on your tax return. This prevents delays in processing your return and issuing refunds. It also safeguards your future social security benefits.

Addresses

Be sure to include any apartment, room, or suite number in the space provided.

P.O. Box

Enter your box number instead of your street address **only** if your post office does not deliver mail to your street address.

Foreign Address

Enter the information in the following order: city, province or state, and country. Follow the country's practice for entering the postal code. Please **do not** abbreviate the country name.

Signature

If you are completing Part II, the owner, an officer, or a representative must sign. An officer is the president, vice president, treasurer, chief accounting officer, etc. A representative is a person who has a valid power of attorney to handle tax matters.

Where To File

Send this form to the **Internal Revenue Service Center** shown below that applies to you.

Filers Who Completed Part I

IF your old home mailing address was in. . .	THEN use this address. . .
Florida, Georgia, South Carolina, West Virginia	Atlanta, GA 39901
Colorado, Idaho, Montana, New Mexico, Oklahoma, Texas, Wyoming	Austin, TX 73301
Delaware, New Jersey, New York (New York City and counties of Nassau, Rockland, Suffolk, and Westchester)	Holtsville, NY 00501
New York (all other counties), Connecticut, Maine, Massachusetts, New Hampshire, Rhode Island, Vermont	Andover, MA 05501
Arizona, California (counties of Alpine, Amador, Butte, Calaveras, Colusa, Contra Costa, Del Norte, El Dorado, Glenn, Humboldt, Lake, Lassen, Marin, Mendocino, Modoc, Napa, Nevada, Placer, Plumas, Sacramento, San Joaquin, Shasta, Sierra, Siskiyou, Solano, Sonoma, Sutter, Tehama, Trinity, Yolo, and Yuba), Nevada, North Dakota, South Dakota, Utah, Washington	Ogden, UT 84201
Alaska, California (all other counties), Hawaii	Fresno, CA 93888
Michigan, Ohio	Cincinnati, OH 45999
District of Columbia, Indiana, Maryland, Pennsylvania, Virginia	Philadelphia, PA 19255
Alabama, Arkansas, Kentucky, Louisiana, Mississippi, Nebraska, North Carolina, Tennessee	Memphis, TN 37501
Illinois, Iowa, Kansas, Minnesota, Missouri, Oregon, Wisconsin	Kansas City, MO 64999
American Samoa	Philadelphia, PA 19255
Guam: Permanent residents	Department of Revenue and Taxation Government of Guam P.O. Box 23607 GMF, GU 96921
Guam: Nonpermanent residents Puerto Rico (or if excluding income under Internal Revenue Code section 933) Virgin Islands: Nonpermanent residents	Philadelphia, PA 19255
Virgin Islands: Permanent residents	V. I. Bureau of Internal Revenue 9601 Estate Thomas Charlotte Amalie St. Thomas, VI 00802
Foreign country: U.S. citizens and those filing Form 2555, Form 2555-EZ, or Form 4563 All APO and FPO addresses	Philadelphia, PA 19255

Filers Who Completed Part II

IF your old business address was in. . .	THEN use this address. . .
Virginia or Outside the United States	Philadelphia, PA 19255
Delaware, District of Columbia, Indiana, Kentucky, Maryland, Michigan, New Jersey, North Carolina, Ohio, Pennsylvania, South Carolina, West Virginia, Wisconsin	Cincinnati, OH 45999
Kansas, New Mexico, Oklahoma	Austin, TX 73301
Alabama, Tennessee	Memphis, TN 37501
Illinois	Kansas City, MO 64999

Alaska, Arizona, Arkansas, California (counties of Alpine, Amador, Butte, Calaveras, Colusa, Contra Costa, Del Norte, El Dorado, Glenn, Humboldt, Lake, Lassen, Marin, Mendocino, Modoc, Napa, Nevada, Placer, Plumas, Sacramento, San Joaquin, Shasta, Sierra, Siskiyou, Solano, Sonoma, Sutter, Tehama, Trinity, Yolo, and Yuba), Colorado, Hawaii, Idaho, Iowa, Louisiana, Minnesota, Mississippi, Missouri, Montana, Nebraska, Nevada, North Dakota, Oregon, South Dakota, Texas, Utah, Washington, Wyoming	Ogden, UT 84201
California (all other counties)	Fresno, CA 93888
Florida, Georgia	Atlanta, GA 39901
New York (New York City and counties of Nassau, Rockland, Suffolk, and Westchester)	Holtsville, NY 00501
New York (all other counties), Connecticut, Maine, Massachusetts, New Hampshire, Rhode Island, Vermont	Andover, MA 05501

Privacy Act and Paperwork Reduction Act Notice. We ask for the information on this form to carry out the Internal Revenue laws of the United States. We may give the information to the Department of Justice and to other Federal agencies, as provided by law. We may also give it to cities, states, the District of Columbia, and U.S. commonwealths or possessions to carry out their tax laws. And we may give it to foreign governments because of tax treaties they have with the United States.

You are not required to provide the information requested on a form that is subject to the Paperwork Reduction Act unless the form displays a valid OMB control number. Books or records relating to a form or its instructions must be retained as long as their contents may become material in the administration of any Internal Revenue law. Generally, tax returns and return information are confidential, as required by Internal Revenue Code section 6103.

The use of this form is voluntary. However, if you fail to provide the Internal Revenue Service with your current mailing address, you may not receive a notice of deficiency or a notice and demand for tax. Despite the failure to receive such notices, penalties and interest will continue to accrue on the tax deficiencies.

The time needed to complete and file this form will vary depending on individual circumstances. The estimated average time is 16 minutes.

If you have comments concerning the accuracy of this time estimate or suggestions for making this form simpler, we would be happy to hear from you. You can write to the Tax Forms Committee, Western Area Distribution Center, Rancho Cordova, CA 95743-0001. **Do not** send the form to this address. Instead, see **Where To File** on this page.

BIRTH OR DEATH CERTIFICATE REQUEST

TO: (Office of Vital Statistics Address)

FROM: (Current name and address)

I request a certified copy of the ❑ birth certificate ❑ death certificate

of _____
(Give full name)

DATE of BIRTH or DEATH _____

PLACE of BIRTH or DEATH _____
(City, town, county, and state)

HOSPITAL _____

SEX _____ RACE _____

NAME OF FATHER _____

NAME OF MOTHER _____ (Include maiden name)

The purpose for which this certificate is needed is: _____

_____

My relationship to the person is ❑ self ❑ Other: _____

ENCLOSED (Do not send cash)

❑ Certified check for $_____ ❑ Money order for $_____

_____
Signature

PASSPORT APPLICATION

UNITED STATES DEPARTMENT OF STATE

APPLICATION FOR ☐ PASSPORT ☐ REGISTRATION
(Type or print all capital letters in blue or black ink in white areas only)

1. NAME (First and Middle)

LAST

2. MAIL PASSPORT TO: STREET / RFD # OR P.O. BOX APT. #

CITY STATE

ZIP CODE COUNTRY / IN CARE OF (If applicable)

☐ 5 Yr. ☐ 10 Yr. Issue Date ___
R D O DP
End. # ___ Exp. ___

3. SEX ☐ M ☐ F **4. PLACE OF BIRTH** (City & State or City & Country) **5. DATE OF BIRTH** Month Day Year **6. SOCIAL SECURITY NUMBER** (SEE FEDERAL TAX LAW NOTICE ON PAGE 2)

7. HEIGHT Feet Inches **8. HAIR COLOR** **9. EYE COLOR** **10. HOME TELEPHONE** ( ) **11. BUSINESS TELEPHONE** ( ) **12. OCCUPATION**

13. PERMANENT ADDRESS (DO NOT LIST P.O. BOX) STREET/RFD # CITY STATE ZIP CODE

14. FATHER'S FULL NAME Last First | BIRTHPLACE | BIRTHDATE | U.S. CITIZEN ☐ Yes ☐ No | **15. MOTHER'S FULL MAIDEN NAME** Last First | BIRTHPLACE | BIRTHDATE | U.S. CITIZEN ☐ Yes ☐ No

16. HAVE YOU EVER BEEN MARRIED? ☐ Yes ☐ No | SPOUSE'S OR FORMER SPOUSE'S FULL NAME AT BIRTH Last First | BIRTHPLACE | BIRTHDATE | U.S. CITIZEN ☐ Yes ☐ No

DATE OF MOST RECENT MARRIAGE Month Day Year | WIDOWED/DIVORCED? ☐ Yes Give Date Month Day Year ☐ No | **17. OTHER NAMES YOU HAVE USED** (1) (2)

18. HAVE YOU EVER BEEN ISSUED A U.S. PASSPORT? ☐ Yes ☐ No IF YES, COMPLETE NEXT LINE AND SUBMIT PASSPORT IF AVAILABLE. **DISPOSITION**
NAME IN WHICH ISSUED | MOST RECENT PASSPORT NUMBER | APPROXIMATE ISSUE DATE Month Day Year | ☐ Submitted ☐ Stolen ☐ Lost ☐ Other ___

It is necessary to submit a statement with an application for a new passport when a previous valid or potentially valid passport cannot be presented. The statement must set forth in detail why the previous passport cannot be presented. Use Form DSP-64.

2x2" FROM 1" TO 1 - 3/8"
STAPLE STAPLE
SUBMIT TWO RECENT IDENTICAL PHOTOS

19. EMERGENCY CONTACT. If you wish, you may supply the name, address and telephone number of a person not traveling with you to be contacted in case of emergency.
NAME
STREET
CITY STATE ZIP CODE
TELEPHONE ( ) RELATIONSHIP

20. TRAVEL PLANS (not mandatory) Month Day Year
Date of Trip
Length of Trip
COUNTRIES TO BE VISITED

21. STOP. DO NOT SIGN APPLICATION UNTIL REQUESTED TO DO SO BY PERSON ADMINISTERING OATH.
I have not, since acquiring United States citizenship, performed any of the acts listed under "Acts or Conditions" on the reverse of this application form (unless explanatory statement is attached). I solemnly swear (or affirm) that the statements made on this application are true and the photograph attached is a true likeness of me.

X ___ | X ___
Parent's/Legal Guardian's Signature if identifying minor child | Applicant's Signature - age 13 or older

22. FOR ACCEPTANCE AGENT'S USE
Subscribed and sworn to (affirmed) before me Month Day Year (SEAL)
(Signature of person authorized to accept application)
☐ Clerk of Court; Location ___
☐ PASSPORT Agent
☐ Postal Employee
☐ (Vice) Consul USA

23. APPLICANT'S IDENTIFYING DOCUMENTS
☐ DRIVER'S LICENSE ISSUE DATE: Month Day Year EXPIRATION DATE: Month Day Year ID No. ___
☐ PASSPORT
☐ OTHER (Specify) ___ PLACE OF ISSUE ___ ISSUED IN THE NAME OF: ___

24. FOR ISSUING OFFICE USE ONLY (Applicant's evidence of citizenship)
☐ Birth Certificate SR CR City Filed/Issued:
☐ Passport Bearer's Name:
☐ Report of Birth
☐ Naturalization/Citizenship Cert. No.: Issued:
☐ Other
☐ Seen & Returned
☐ Attached

APPLICATION APPROVAL
25.
FEE ___ EXEC. ___ EF ___ OTHER ___

Page 1

FORM DSP-11 (12-97) (SEE INSTRUCTIONS ON PAGE 2) Form Approved OMB No. 1405-0004 (Exp. 3/31/08) Estimated Burden - 20 Minutes*

136

UNITED STATES DEPARTMENT OF STATE

PASSPORT APPLICATION
HOW TO APPLY FOR A U.S. PASSPORT

FOR INQUIRIES (A fee is charged for this service.): National Passport Information Center, 1-900-225-5674, For TDD: 1-900-225-7778 **OR** For Credit Card Users: 1-888-362-8668, For TDD: 1-888-498-3648

U.S. passports are issued only to U.S. citizens or nationals. Each person must obtain his or her own passport. IF YOU ARE A FIRST-TIME APPLICANT, please complete and submit this application in person. (Applicants under 13 years of age usually need not appear in person unless requested. A parent or guardian may execute the application on the child's behalf.) Each application must be accompanied by (1) PROOF OF U.S. CITIZENSHIP, (2) PROOF OF IDENTITY, (3) TWO PHOTOGRAPHS, (4) FEES (as explained below) to one of the following acceptance agents: a clerk of any Federal or State court of record or a judge or clerk of any probate court accepting applications; a designated municipal or county official; a designated postal employee at an authorized post office; or an agent at a Passport Agency in Boston, Chicago, Honolulu, Houston, Los Angeles, Miami, New Orleans, New York, Philadelphia, San Francisco, Seattle, Stamford, or Washington, D.C.; or a U.S. consular official.

IF YOU HAVE HAD A PREVIOUS PASSPORT, inquire about eligibility to use Form DSP-82 (mail-in application). Address requests for passport amendment, extension of validity, or additional visa pages to a Passport Agency or a U.S. Consulate or Embassy abroad. Check visa requirements with consular officials of countries to be visited well in advance of your departure.

(1) PROOF OF U.S. CITIZENSHIP.
(a) APPLICANTS BORN IN THE UNITED STATES. Submit previous U.S. passport or **certified** birth certificate. A birth certificate must include your given name and surname, date and place of birth, date the birth record was filed, and seal or other certification of the official custodian of such records. A record filed more than 1 year after the birth is acceptable if it is supported by evidence described in the next paragraph.

IF NO BIRTH RECORD EXISTS, submit registrar's notice to that effect. Also submit an early baptismal or circumcision certificate, hospital birth record, early census, school, or family Bible records, newspaper or insurance files, or notarized affidavits of persons having knowledge of your birth (preferably with at least one record listed above). Evidence should include your given name and surname, date and place of birth, and seal or other certification of office (if customary) and signature of issuing official.

(b) APPLICANTS BORN OUTSIDE THE UNITED STATES. Submit previous U.S. passport or Certificate of Naturalization, or Certificate of Citizenship, or a Report of Birth Abroad, or evidence described below.

IF YOU CLAIM CITIZENSHIP THROUGH NATURALIZATION OF PARENT(S), submit the Certificate(s) of Naturalization of your parent(s), your foreign birth certificate, and proof of your admission to the United States for permanent residence.

IF YOU CLAIM CITIZENSHIP THROUGH BIRTH ABROAD TO U.S. CITIZEN PARENT(S), submit a Consular Report of Birth (Form FS-240) or Certification of Birth (Form DS-1350 or FS-545), or your foreign birth certificate, parents' marriage certificate, proof of citizenship of your parent(s), and affidavit of U.S. citizen parent(s) showing all periods and places of residence/physical presence in the United States and abroad before your birth.

(2) PROOF OF IDENTITY. If you are not personally known to the acceptance agent, you must establish your identity to the agent's satisfaction. You may submit items such as the following containing your signature AND physical description or photograph that is a good likeness of you: previous U.S. passport; Certificate of Naturalization or of Citizenship; driver's license (not temporary or learner's license); or government (Federal, State, municipal) identification card or pass. Temporary or altered documents are not acceptable.

IF YOU CANNOT PROVE YOUR IDENTITY as stated above, you must appear with an IDENTIFYING WITNESS who is a U.S. citizen or permanent resident alien who has known you for at least 2 years. Your witness must prove his or her identity and complete and sign an Affidavit of Identifying Witness (Form DSP-71) before the acceptance agent. You must also submit some identification of your own.

(3) TWO PHOTOGRAPHS. Submit two identical photographs of you alone, sufficiently recent to be a good likeness (normally taken within the last 6 months), 2 x 2 inches in size, with an image size from bottom of chin to top of head (including hair) of between 1 and 1-3/8 inches. Photographs must be clear, front view, full face, taken in normal street attire without a hat or dark glasses, and printed on thin paper with a plain light (white or off-white) background. They may be black and white or color. They must be capable of withstanding a mounting temperature of 225° Fahrenheit (107° Celsius). Photographs retouched so that your appearance is changed are unacceptable. Snapshots, most vending machine prints, and magazine or full-length photographs are unacceptable.

(4) FEES. Submit $60 if you are 16 years of age or older. The passport fee is $45. In addition, a fee of $15 is charged for the execution of the application. Your passport will be valid for 10 years from the date of issue except where limited by the Secretary of State to a shorter period. Submit $40 if you are 15 years of age or younger. The passport fee is $25 and the execution fee is $15. Your passport will be valid for 5 years from the date of issue, except where limited as above.

Expedited service is available only in the United States. Expedite requests will be processed in 3 workdays from receipt at a Passport Agency. This service is available only for early departure, generally with proof of travel. The additional fee is $35.

Pay the passport and execution fees in one of the following forms: Checks-personal, certified, traveler's; bank draft or cashier's check; money order-U.S. Postal, international, currency exchange; or if abroad, the foreign currency equivalent, or a check drawn on a U.S. bank.

Make passport and execution fees payable to Passport Services (except if applying at a designated acceptance facility, such as a State court or municipal office, pay execution fee as required) or the appropriate Embassy or Consulate, if abroad. Pay special postage if applicable.

An additional adjudication fee of $100 will be charged to previously undocumented passport customers who were born outside the United States and who have not been issued any of the following documents: a U.S. passport, a Consular Report of Birth Abroad, a Certification of Report of Birth, a Certificate of Naturalization or a Certificate of Citizenship.

An additional $15 fee will be charged when, upon request, the Department of State verifies issuance of a previous U.S. passport or Consular Report of Birth Abroad because the customer is unable to submit evidence of U.S. citizenship.

No fee is charged to applicants with U.S. Government or military authorization for no-fee passports (except designated acceptance facilities may collect the execution fee).

FEDERAL TAX LAW:
26 U.S.C. 6039E (Internal Revenue Code) requires a passport applicant to provide his/her name and social security number. If you have not been issued a social security number, enter zeros in box #6. The Department of State must provide this information to the Internal Revenue Service routinely. Any applicant who fails to provide the required information is subject to a **$500** penalty enforced by the IRS. All questions on this matter should be referred to the nearest IRS office.

ACTS OR CONDITIONS
(If any of the below-mentioned acts or conditions have been performed by or apply to the applicant, the portion which applies should be lined out, and a supplementary explanatory statement under oath (or affirmation) by the applicant should be attached and made a part of this application.) I have not, since acquiring United States citizenship, been naturalized as a citizen of a foreign state; taken an oath or made an affirmation or other formal declaration of allegiance to a foreign state; entered or served in the armed forces of a foreign state; accepted or performed the duties of any office, post, or employment under the government of a foreign state or political subdivision thereof; made a formal renunciation of nationality either in the United States, or before a diplomatic or consular officer of the United States in a foreign state; or been convicted by a court or court martial of competent jurisdiction of committing any act of treason against, or attempting by force to overthrow, or bearing arms against, the United States, or conspiring to overthrow, put down, or to destroy by force, the Government of the United States.
WARNING: False statements made knowingly and willfully in passport applications or in affidavits or other supporting documents submitted therewith are punishable by fine and/or imprisonment under provisions of 18 USC 1001 and/or 18 USC 1542. Alteration or mutilation of a passport issued pursuant to this application is punishable by fine and/or imprisonment under the provisions of 18 USC 1543. The use of a passport in violation of the restrictions contained therein or of the passport regulations is punishable by fine and/or imprisonment under 18 USC 1544. All statements and documents submitted are subject to verification.

PRIVACY ACT STATEMENT:
AUTHORITIES: The information solicited on this form is requested pursuant to provisions in Titles 8, 18, and 22 of the United States Code, whether or not codified, including specifically 22 USC 211a, 212, 213, and all regulations issued pursuant to Executive Order 11295 (August 5, 1966), including Part 51, Title 22, Code of Federal Regulations (CFR). Also, as noted, 26 USC 6039E.
PURPOSE: The primary purpose for soliciting the information is to establish citizenship, identity and entitlement to issuance of a U.S. passport. The information may also be used in connection with issuing other travel documents or evidence of citizenship, and in furtherance of the Secretary's responsibility for the protection of U.S. nationals abroad. Social Security information is collected for the IRS (see above).
ROUTINE USES: The information is made available as a routine use on a need-to-know basis to personnel of the Department of State. The principal users of this information are offices within the Bureau of Consular Affairs. Information may also be provided to other government agencies having statutory or other lawful authority to gain access to such information in the performance of their official duties, pursuant to a court order, and as set forth in Part 171, Title 22 CFR.

The submission of this form is mandatory in order to obtain a U.S. passport. Individuals who fail to submit this form or who do not provide all the requested information, except that which is marked "Not Mandatory", may be denied a passport, related document, or service.

*Public reporting burden for this collection of information is estimated to average 20 minutes per response, including time required for searching existing data sources, gathering the necessary data, providing the information required, and reviewing the final collection. Send comments on the accuracy of this estimate of the burden and recommendations for reducing it to: Department of State (OIS/RA/DIR) Washington, D.C. 20520-0264, and to the Office of Information and Regulatory Affairs, Office of Management and Budget, Paperwork Reduction Project (1405-0004), Washington, D.C. 20503.

PAGE 2

form 18

PASSPORT RENEWAL APPLICATION

UNITED STATES DEPARTMENT OF STATE
APPLICATION FOR PASSPORT BY MAIL

TYPE OR PRINT IN BLUE OR BLACK INK IN WHITE AREAS ONLY   USE BLOCK LETTERS/NUMBERS

NAME	FIRST	MIDDLE
	LAST	

MAIL PASSPORT TO

STREET / RFD # OR P.O. BOX		APT. #
CITY	STATE	ZIP CODE

IN CARE OF *(IF APPLICABLE)*

Issue Date _____

R   D   O   DP

End. # _____   Exp. _____

SEX	PLACE OF BIRTH	DATE OF BIRTH			SOCIAL SECURITY NUMBER
☐ Male ☐ Female	City & State or City & Country	Month	Day	Year	(SEE FEDERAL TAX LAW NOTICE ON REVERSE SIDE)

HEIGHT	HAIR COLOR	EYE COLOR	HOME TELEPHONE	BUSINESS TELEPHONE
Feet	Inches			( )	( )

NOTE: Most recent passport MUST be enclosed!

PASSPORT NUMBER	ISSUE DATE			PLACE OF ISSUANCE	OCCUPATION *(Not Mandatory)*
	Month	Day	Year		

DEPARTURE DATE	18. TRAVEL PLANS *(Not Mandatory)* COUNTRIES TO BE VISITED	LENGTH OF STAY *(Not Mandatory)*

PERMANENT ADDRESS (Do not list P.O. Box)

STREET / R.F.D. #	CITY	STATE	ZIP CODE

EMERGENCY CONTACT. If you wish, you may supply the name, address and telephone number of a person not traveling with you to be contacted in case of emergency.

NAME

STREET

CITY	STATE	ZIP CODE

TELEPHONE	RELATIONSHIP

OATH AND SIGNATURE (If any of the below-mentioned acts or conditions have been performed by or apply to the applicant, the portion which applies should be lined out, and a supplementary explanatory statement should be attached, signed, and made part of this application.)

I have not, since acquiring United States citizenship, been naturalized as a citizen of a foreign state; taken an oath, or made an affirmation or other formal declaration of allegiance to a foreign state; entered or served in the armed forces of a foreign state; accepted or performed the duties of any office, post, or employment under the Government of a foreign state or political subdivision thereof; made a formal renunciation of nationality either in the United States or before a diplomatic or consular officer of the United States in a foreign state; or been convicted by a court or court martial of competent jurisdiction of committing any act of treason against, or attempting by force to overthrow, or bearing arms against the United States, or conspiring to overthrow, put down or destroy by force the Government of the United States.

2" x 2" / FROM 1" TO 1 – 3/8"

SUBMIT TWO RECENT IDENTICAL PHOTOS WITH LIGHT, PLAIN BACKGROUND

WARNING: False statements made knowingly and willfully in passport applications or affidavits or other supporting documents are punishable by fine and/or imprisonment under provisions of 18 USC 1001 and/or 18 USC 1542. The alteration or mutilation of a passport issued pursuant to this application is punishable by fine and/or imprisonment under 18 USC 1543. The use of a passport in violation of the restrictions therein is punishable by fine and/or imprisonment under 18 USC 1544.

DECLARATION: I declare that the statements made in this application are true and complete to the best of my knowledge and belief, that the attached photographs are a true likeness of me, and that I have not been issued a passport subsequent to the one submitted herein.

➡ NOTE: APPLICANT MUST SIGN & DATE

SIGNATURE	DATE

DO NOT WRITE BELOW THIS SPACE · FOR PASSPORT SERVICES USE ONLY · DO NOT WRITE BELOW THIS SPACE

Application Approval	Evidence of Name Change	Fees
	☐ Marriage Cert. ☐ Court Order	
	Date _____	
	Place _____	
	From _____	
	To _____	

FORM DSP-82 (12-97)

OMB No. 1405-0020 (Exp. 2/28/98) Estimated Burden 15 Minutes*

WHAT DO I NEED TO SEND WITH THE APPLICATION FORM?

1. **Your most recent passport.**
2. **A marriage certificate or court order if your name has changed.**
3. **Passport fee of $40.**
4. **Two recent (taken within the last 6 months) identical photographs with a light, plain background.**

For detailed information on the items to be included, see below.

1. YOUR MOST RECENT PASSPORT.
Issued at age 16 or older in your current name (or see item #2 below) and issued within the past 12 years. If your passport is mutilated or damaged, you must apply on the DSP-11 Application form as specified below.

2. A MARRIAGE CERTIFICATE OR COURT ORDER.
If the name you are currently using differs from the name on your most recent passport, you must submit a marriage certificate or court order showing the change of name. The name change document MUST bear the official seal of the issuing authority. Uncertified copies or notarized documents cannot be accepted. All documents will be returned to you with your passport. If you are unable to document your name change in this manner, you must apply on the DSP-11 Application form by making a personal appearance at (1) a passport agency; (2) any Federal or State court of record or any probate court accepting passport applications; or (3) a Post Office which has been selected to accept passport applications.

3. THE PASSPORT FEE OF $40.
Enclose the $40 passport fee in the form of a personal check or money order. DO NOT SEND CASH. Passport Services cannot be responsible for cash sent through the mail. If you desire special postage other than first class (registered, special delivery, etc.) include the appropriate fee on the check. THE FULL NAME AND DATE OF BIRTH OF THE APPLICANT MUST BE TYPED OR PRINTED ON THE FRONT OF THE CHECK. MAKE CHECKS PAYABLE TO PASSPORT SERVICES. Expedited service is available only in the United States. Expedite requests will be processed in 3 workdays from receipt at a Passport Agency. This service is available only for early departure, generally with proof of travel. The additional fee is $35.

4. TWO RECENT IDENTICAL PHOTOGRAPHS.
The photographs must have been taken within the past six months and be a good likeness of you. The photographs must be clear with a full front view of your face and taken on a light (white or off-white) background. Photographs may be in color or black and white and the image size must correspond to the dimensions on the diagram on the front of this form. Photographs must be taken in normal street attire, showing you without headcovering unless a signed statement is submitted indicating that the headcovering is worn daily for religious or medical reasons. Dark glasses may not be worn in passport photographs unless a doctor's statement is submitted supporting the wearing of dark glasses for medical reasons.

MAIL THIS FORM TO:	DELIVERY - Other Than U.S. Postal Service	FOR INQUIRIES CONTACT:
National Passport Center **P.O. Box 371971** **Pittsburgh, Pa. 15250-7971**	**Passport Services Lockbox** **Attn: Passport Supervisor, 371971** **3 Mellon Bank Center, Rm. 153-2723** **Pittsburgh, Pa. 15259-0001**	**National Passport Information Center** **1-900-225-5674** **FOR TDD: 1-900-225-7778** **FOR CREDIT CARD USERS: 1-888-362-8668** **FOR TDD: 1-888-498-3648** **(A fee is charged for this service.)**

NOTICE TO APPLICANTS RESIDING ABROAD

United States citizens residing abroad CANNOT submit this form to the Passport Facility listed above. Such applicants should contact the nearest United States Embassy or Consulate for procedures to be followed when applying overseas.

NOTICE TO APPLICANTS FOR OFFICIAL, DIPLOMATIC, OR NO-FEE PASSPORTS

You may use this application if you meet all of the provisions listed above. Submit your U.S. Government or military authorization for a no-fee passport with your application in lieu of the passport fee. CONSULT YOUR SPONSORING AGENCY FOR INSTRUCTIONS ON PROPER ROUTING PROCEDURES BEFORE FORWARDING THIS APPLICATION. Your completed passport will be released to your sponsoring agency for forwarding to you.

FEDERAL TAX LAW

26 U.S.C. 6039E (Internal Revenue Code) requires a passport applicant to provide his/her name and social security number. If you have not been issued a social security number, enter zeros in box. The Department of State must provide this information to the Internal Revenue Service routinely. Any applicant who fails to provide the required information is subject to a $500 penalty enforced by the IRS. All questions on this matter should be referred to the nearest IRS office.

PRIVACY ACT STATEMENT

AUTHORITIES: The information solicited on this form is requested pursuant to provisions in Titles 8, 18, and 22 of the United States Code, whether or not codified, including specifically 22 U.S.C. 211a, 212, 213, and all regulations issued pursuant to Executive Order 11295 (August 5, 1966), including 22 C.F.R Part 51. Also, as noted, 26 U.S.C. 6039E.
PURPOSE: The primary purpose for soliciting the information is to establish citizenship, identity and entitlement to issuance of a U.S. passport. The information may also be used in connection with issuing other travel documents or evidence of citizenship, and in furtherance of the Secretary's responsibility for the protection of U.S. nationals abroad. Social Security information is collected for the IRS (see above).
ROUTINE USES: The information is made available as a routine use on a need-to-know basis to personnel of the Department of State. The principal users of this information are offices within the Bureau of Consular Affairs. Information may also be provided to other government agencies having statutory or other lawful authority to gain access to such information in the performance of their official duties, pursuant to a court order, and as set forth in Part 171, Title 22 C.F.R.
The submission of this form is mandatory in order to obtain a U.S. passport. Individuals who fail to submit this form or who do not provide all the requested information, except that which is marked "Not Mandatory", may be denied a passport, related document, or service.

APPLICATION FOR A SOCIAL SECURITY NUMBER

SOCIAL SECURITY ADMINISTRATION
Application for a Social Security Card

Applying for a Social Security Card is easy AND it is FREE!

If you DO NOT follow these instructions, we CANNOT process your application!

STEP 1   Complete and sign the application with BLUE or BLACK ink.
Do NOT use pencil! Follow instructions below.

STEP 2   See Page 2 to determine what evidence we need.

STEP 3   Submit the application and evidence to any Social Security office. Follow instructions below.

HOW TO COMPLETE THE APPLICATION

Most items on the form are self-explanatory. Those that need explanation are discussed below. The numbers match the numbered items on the form. If you are completing this form for someone else, please complete the items as they apply to that person.

2. Show an address where you can receive the card 10 to 14 days from now.

3. If you check "other" for CITIZENSHIP, provide a document from the Federal/State or local agency explaining why you need a Social Security number and that you meet all the requirements for the benefit or service except for a number.

5. You do not have to complete this item about race/ethnic background. We use this information for statistical reports on how Social Security programs affect people. We do not reveal the identities of individuals.

6. Show the month, day, and full (4-digit) year of birth, for example, "1998" for year of birth.

8. You **must** enter the mother's Social Security number in item 8B. if you are applying for a number for a child under age 18.

9. You **must** enter the father's Social Security number in item 9B. if you are applying for a number for a child under age 18.

13. If the date of birth you show in item 6 is different from the date of birth you used on a prior application for a Social Security number card, show the date of birth you used on the prior application and submit evidence of age to support the date of birth in item 6.

16. You **must** sign the application if you are age 18 or older and are physically and mentally capable. If you are under age 18, you may also sign the application if you are physically and mentally capable. If you cannot sign your name, you should sign with an "X" mark and have two people sign as witnesses in the space beside the mark. If you are physically or mentally incapable, generally a parent, close relative, or legal guardian may sign the application. Call us if you need clarification about who can sign.

HOW TO SUBMIT THE APPLICATION

Mail the form and your evidence documents to the nearest Social Security office. We will return your documents to you. If you do not want to mail your original documents, take them to the nearest Social Security office with this application.

If you are age 18 or older and have never been assigned a number before, you must apply in person.

Form **SS-5** Internet (2-98) Destroy Prior Editions   Page 1

EVIDENCE WE NEED

CAUTION: We cannot accept photocopies of documents. You must submit original documents or copies certified by the custodian of the record. **Notarized copies are not acceptable.** If your documents do not meet this requirement, we cannot process your application. We will return your documents. IF YOU DO NOT WANT TO MAIL YOUR ORIGINAL DOCUMENTS, TAKE THEM TO ANY SOCIAL SECURITY OFFICE.

If you need an **ORIGINAL CARD** (you have NEVER been assigned a Social Security number before), you must show us proof of :

> **AGE,**
> **IDENTITY, and**
> **U.S. CITIZENSHIP or LAWFUL ALIEN STATUS**

If you need a **DUPLICATE CARD** (no name change), you must show us proof of **IDENTITY**.

IMPORTANT: If you were born outside the U.S., you must also show us proof of **U.S. CITIZENSHIP or LAWFUL ALIEN STATUS.**

If you need a **CORRECTED CARD** because of a name change, you must show us proof of **IDENTITY**.

To **CHANGE YOUR NAME** on our records, we need one or more documents identifying you by your OLD NAME on our records and your NEW NAME.

IMPORTANT: If you were born outside the U.S., you must also show us proof of **U.S. CITIZENSHIP or LAWFUL ALIEN STATUS.**

AGE: We prefer to see your birth certificate. However, we can accept other documents such as a hospital record of your birth made before you were age 5 or a religious record made before you were three months old. If you were born outside the U.S., we can accept your passport. Call us for advice if you cannot obtain any of these documents.

IDENTITY: We must see a document in the name you want shown on the card. We can generally accept a current document that has enough information to identify you (e.g., signature, name, age, date of birth, parents' names). **We CANNOT ACCEPT a BIRTH CERTIFICATE, HOSPITAL BIRTH RECORD, SSN CARD, SSN CARD STUB, OR SSA RECORD.** Some documents that we can accept are:

- Driver's license
- Employer ID card
- Passport
- Marriage or divorce record
- Adoption record
- Health Insurance card (not a Medicare card)
- Military records
- Insurance policy
- School ID card

IMPORTANT: If you are applying for a card on behalf of someone else, we must see proof of identity for both you and the person to whom the card will be issued.

NAME CHANGE: If your name is now different from the name shown on your card, we need an identity document that identifies you by BOTH your old name AND your new name. Examples include a marriage certificate, divorce decree, or a court order that changes your name. Or we can accept two identity documents—one in your old name and one in your new name. (See IDENTITY for examples of identity documents.)

U.S. CITIZENSHIP: We can accept most documents that show you were born in the U.S. If you are a U.S. citizen born outside the U.S., show us a U.S. consular report of birth, a U.S. passport, a Certificate of Citizenship, or a Certificate of Naturalization.

ALIEN STATUS: We need to see a current document issued to you by the U.S. Immigration and Naturalization Service (INS), such as Form I-551, I-94, I-688B, or I-766. We CANNOT accept a receipt showing you applied for the document. If you are not authorized to work in the U.S., we can issue you a Social Security card if you are lawfully here and need the number for a valid nonwork reason. Your card will be marked to show you cannot work, and, if you do, we will notify INS.

IF YOU HAVE ANY QUESTIONS: If you have any questions about this form, or about the documents you need to show us, please contact any Social Security office. A telephone call will help you make sure you have everything you need to apply for a card.

THE PAPERWORK/PRIVACY ACT AND YOUR APPLICATION

The Privacy Act of 1974 requires us to give each person the following notice when applying for a Social Security number.

Sections 205(c) and 702 of the Social Security Act allow us to collect the facts we ask for on this form.

We use the facts you provide on this form to assign you a Social Security number and to issue you a Social Security card. You do not have to give us these facts, however, without them we cannot issue you a Social Security number or a card. Without a number, you may not be able to get a job and could lose Social Security benefits in the future.

The Social Security number is also used by the Internal Revenue Service for tax administration purposes as an identifier in processing tax returns of persons who have income which is reported to the Internal Revenue Service and by persons who are claimed as dependents on someone's Federal income tax return.

We may disclose information as necessary to administer Social Security programs, including to appropriate law enforcement agencies to investigate alleged violations of Social Security law; to other government agencies for administering entitlement, health, and welfare programs such as Medicaid, Medicare, veterans benefits, military pension, and civil service annuities, black lung, housing, student loans, railroad retirement benefits, and food stamps; to the Internal Revenue Service for Federal tax administration; and to employers and former employers to properly prepare wage reports. We may also disclose information as required by Federal law, for example, to the Department of Justice, Immigration and Naturalization Service, to identify and locate aliens in the U.S.; to the Selective Service System for draft registration; and to the Department of Health and

Human Services for child support enforcement purposes. We may verify Social Security numbers for State motor vehicle agencies that use the number in issuing drivers licenses, as authorized by the Social Security Act. Finally, we may disclose information to your Congressional representative if they request information to answer questions you ask him or her.

We may use the information you give us when we match records by computer. Matching programs compare our records with those of other Federal, State, or local government agencies to determine whether a person qualifies for benefits paid by the Federal government. The law allows us to do this even if you do not agree to it.

Explanations about these and other reasons why information you provide us may be used or given out are available in Social Security offices. If you want to learn more about this, contact any Social Security office.

The Paperwork Reduction Act of 1995 requires us to notify you that this information collection is in accordance with the clearance requirements of section 3507 of the Paperwork Reduction Act of 1995. We may not conduct or sponsor, and you are not required to respond to, a collection of information unless it displays a valid OMB control number.

TIME IT TAKES TO COMPLETE THIS FORM

We estimate that it will take you about 8.5 to 9 minutes to provide the information. This includes the time it will take to read the instructions, gather the necessary facts and provide the information. All requests for Social Security cards and other claims-related information **should be sent to your local Social Security office**, whose address is listed under Social Security Administration in the U.S. Government section of your telephone directory. Comments or suggestions on our "Time it Takes" estimate are welcome and should be addressed to: Social Security Administration, ATTN: Reports Clearance Officer, 1-A-21 Operations Building, Baltimore, MD 21235-0001. SEND ONLY COMMENTS ON OUR "TIME IT TAKES" ESTIMATE TO THIS ADDRESS.

SOCIAL SECURITY ADMINISTRATION Application for a Social Security Card

Form Approved
OMB No. 0960-0066

1	**NAME** TO BE SHOWN ON CARD ➜	First	Full Middle Name	Last
	FULL NAME AT BIRTH IF OTHER THAN ABOVE ➜	First	Full Middle Name	Last
	OTHER NAMES USED ➜			

2	**MAILING ADDRESS** ➜ Do Not Abbreviate	Street Address, Apt. No., PO Box, Rural Route No.
		City State Zip Code

3 **CITIZENSHIP** (Check One) ➜
☐ U.S. Citizen   ☐ Legal Alien Allowed To Work   ☐ Legal Alien **Not** Allowed To Work   ☐ Other (See Instructions On Page 1)

4 **SEX** ➜   ☐ Male   ☐ Female

5 **RACE/ETHNIC DESCRIPTION** (Check One Only—Voluntary) ➜
☐ Asian Asian-American or Pacific Islander   ☐ Hispanic   ☐ Black (Not Hispanic)   ☐ North American Indian or Alaskan Native   ☐ White (Not Hispanic)

6 **DATE OF BIRTH** _____ Month, Day, Year

7 **PLACE OF BIRTH** (Do Not Abbreviate)   City   State or Foreign Country   FCI   Office Use Only

8 **A. MOTHER'S MAIDEN NAME** ➜   First   Full Middle Name   Last Name At Her Birth

B. MOTHER'S SOCIAL SECURITY NUMBER (Complete only if applying for a number for a child under age 18.) ➜ ☐☐☐–☐☐–☐☐☐☐

9 **A. FATHER'S NAME** ➜   First   Full Middle Name   Last

B. FATHER'S SOCIAL SECURITY NUMBER (Complete only if applying for a number for a child under age 18.) ➜ ☐☐☐–☐☐–☐☐☐☐

10 Has the applicant or anyone acting on his/her behalf ever filed for or received a Social Security number card before?

☐ Yes (If "yes", answer questions 11-13.)   ☐ No (If "no", go on to question 14.)   ☐ Don't Know (If "don't know", go on to question 14.)

11 Enter the Social Security number previously assigned to the person listed in item 1. ➜ ☐☐☐–☐☐–☐☐☐☐

12 Enter the name shown on the most recent Social Security card issued for the person listed in item 1. ➜   First   Middle   Last

13 Enter any different date of birth if used on an earlier application for a card. ➜ _____ Month, Day, Year

14 **TODAY'S DATE** _____ Month, Day, Year

15 **DAYTIME PHONE NUMBER** ( )   Area Code   Number

DELIBERATELY FURNISHING (OR CAUSING TO BE FURNISHED) FALSE INFORMATION ON THIS APPLICATION IS A CRIME PUNISHABLE BY FINE OR IMPRISONMENT, OR BOTH.

16 **YOUR SIGNATURE** ▶

17 **YOUR RELATIONSHIP TO THE PERSON IN ITEM 1 IS:**
☐ Self   ☐ Natural or Adoptive Parent   ☐ Legal Guardian   ☐ Other (Specify)

DO NOT WRITE BELOW THIS LINE (FOR SSA USE ONLY)					
NPN		DOC	NTI	CAN	ITV
PBC	EVI	EVA	EVC	PRA	NWR	DNR	UNIT

EVIDENCE SUBMITTED	SIGNATURE AND TITLE OF EMPLOYEE(S) REVIEWING EVIDENCE AND/OR CONDUCTING INTERVIEW
	DATE
	DCL DATE

Form **SS-5** Internet (2-98) Destroy Prior Editions   Page 5

WHEN YOU APPLY FOR A CHILD'S SOCIAL SECURITY NUMBER

You may need this additional information to complete items 8.B. and 9.B. on Form SS-5, Application for a Social Security Card.

When you apply for a Social Security number for a child under age 18, you need to provide each parent's Social Security number **unless** the-
* parent does not have a Social Security number;
* parent's Social Security number is not known.

If you can't provide the parent's Social Security number for one of the reasons listed above, we'll still be able to assign the child a Social Security number.

^^^

CUANDO USTED SOLICITA UN NÚMERO DE SEGURO SOCIAL PARA UN NIÑO

Usted podría necesitar esta información adicional para completar los artículos 8.B. y 9.B. en el formulario SS-5, *Solicitud para una tarjeta de Seguro Social.*

Cuando usted solicita un número de Seguro Social para un niño menor de 18 años, necesita proveer los números de Seguro Social de cada padre **a menos que-**
* los padres no tengan números de Seguro Social;
* los números de Seguro Social de los padres sean desconocidos.

Si usted no puede proveer los números de Seguro Social de los padres por una de las razones mencionadas arriba, todavía podremos asignar un número de Seguro Social al niño(a).

Form **SS-5-SUP** (05-2000)

Last Will and Testament

I, _____ a resident of _____
County, _____ do hereby make, publish, and declare this to be my Last Will
and Testament, hereby revoking any and all Wills and Codicils heretofore made by me.

FIRST: I direct that all my just debts and funeral expenses be paid out of my estate as soon
after my death as is practicable.

SECOND: I give, devise, and bequeath the following specific gifts:

_____

_____

_____

_____

_____

_____

_____

_____

_____

_____

THIRD: I give, devise, and bequeath all my estate, real, personal, and mixed, of whatever
kind and wherever situated, of which I may die seized or possessed, or in which I may have any
interest or over which I may have any power of appointment or testamentary disposition, to my
spouse, _____. If my said spouse does not survive me,
I give, and bequeath the said property to my children _____

_____

_____,
plus any afterborn or adopted children in equal shares or their lineal descendants, per stirpes.

FOURTH: In the event that any beneficiary fails to survive me by thirty days, then this will
shall take effect as if that person had predeceased me.

FIFTH: Should my spouse not survive me, I hereby nominate, constitute, and appoint
_____ as guardian over the person and estate of any of
my children who have not reached the age of majority at the time of my death. In the event that said
guardian is unable or unwilling to serve, then I nominate, constitute, and appoint
_____ as guardian. Said guardian shall serve without bond
or surety.

SIXTH: I hereby nominate, constitute, and appoint _____
as Executor or Personal Representative of this, my Last Will and Testament. In the event that such

named person is unable or unwilling to serve at any time or for any reason, then I nominate, constitute, and appoint _____ as Executor or Personal Representative in the place and stead of the person first named herein. It is my will and I direct that my Executor or Personal Representative shall not be required to furnish a bond for the faithful performance of his or her duties in any jurisdiction, any provision of law to the contrary notwithstanding, and I give my Executor or Personal Representative full power to administer my estate, including the power to settle claims, pay debts, and sell, lease or exchange real and personal property without court order.

     IN WITNESS WHEREOF I declare this to be my Last Will and Testament and execute it willingly as my free and voluntary act for the purposes expressed herein and I am of legal age and sound mind and make this under no constraint or undue influence, this _____ day of _____, 20___ at _____ State of _____.

_____

     The foregoing instrument was on said date subscribed at the end thereof by _____, the above named Testator who signed, published, and declared this instrument to be his/her Last Will and Testament in the presence of us and each of us, who thereupon at his/her request, in his/her presence, and in the presence of each other, have hereunto subscribed our names as witnesses thereto. We are of sound mind and proper age to witness a will and understand this to be his/her will, and to the best of our knowledge testator is of legal age to make a will, of sound mind, and under no constraint or undue influence.

_____residing at_____

_____residing at_____

_____residing at_____

Last Will and Testament

I, _____ a resident of _____
County, _____ do hereby make, publish, and declare this to be my Last Will
and Testament, hereby revoking any and all Wills and Codicils heretofore made by me.

FIRST: I direct that all my just debts and funeral expenses be paid out of my estate as soon
after my death as is practicable.

SECOND: I give, devise, and bequeath the following specific gifts:

_____
_____
_____
_____
_____
_____
_____
_____
_____
_____

THIRD: I give, devise, and bequeath all my estate, real, personal, and mixed, of whatever
kind and wherever situated, of which I may die seized or possessed, or in which I may have any
interest or over which I may have any power of appointment or testamentary disposition, to my
spouse, _____. If my said spouse does not survive me,
I give, and bequeath the said property to _____
_____
_____,
or to their lineal descendants, per stirpes.

FOURTH: In the event that any beneficiary fails to survive me by thirty days, then this will
shall take effect as if that person had predeceased me.

FIFTH: I hereby nominate, constitute, and appoint _____
as Executor or Personal Representative of this, my Last Will and Testament. In the event that such
named person is unable or unwilling to serve at any time or for any reason, then I nominate,
constitute, and appoint _____ as Executor or Personal
Representative in the place and stead of the person first named herein. It is my will and I direct that
my Executor or Personal Representative shall not be required to furnish a bond for the faithful
performance of his or her duties in any jurisdiction, any provision of law to the contrary
notwithstanding, and I give my Executor or Personal Representative full power to administer my

estate, including the power to settle claims, pay debts, and sell, lease or exchange real and personal property without court order.

IN WITNESS WHEREOF I declare this to be my Last Will and Testament and execute it willingly as my free and voluntary act for the purposes expressed herein and I am of legal age and sound mind and make this under no constraint or undue influence, this _____ day of _____, 20___ at _____ State of _____.

_____

The foregoing instrument was on said date subscribed at the end thereof by _____, the above named Testator who signed, published, and declared this instrument to be his/her Last Will and Testament in the presence of us and each of us, who thereupon at his/her request, in his/her presence, and in the presence of each other, have hereunto subscribed our names as witnesses thereto. We are of sound mind and proper age to witness a will and understand this to be his/her will, and to the best of our knowledge testator is of legal age to make a will, of sound mind, and under no constraint or undue influence.

_____residing at_____

_____residing at_____

_____residing at_____

Last Will and Testament

I, _____ a resident of _____
County, _____ do hereby make, publish, and declare this to be my Last Will
and Testament, hereby revoking any and all Wills and Codicils heretofore made by me.

FIRST: I direct that all my just debts and funeral expenses be paid out of my estate as soon
after my death as is practicable.

SECOND: I give, devise, and bequeath the following specific gifts:

_____
_____
_____
_____
_____
_____
_____
_____
_____
_____
_____

THIRD: I give, devise, and bequeath all my estate, real, personal, and mixed, of whatever
kind and wherever situated, of which I may die seized or possessed, or in which I may have any
interest or over which I may have any power of appointment or testamentary disposition, to my
children _____
_____
_____,
plus any afterborn or adopted children in equal shares or to their lineal descendants per stirpes.

FOURTH: In the event that any beneficiary fails to survive me by thirty days, then this will
shall take effect as if that person had predeceased me.

FIFTH: In the event any of my children have not attained the age of 18 years at the time of
my death, I hereby nominate, constitute, and appoint _____ as
guardian over the person and estate of any of my children who have not reached the age of majority
at the time of my death. In the event that said guardian is unable or unwilling to serve, then I
nominate, constitute, and appoint _____ as guardian. Said
guardian shall serve without bond or surety.

SIXTH: I hereby nominate, constitute, and appoint _____ as
Executor or Personal Representative of this, my Last Will and Testament. In the event that such named
person is unable or unwilling to serve at any time or for any reason, then I nominate, constitute, and

appoint _____ as Executor or Personal Representative in the place and stead of the person first named herein. It is my will and I direct that my Executor or Personal Representative shall not be required to furnish a bond for the faithful performance of his or her duties in any jurisdiction, any provision of law to the contrary notwithstanding, and I give my Executor or Personal Representative full power to administer my estate, including the power to settle claims, pay debts, and sell, lease or exchange real and personal property without court order.

IN WITNESS WHEREOF I declare this to be my Last Will and Testament and execute it willingly as my free and voluntary act for the purposes expressed herein and I am of legal age and sound mind and make this under no constraint or undue influence, this _____ day of _____, 20___ at _____ State of _____.

_____

The foregoing instrument was on said date subscribed at the end thereof by _____, the above named Testator who signed, published, and declared this instrument to be his/her Last Will and Testament in the presence of us and each of us, who thereupon at his/her request, in his/her presence, and in the presence of each other, have hereunto subscribed our names as witnesses thereto. We are of sound mind and proper age to witness a will and understand this to be his/her will, and to the best of our knowledge testator is of legal age to make a will, of sound mind, and under no constraint or undue influence.

_____ residing at_____

_____ residing at_____

_____ residing at_____

Last Will and Testament

I, _____ a resident of
_____ County, _____ do hereby make, publish, and
declare this to be my Last Will and Testament, hereby revoking any and all Wills and Codicils
heretofore made by me.

FIRST: I direct that all my just debts and funeral expenses be paid out of my estate as soon
after my death as is practicable.

SECOND: I give, devise, and bequeath the following specific gifts:

_____
_____
_____
_____
_____
_____
_____
_____
_____

THIRD: I give, devise, and bequeath all my estate, real, personal, and mixed, of whatever
kind and wherever situated, of which I may die seized or possessed, or in which I may have any interest
or over which I may have any power of appointment or testamentary disposition, to the following:

_____
_____
_____,
in equal share, or to the survivor of them.

FOURTH: In the event that any beneficiary fails to survive me by thirty days, then this will
shall take effect as if that person had predeceased me.

FIFTH: I hereby nominate, constitute, and appoint _____ as
Executor or Personal Representative of this, my Last Will and Testament. In the event that such named
person is unable or unwilling to serve at any time or for any reason, then I nominate, constitute, and
appoint _____ as Executor or Personal Representative in the place
and stead of the person first named herein. It is my will and I direct that my Executor or Personal
Representative shall not be required to furnish a bond for the faithful performance of his or her
duties in any jurisdiction, any provision of law to the contrary notwithstanding, and I give my

Executor or Personal Representative full power to administer my estate, including the power to settle claims, pay debts, and sell, lease or exchange real and personal property without court order.

IN WITNESS WHEREOF I declare this to be my Last Will and Testament and execute it willingly as my free and voluntary act for the purposes expressed herein and I am of legal age and sound mind and make this under no constraint or undue influence, this _____ day of _____, 20___ at _____ State of _____.

_____

The foregoing instrument was on said date subscribed at the end thereof by _____, the above named Testator who signed, published, and declared this instrument to be his/her Last Will and Testament in the presence of us and each of us, who thereupon at his/her request, in his/her presence, and in the presence of each other, have hereunto subscribed our names as witnesses thereto. We are of sound mind and proper age to witness a will and understand this to be his/her will, and to the best of our knowledge testator is of legal age to make a will, of sound mind, and under no constraint or undue influence.

_____residing at_____

_____residing at_____

_____residing at_____

First Codicil to the Will of

_____

I, _____, a resident of _____
County, _____ declare this to be the first codicil to my Last Will and Testament
dated _____, 20____.

FIRST: I hereby revoke the clause of my Will which reads as follows:
_____
_____
_____
_____.

SECOND: I hereby add the following clause to my Will: _____
_____
_____
_____
_____.

THIRD: In all other respects I hereby confirm and republish my Last Will and Testament
dated _____, _____.

IN WITNESS WHEREOF, I have signed, published, and declared the foregoing instrument
as and for a codicil to my Last Will and Testament, this _____ day of _____, 20____.

_____

The foregoing instrument was on the _____day of _____, 20____,
signed at the end thereof, and at the same time published and declared by
_____, as and for a codicil to his/her Last Will and Testament,
dated _____, 20_____, in the presence of each of us, who, this attestation clause
having been read to us, did at the request of the said testator/testatrix, in his/her presence and in the
presence of each other signed our names as witnesses thereto.

_____residing at_____

_____residing at_____

_____residing at_____

Declaration of Joint property

The undersigned, in consideration of the mutual agreement herein contained, agree that all property owned by them and located in their place of residence, shall be owned in joint tenancy with full rights of survivorship, except the following items which shall remain separate property for all purposes:

In addition to the property located at the residence, the following property shall also be owned in joint tenancy with full rights of survivorship:

In witness whereof, the parties affix their signatures and seals this _____ day of _____, 20___.

_____(seal)

_____(seal)

155

DECLARATION OF SEPARATE PROPERTY

The undersigned, in consideration of the mutual agreement herein contained, agree that all property owned by them and located in their place of residence, shall be owned as separate property of the person by whom it was purchased, except the following items which are owned as joint property with full rights of survivorship.

In addition to the property located at the residence, the following property shall also be owned as separate property:

In witness whereof, the parties affix their signatures and seals this _____ day of _____, 20____.

_____(seal)

_____(seal)

LIVING TRUST - SCHEDULE OF ASSETS

This Schedule of Assets of Living Trust is attached and made part of the _____ Revocable Living Trust, dated _____, 20____.
The following assets are made part of this Living Trust:

LIVING TRUST - AMENDMENT

AMENDMENT
TO THE

_____

REVOCABLE LIVING TRUST

  This Amendment to the _____ Revocable Living Trust, dated _____, 20____, is made by _____, Grantor, on _____, 20____.

The Grantor hereby amends the Trust as follows:

State of _____
County of _____

  On _____, 20_____, before me personally appeared _____, who is personally known to me or who provided _____ as identification, and signed the above document in my presence.

_____
Notary Public
My Commission expires:

LIVING TRUST - TERMINATION

I, _____, of _____
_____, hereby revoke
the Living Trust, dated _____, 20____.

Dated: _____, 20____

_____
Grantor

State of _____
County of _____

On _____, 20_____, before me personally appeared
_____, who is personally known to me or who provided
_____ as identification, and
signed the above document in my presence.

_____
Notary Public
My Commission expires:

LIVING TRUST

THE

_____

REVOCABLE LIVING TRUST

I, _____, of _____
_____, hereby make
and declare this Living Trust, as Grantor and Trustee, on _____, 20____.

This Trust shall be known as the _____ Revocable
Living Trust. I, _____ will be trustee of this trust. Upon
my death or if I am unable to manage this trust and my financial affairs, I appoint
_____, my _____, of
_____ _____ as successor
trustee, to serve without bond. In addition to any powers, authority and discretion granted
by law, I grant such Trustee and Successor Trustee any and all powers to perform any acts, in
his or her sole discretion and without court approval, for the management and distribution
of this trust.

TRANSFER OF PROPERTY. I hereby transfer to this trust the property listed on the
attached Schedule of Assets which is made a part of this trust. I shall have the right at any
time to add property to the trust or delete property from the trust.

DISPOSITION OF INCOME AND PRINCIPAL. During my lifetime, the Trustee
shall pay so much or all of the net income and principal of the trust as I from time to time
may request to me. Upon my death, the successor trustee shall pay all claims, expenses and
taxes and shall distribute the trust estate to the following beneficiary or beneficiaries who
shall survive me:

_____
_____
_____
_____

The share of a beneficiary who is under ____ years of age shall not be paid to such beneficiary but shall be held in trust by the Trustee. The Trustee shall pay so much or all of the net
income and principal of such trust to the beneficiary as he thinks necessary for his or her
support, welfare and education. The Trustee shall pay the beneficiary the remaining principal, if any, when he or she attains the age of ____ years.

In case a beneficiary for whom a share is held in trust dies before receiving the remaining principal, it shall be paid to his or her living child or children or, if none, to my then living descendants.

This trust shall terminate twenty-one (21) years after the death of the last beneficiary named in the trust.

REVOCATION AND AMENDMENT. I may, by signed instrument delivered to the Trustee, revoke or amend this Trust Agreement in whole or in part.

GOVERNING LAW. This Trust will be governed under the laws of the State of _____.

In Witness Whereof, I as Grantor and Trustee have executed this Agreement on the date above written.

_____   _____
Witness   Grantor

_____   _____
Witness   Trustee

STATE OF   )
COUNTY OF   )

The foregoing instrument was acknowledged before me this ____ day of _____, 20____, by _____, as Grantor and Trustee, who is personally known to me or who has produced _____ as identification.

_____
Notary Public
My Commission Expires:

POWER OF ATTORNEY - GENERAL

_____ (the "Grantor")
hereby grants to _____(the "Agent") a
general power of attorney. As the Grantor's attorney in fact, the Agent shall have full power and authority to undertake any and all acts which may be lawfully undertaken on behalf of the grantor including
but not limited to the right to buy, sell, lease, mortgage, assign, rent or otherwise dispose of any real or
personal property belonging to the Grantor; to execute, accept, undertake and perform contracts in the
name of the Grantor; to deposit, endorse, or withdraw funds to or from any bank depository of the
Grantor; to initiate, defend or settle legal actions on behalf of the Grantor; and to retain any accountant, attorney or other advisor deemed by the Agent to be necessary to protect the interests of the
Grantor in relation to such powers.

By accepting this grant, the Agent agrees to act in a fiduciary capacity consistent with the reasonable best interests of the Grantor. This power of attorney may be revoked by the Grantor at any
time; however, any person dealing with the Agent as attorney in fact may rely on this appointment
until receipt of actual notice of termination.

IN WITNESS WHEREOF, the undersigned grantor has executed this power of attorney
under seal as of the date stated above.

_____(Seal)
, Grantor

STATE OF
COUNTY OF

I certify that _____ ,who ❑ is personally
known to me to be the person whose name is subscribed to the foregoing instrument ❑ produced _____ as identification, personally appeared
before me on _____, 20_____, and acknowledged the execution of the
foregoing instrument.

_____
Notary Public, State of

Notary's commission expires:

I hereby accept the foregoing appointment as attorney in fact on _____, 20____.

_____
Attorney in Fact

POWER OF ATTORNEY - SPECIFIC

_____ (the "Grantor") hereby grants to _____ (the "Agent") a limited power of attorney. As the Grantor's attorney in fact, the Agent shall have full power and authority to undertake and perform the following on behalf of the Grantor:

By accepting this grant, the Agent agrees to act in a fiduciary capacity consistent with the reasonable best interests of the Grantor. This power of attorney may be revoked by the Grantor at any time; however, any person dealing with the Agent as attorney in fact may rely on this appointment until receipt of actual notice of termination.

IN WITNESS WHEREOF, the undersigned grantor has executed this power of attorney under seal as of the date stated above.

_____(Seal)
, Grantor

STATE OF
COUNTY OF

I certify that _____ ,who ❏ is personally known to me to be the person whose name is subscribed to the foregoing instrument ❏ produced _____ as identification, personally appeared before me on _____, 20_____, and acknowledged the execution of the foregoing instrument.

_____
Notary Public, State of

Notary's commission expires:

I hereby accept the foregoing appointment as attorney in fact on _____, 20____.

_____
Attorney in Fact

REVOCATION OF POWER OF ATTORNEY

_____ (the "Grantor") of a Power of Attorney to _____ (the "Agent") dated _____, hereby revokes said power of attorney as of _____, 20___.

IN WITNESS WHEREOF, the undersigned grantor has executed this power of attorney under seal as of the date stated above.

_____(Seal)

LIVING WILL

I, _____, being of sound mind willfully and voluntarily make known my desires regarding my medical care and treatment under the circumstances as indicated below:

_____ 1. If I should have an incurable or irreversible condition that will cause my death within a relatively short time, and if I am unable to make decisions regarding my medical treatment, I direct my attending physician to withhold or withdraw procedures that merely prolong the dying process and are not necessary to my comfort or to alleviate pain. This authorization includes, but is not limited to, the withholding or the withdrawal of the following types of medical treatment (subject to any special instructions in paragraph 5 below):

_____ a. Artificial feeding and hydration.
_____ b. Cardiopulmonary resuscitation (this includes, but is not limited to, the use of drugs, electric shock, and artificial breathing).
_____ c. Kidney dialysis.
_____ d. Surgery or other invasive procedures.
_____ e. Drugs and antibiotics.
_____ f. Transfusions of blood or blood products.
_____ g. Other: _____
_____

_____ 2. If I should be in an irreversible coma or persistent vegetative state that my attending physician reasonably believes to be irreversible or incurable, I direct my attending physician to withhold or withdraw medical procedures and treatment other than such medical procedures and treatment necessary to my comfort or to alleviate pain. This authorization includes, but is not limited to, the withholding or withdrawal of the following types of medical treatment (subject to any special instructions in paragraph 5 below):

_____ a. Artificial feeding and hydration.
_____ b. Cardiopulmonary resuscitation (this includes, but is not limited to, the use of drugs, electric shock, and artificial breathing).
_____ c. Kidney dialysis.
_____ d. Surgery or other invasive procedures.
_____ e. Drugs and antibiotics.
_____ f. Transfusions of blood or blood products.
_____ g. Other: _____
_____

_____ 3. If I have a medical condition where I am unable to communicate my desires as to treatment and my physician determines that the burdens of treatment outweigh the expected benefits, I direct my attending physician to withhold or withdraw medical procedures and treatment other than such medical procedures and treatment necessary to my comfort or to alleviate pain. This authorization includes, but is not limited to, the withholding or withdrawal of the following types of medical treatment (subject to any special instructions in paragraph 5 below):

_____ a. Artificial feeding and hydration.
_____ b. Cardiopulmonary resuscitation (this includes, but is not limited to, the use of drugs, electric shock, and artificial breathing).
_____ c. Kidney dialysis.
_____ d. Surgery or other invasive procedures.

    _____   e.   Drugs and antibiotics.

    _____   f.   Transfusions of blood or blood products.

    _____   g.   Other: _____

                                     _____

_____   4.   I want my life prolonged to the greatest extent possible (subject to any special instructions in paragraph 5 below).

_____   5.   Special instructions (if any) _____

                                     _____

                                     _____

                                     _____

Signed this _____ day of _____,20____.

Signature _____

Address:_____

            _____

The declarant is personally known to me and voluntarily signed this document in my presence.

Witness:_____   Witness_____

Name:_____   Name:_____

Address:_____   Address:_____

_____   _____

State of _____)
County of _____)

    On this _____ day of _____, 20_____, before me, personally appeared _____, principal, and _____ and _____, witnesses, who are personally known to me or who provided _____

_____

as identification, and signed the foregoing instrument in my presence.

_____
Notary Public

ANATOMICAL GIFTS

UNIFORM DONOR CARD

The undersigned hereby makes this anatomical gift, if medically acceptable, to take effect on death. The words and marks below indicate my desires:

I give:

        (a) ____ any needed organs or parts;

        (b) ____ only the following organs or parts

_____

for the purpose of transplantation, therapy, medical research, or education;

        (c) ____ my body for anatomical study if needed.

Limitations or special wishes, if any:

_____

Signed by the donor and the following witnesses in the presence of each other:

_____   _____
Signature of Donor   Date of birth

_____   _____
Date signed   City & State

_____   _____
Witness   Witness

_____   _____
Address   Address

UNIFORM DONOR CARD

The undersigned hereby makes this anatomical gift, if medically acceptable, to take effect on death. The words and marks below indicate my desires:

I give:

        (a) ____ any needed organs or parts;

        (b) ____ only the following organs or parts

_____

for the purpose of transplantation, therapy, medical research, or education;

        (c) ____ my body for anatomical study if needed.

Limitations or special wishes, if any:

_____

Signed by the donor and the following witnesses in the presence of each other:

_____   _____
Signature of Donor   Date of birth

_____   _____
Date signed   City & State

_____   _____
Witness   Witness

_____   _____
Address   Address

UNIFORM DONOR CARD

The undersigned hereby makes this anatomical gift, if medically acceptable, to take effect on death. The words and marks below indicate my desires:

I give:

        (a) ____ any needed organs or parts;

        (b) ____ only the following organs or parts

_____

for the purpose of transplantation, therapy, medical research, or education;

        (c) ____ my body for anatomical study if needed.

Limitations or special wishes, if any:

_____

Signed by the donor and the following witnesses in the presence of each other:

_____   _____
Signature of Donor   Date of birth

_____   _____
Date signed   City & State

_____   _____
Witness   Witness

_____   _____
Address   Address

UNIFORM DONOR CARD

The undersigned hereby makes this anatomical gift, if medically acceptable, to take effect on death. The words and marks below indicate my desires:

I give:

        (a) ____ any needed organs or parts;

        (b) ____ only the following organs or parts

_____

for the purpose of transplantation, therapy, medical research, or education;

        (c) ____ my body for anatomical study if needed.

Limitations or special wishes, if any:

_____

Signed by the donor and the following witnesses in the presence of each other:

_____   _____
Signature of Donor   Date of birth

_____   _____
Date signed   City & State

_____   _____
Witness   Witness

_____   _____
Address   Address

One of these cards should be cut out and carried in your wallet or purse.

167

RECEIPT

The undersigned hereby acknowledges receipt of the sum of _____
_____($_____) in the form of

❏ cash

❏ a check numbered _____, dated _____, 20_____

as payment for: _____
_____
_____
_____
_____

Balance due: _____($_____)

Date _____, 20_____

_____

PROMISSORY NOTE - LUMP PAYMENT

$_____   Date:_____, 20____

_____ hereby
promises to pay to the order of _____
_____ the sum of $_____,
with interest thereon from the date of this note to the date of payment at the rate of _____
per annum.

This note is due and payable in full on _____, 20___, if not paid
sooner. The principal and interest shall be payable when due at _____
_____ or at a place
of which the undersigned may be notified in writing by the holder of this note.

This note is not assumable without the written consent of the lender. This note may
be paid in whole or in part at any time prior without penalty. The borrower waives demand,
presentment, protest, and notice. This note shall be fully payable upon demand of any holder
in the event the undersigned shall default on the terms of this note or any agreement securing the payment of this note. In the event of default, the undersigned agrees to pay all costs
of collection including reasonable attorneys fees.

IN WITNESS WHEREOF, the undersigned has executed this note under seal as of the
date stated above (if the undersigned is a corporation, this note has been executed under seal
and by authority of its board of directors).

_____

_____

PROMISSORY NOTE - AMORTIZED
WITH GUARANTY

$_____   Date:_____, 20___

_____ hereby
promises to pay to the order of _____
_____ the sum of $_____, with
interest thereon from the date of this note to the date of payment at the rate of _____ per annum.

This note is payable $_____ per _____ including principal and
interest until paid in full. The principal and interest shall be payable when due at _____
_____ or
at a place of which the undersigned may be notified in writing by the holder of this note.

This note is not assumable without the written consent of the lender. This note may
be paid in whole or in part at any time prior without penalty. The borrower waives demand,
presentment, protest, and notice. This note shall be fully payable upon demand of any holder
in the event the undersigned shall default on the terms of this note or any agreement securing the payment of this note. In the event of default, the undersigned agrees to pay all costs
of collection including reasonable attorneys fees.

IN WITNESS WHEREOF, the undersigned has executed this note under seal as of the
date stated above (if the undersigned is a corporation, this note has been executed under seal
and by authority of its board of directors).

_____

_____

Guaranty

The undersigned, to induce the acceptance of the above Promissory Note hereby uncondi-
tionally guarantees the payment of this note according to its terms. The undersigned waives
presentment, demand for payment, protest and notice of nonpayment, dishonor or protest.
This guaranty shall inure to the benefit of all subsequent holders of this note.

_____

_____

PROMISSORY NOTE - PAYABLE ON DEMAND

$_____   Date:_____, 20___

_____ hereby
promises to pay to the order of _____
_____ the sum of $_____,
with interest thereon from the date of this note to the date of payment at the rate of _____
per annum.

    This note is payable upon demand of the holder. The principal and interest shall be
payable when due at _____
or at a place of which the undersigned may be notified in writing by the holder of this note.

    This note is not assumable without the written consent of the lender. This note may
be paid in whole or in part at any time prior without penalty. The borrower waives demand,
presentment, protest, and notice. This note shall be fully payable upon demand of any holder
in the event the undersigned shall default on the terms of this note or any agreement securing the payment of this note. In the event of default, the undersigned agrees to pay all costs
of collection including reasonable attorneys fees.

    IN WITNESS WHEREOF, the undersigned has executed this note under seal as of the
date stated above (if the undersigned is a corporation, this note has been executed under seal
and by authority of its board of directors).

                                                                        _____

                                                                        _____

AUTHORIZATION TO CHECK CREDIT

To:

The undersigned hereby authorizes you to release my credit report to:

_____

_____

_____

_____
Signature

REQUEST FOR CREDIT REPORT

Re: Disclosure of Credit Information

   In accordance with the Federal Fair Credit Reporting Act, I hereby request a full and complete disclosure of my personal credit file. This disclosure should include the names and addresses of all parties who have received a copy of my credit report and the names and addresses of all parties who have provided information that is contained in my credit report.

   ❑ I enclose the sum of $ _____ for this report.
Thank you for your cooperation.

   ❑ I was recently denied credit based upon a report issued by your agency. As required by law, please provide me with a copy of my credit report.

Name:_____   Soc. Sec. No.:_____

Address:_____

Thank you,

_____

REQUEST FOR CORRECTION OF CREDIT REPORT

To:

From: _____

Address: _____

_____

Social Security No _____

Your report on my credit history contains the following error(s):

Kindly correct these errors and provide me with a corrected copy of my report.

Thank you,

_____

DENIAL OF DEBT

To:

Re: _____
Amount $_____

The records of your company regarding the above debt are in error for the following reasons:

Kindly correct your records accordingly.

Thank you,

_____

REQUEST TO STOP HARASSMENT ON DEBT

To:

Re: _____

Amount $_____

Please do not continue to contact me regarding the above debt.

Thank you,

_____

SATISFACTION AND RELEASE OF JUDGMENT

The Plaintiff, _____ hereby acknowledges that the judgment in this action rendered on _____ has been fully satisfied by Defendant, _____ and hereby releases and discharges said Defendant from any and all further liability for said judgment.

Dated: _____, 20____

_____

This document is signed by _____ , (insert: "individually" or "as agent of Plaintiff corporation")_____ on_____, 20____ .

Plaintiff, _____ , to acknowledge full payment of the judgment signed by the Judge on _____, 20____ . Plaintiff agrees that Defendant(s) do(es) not owe the Plaintiff any more monies for the judgment.

Notice of Lost Credit Card

To:

Re: Credit Card #_____

The referenced credit card was lost or stolen on or about _____, 20___. Any charges incurred after that date were not made by me. Please cancel this card and issue me a new one.

Thank you,

_____

Address:

REQUEST TO CANCEL CREDIT CARD

To:

Re: Credit Card #_____

Please cancel the above-referenced credit card account and report to the credit bureaus that the account has been closed. The card(s) issued for the account ❑ are enclosed ❑ have been destroyed.

Thank you,

_____

Address:

REQUEST FOR FORBEARANCE ON LOAN

Direct Loans
William D. Ford Federal Direct Loan Program

General Forbearance Request
William D. Ford Federal Direct Loan Program
Federal Direct Stafford/Ford Loans, Federal Direct Unsubsidized Stafford/Ford Loans, Federal Direct PLUS Loans, Federal Direct Consolidation Loans

OMB No. 1840-0725
Form Approved
Exp. Date 12/31/99

GFB
General

WARNING: Any person who knowingly makes a false statement or misrepresentation on this form shall be subject To penalties which may include fines, imprisonment or both, under the U.S. Criminal Code and 20 U.S.C. 1097.

Borrower's Information   *Please print*

Last Name	First Name	Middle Initial	Social Security Number

Street Address	Home Area Code/Telephone Number ( )

City	State	Zip Code	

Section 1: Forbearance Request   *Must be completed by borrower*

Forbearance means an arrangement to postpone or reduce the amount of a borrower's monthly payment for a limited and specific time period. The borrower is charged interest during a forbearance. A forbearance is available to a borrower or an endorser who is willing but unable to make currently scheduled Direct Loan payments due to a temporary financial hardship.

To request a forbearance, please complete the items below, sign and date this form, and return it to the Direct Loan Servicing Center. (Please note that all references to "borrower" apply to an endorser on a Federal Direct PLUS Loan.)

I am willing but unable to make my current Direct Loan payments due to a temporary financial hardship.

If this forbearance is approved, I choose to (check one):

❑ temporarily stop making payments;   ❑ make smaller payments than previously scheduled. I would like to pay $_____ per month.

I am requesting this forbearance because: _____

_____

_____

I am requesting that the U.S. Department of Education (ED) grant a forbearance on my loan(s) beginning (MM-DD-YY) ⌷⌷⌷⌷⌷⌷ and ending

(MM-DD-YY) ⌷⌷⌷⌷⌷⌷ for a period not to exceed one year. At the end of one year, I may reapply to renew the forbearance if I am still

experiencing financial hardship.

Borrower Understandings and Certifications

I understand that: (1) I will continue to receive billing statements for my current payment amount which I must pay until I am notified by the Direct Loan Servicing Center that my forbearance request has been granted; (2) ED will not grant this forbearance request unless all items on this form are completed and any additional required documentation is provided; (3) during the forbearance period, principal and interest payments may be forborne, but interest will continue to accrue whether or not my loan(s) is subsidized by the federal government; (4) if I requested a temporary suspension of payments, I will receive a quarterly statement detailing the interest that has accrued during the prior period, and unless I choose to pay this interest, ED will add the interest to the principal balance of my loan(s) at the end of the forbearance period (this is called capitalization); (5) if I requested a reduced payment forbearance, I will receive a monthly bill for the requested payment amount until the forbearance ends, and any unpaid interest that has accrued during the period will be added to the principal balance of my loan(s) (capitalized) at the end of the forbearance period.

I certify that: (1) The information I have provided above is true and correct; (2) I will provide additional documentation, as required, to ED to support my continued forbearance status; (3) I will notify ED immediately when the condition(s) that qualified me for the forbearance ends; (4) I have read, understand, and meet the terms and conditions of the forbearance for which I have applied; and (5) I agree, upon termination of this forbearance, to repay this loan according to the terms of my promissory note and repayment schedule.

Signature of Borrower:_____ Date_____

GFB (SCH)   Revised 6/97

Privacy Act Disclosure Notice

The Privacy Act of 1974 (5 U.S.C. 552a) requires that we disclose to you the following information:

The authority for collecting this information is §451 et seq. of the Higher Education Act of 1965 as amended (the HEA) (20 U.S.C. § 1087a et. seq.). The principal purpose for collecting this information is to determine whether you are eligible for a forbearance on your loan(s) under the William D. Ford Federal Direct Loan (Direct Loan) Program.

We ask that you provide the information requested on this Direct Loan forbearance form on a voluntary basis. However, you must provide all of the requested information that is available to you so the Department can determine whether you qualify for a forbearance.

The information in your file may be disclosed to third parties as authorized under routine uses in the Privacy Act notices called "Title IV Program Files" (originally published on April 12, 1994, Federal Register, Vol. 59 p. 17531) and "National Student Loan Data System" (originally published on December 20, 1994, Federal Register, Vol. 59 p. 65532). Thus, this information may be disclosed to parties that we authorize to assist us in administering the Federal student aid programs, including contractors that are required to maintain safeguards under the Privacy Act. Disclosures may also be made for verification of information, determination of eligibility, enforcement of conditions of the loan or grant, debt collection, and the prevention of fraud, waste, and abuse of these disclosures may be made through computer matching programs with other Federal agencies. Disclosures may be made to determine the feasibility of entering into computer matching agreements. We may send information to members of Congress if you ask them in writing to help you with Federal student aid questions. If we are involved in litigation, we may send information to the Department of Justice (DOJ), a court adjudicative body, counsel, or witness if the disclosure is related to financial aid and certain other conditions are met. If this information, either alone or with other information, indicates a potential violation of law, we may send it to the appropriate authority for consideration of action and we may disclose to DOJ to get its advice related to the Title IV, HEA programs or questions under the Freedom of Information Act. Disclosures may be made to qualified researchers under Privacy Act safeguards. In some circumstances involving employment decisions, grievances, or complaints involving decisions regarding the letting of a contract or making of a grant, license or other benefit, we may send information to an appropriate authority. In limited circumstances, we may disclose to a Federal labor organization recognized under 5 U.S.C. Chapter 71.

Because we request your social security number (SSN), we must inform you that we collect your SSN on a voluntary basis, but section 484(a)(4) of the HEA (20 U.S.C. 1091(a)(4)) provides that, in order to receive any grant, loan, or work assistance under Title IV of the HEA, a student must provide his or her SSN. Your SSN is used to verify your identity, and as an account number (identifier) throughout the life of your loan(s) so that data may be recorded accurately.

Privacy Act Notice

The Privacy Act of 1974 (5 U.S.C. 552a) requires that the following notice be provided to you. The authority for collecting the information requested on this form is §451 et seq. of the Higher Education Act of 1965 as amended. Your disclosure of this information is voluntary. However, if you do not provide this information, you cannot repay your Federal Direct Student Loan through the use of an Electronic Debit Account. The information you provide may be disclosed to federal and state agencies, private parties such as relatives, present and former employers and creditors, and contractors of the Department of Education for purposes of administration of the student financial assistance program, for enforcement purposes, for litigation where such disclosure is compatible with the purposes for which the records were collected, for use by federal, state, local, or foreign agencies in connection with employment matters or the issuance of a license, grant or other benefit, for use in any employee grievance or discipline proceeding in which the Federal Government is a party, for use in connection with audits or other investigations, for research purposes, for purposes of determining whether particular records are required to be disclosed under the Freedom of Information Act, and to a Member of Congress in response to an inquiry from the congressional office made at your written request.

Return this form and any required documentation to:

Direct Loan Servicing Center
Borrower Services Department
P.O. Box 4609
Utica, NY 13504-4609

If assistance is needed in completing this form call: 1 (800) 848-0979

Paperwork Reduction Notice

The time required to complete this information collection is estimated to average 0.2 hours (12 minutes) per response, including the time to review instructions, search existing data resources, gather and maintain the data needed, and complete and review the information collection. **If you have any comments concerning the accuracy of the time estimates(s) or suggestions for improving this form, please write to:** U.S. Department of Education, Washington, DC 20202-4651. **If you have any comments or concerns regarding the status of** *your individual submission* **of this form, write directly to:**

Direct Loan Servicing Center
Borrower Services Department
P.O. Box 4609
Utica, NY 13504-4609

REQUEST FOR CONSOLIDATION OF LOANS

To:

I wish to consolidate the following loans with a new loan from your institution:

Please let me know if this will be possible and if so send information on the terms available and any application forms which need to be completed.

Thank you,

_____

Address:

NOTICE OF DEATH OF DEBTOR

To:

Re: Name: _____

Social Security number: _____

Date of Death: _____

Account Number: _____

The above-referenced debtor is deceased.

❑ No probate proceedings are planned

❑ Probate proceedings have been filed in the following court:

_____

File No. _____

Very truly yours,

_____

Address:

REQUEST FOR QUOTATION

To:

We are considering the purchase of the following:

If you are able to provide this as specified, kindly provide us with a quotation of total price and completion or delivery date.

Thank you,

_____

RECEIPT FOR PERSONAL PROPERTY

The undersigned hereby certifies and acknowledges that on _____, 20____, (s)he received from _____ the following personal property:

The purpose for which such items were received was _____
_____.

These items shall be returned _____

In consideration for use of the property the undersigned agrees to be fully responsible for its use and to hold the owner harmless from any claims resulting from the undersigned's use of the property. The undersigned understands that the owner has made no representations or warranties as to the condition of the property or its fitness for any use.

_____

BILL OF SALE

For $\rule{2cm}{0.15mm}$, the receipt of which is hereby acknowledged, the undersigned hereby sells and transfers to $\rule{8cm}{0.15mm}$ all of the undersigned's rights in the following property:

Executed under seal on $\rule{5cm}{0.15mm}$, 20$\rule{1.5cm}{0.15mm}$.

$\rule{10cm}{0.15mm}$

$\rule{10cm}{0.15mm}$

BILL OF SALE - WITH WARRANTY

For valuable consideration, the receipt and sufficiency of which is hereby acknowledged, the undersigned hereby sells and transfers to _____ the following:

The undersigned warrants and represents that it has good title to and full authority to sell and transfer the same and that the property is sold and transferred free and clear of all liens, claims and encumbrances except:

The undersigned warrants that, subject to the exceptions stated above, it will indemnify the Buyer, and defend title to the property, against the adverse claims of all persons.

Executed under seal on _____, 20_____.

_____

_____

CHATTEL MORTGAGE

Date:_____

FOR VALUE RECEIVED, receipt of which is hereby acknowledged, the undersigned debtor hereby grants a security interest in the following property _____

_____ to

_____as secured party.

This security agreement is to secure indebtedness in the amount of _____

_____ Dollars ($_____) evidenced by a promissory note of even date.

The undersigned warrants that he/she is the owner of all interest in said property and that such interest is subject to no other liens, charges encumbrances or claims.

This agreement shall be secured with a UCC financing statement. A copy of this security agreement and the UCC financing statement shall be lodged with the trustee of said land trust and the undersigned consents that no further pledge of the beneficial interest shall be made, or conveyance or encumbrance of the real property of the trust without the consent of the secured party.

Upon default the secured party shall have all the rights and remedies provided a secured party under the Florida Uniform Commercial Code, including the right to sell the beneficial interest at a public or private sale, with or without advertising. The undersigned agrees that the requirements of the UCC shall be met if notice is mailed to the undersigned address at the address below not less than five days prior to the sale or other disposition.

Default shall be any failure to pay principal or interest under the promissory note as it comes due, breach of any warranty made by the debtor, attachment, seizure, foreclosure, forfeiture or levy on the beneficial interest of the trust or the real property held by the trust, institution of any action in bankruptcy by or against debtor, or any reasonable insecurity of the secured party.

The undersigned acknowledges receipt of a completed copy of this security agreement.

Secured party: Debtor:

_____   _____

_____   _____

Address: Address:

_____   _____

_____   _____

UCC-1 Financing Statement

THIS SPACE FOR USE OF FILING OFFICER

FINANCING STATEMENT — FOLLOW INSTRUCTIONS CAREFULLY
This Financing Statement is presented for filing pursuant to the Uniform Commercial Code
and will remain effective, with certain exceptions, for 5 years from date of filing.

A. NAME & TEL. # OF CONTACT AT FILER (optional)	B. FILING OFFICE ACCT. # (optional)

C. RETURN COPY TO: (Name and Mailing Address)

D. OPTIONAL DESIGNATION (if applicable): ☐ LESSOR/LESSEE ☐ CONSIGNOR/CONSIGNEE ☐ NON-UCC FILING

1. DEBTOR'S EXACT FULL LEGAL NAME - insert only one debtor name (1a or 1b)

1a. ENTITY'S NAME

OR

1b. INDIVIDUAL'S LAST NAME	FIRST NAME	MIDDLE NAME	SUFFIX

1c. MAILING ADDRESS	CITY	STATE	COUNTRY	POSTAL CODE

1d. S.S. OR TAX I.D.#	OPTIONAL ADD'NL INFO RE ENTITY DEBTOR	1e. TYPE OF ENTITY	1f. ENTITY'S STATE OR COUNTRY OF ORGANIZATION	1g. ENTITY'S ORGANIZATIONAL I.D.#, if any ☐ NONE

2. ADDITIONAL DEBTOR'S EXACT FULL LEGAL NAME - insert only one debtor name (2a or 2b)

2a. ENTITY'S NAME

OR

2b. INDIVIDUAL'S LAST NAME	FIRST NAME	MIDDLE NAME	SUFFIX

2c. MAILING ADDRESS	CITY	STATE	COUNTRY	POSTAL CODE

2d. S.S. OR TAX I.D.#	OPTIONAL ADD'NL INFO RE ENTITY DEBTOR	2e. TYPE OF ENTITY	2f. ENTITY'S STATE OR COUNTRY OF ORGANIZATION	2g. ENTITY'S ORGANIZATIONAL I.D.#, if any ☐ NONE

3. SECURED PARTY'S (ORIGINAL S/P or ITS TOTAL ASSIGNEE) EXACT FULL LEGAL NAME - insert only one secured party name (3a or 3b)

3a. ENTITY'S NAME

OR

3b. INDIVIDUAL'S LAST NAME	FIRST NAME	MIDDLE NAME	SUFFIX

3c. MAILING ADDRESS	CITY	STATE	COUNTRY	POSTAL CODE

4. This FINANCING STATEMENT covers the following types or items of property:

5. CHECK BOX (if applicable) ☐ This FINANCING STATEMENT is signed by the Secured Party instead of the Debtor to perfect a security interest (a) in collateral already subject to a security interest in another jurisdiction when it was brought into this state, or when the debtor's location was changed to this state, or (b) in accordance with other statutory provisions (additional data may be required)

7. If filed in Florida (check one) ☐ Documentary stamp tax paid ☐ Documentary stamp tax not applicable

6. REQUIRED SIGNATURE(S)

8. ☐ This FINANCING STATEMENT is to be filed (for record) (or recorded) in the REAL ESTATE RECORDS Attach Addendum (if applicable)

9. Check to REQUEST SEARCH CERTIFICATE(S) on Debtor(s) (ADDITIONAL FEE) (optional) ☐ All Debtors ☐ Debtor 1 ☐ Debtor 2

(1) FILING OFFICER COPY — NATIONAL FINANCING STATEMENT (FORM UCC1) (TRANS) (REV. 12/18/95)

General Instructions for National Financing Statement (Form UCC1) (Trans)

Please type or laser-print this form. Be sure it is completely legible. Read all Instructions.

Fill in form very carefully; mistakes may have important legal consequences. Follow Instructions completely. If you have questions, consult your attorney. Filing officer cannot give legal advice.

Do not insert anything in the open space in the upper portion of this form; it is reserved for filing officer use.

When properly completed, send Filing Officer Copy, with required fee, to filing officer. If you want an acknowledgment, also send Acknowledgment Copy, otherwise detach. If you want to make a search request, complete item 9 and send Search Request Copy, otherwise detach. Always detach Debtor and Secured Party Copies.

If you need to use attachments, use 8-1/2 X 11 inch sheets and put at the top of each additional sheet the name of the first Debtor, formatted exactly as it appears in item 1 of this form; you are encouraged to use Addendum (Form UCC1Ad).

Item Instructions

1. **Debtor name**: Enter only one Debtor name in item 1, an entity's name (1a) or an individual's name (1b). Enter Debtor's exact full legal name. Don't abbreviate.

1a. Entity Debtor. "Entity" means an organization having a legal identity separate from its owner. A partnership is an entity; a sole proprietorship is not an entity, even if it does business under a trade name. If Debtor is a partnership, enter exact full legal name of partnership; you need not enter names of partners as additional Debtors. If Debtor is a registered entity (e.g., corporation, limited partnership, limited liability company), it is advisable to examine Debtor's current filed charter documents to determine correct name, entity type, and state of organization.

1b. Individual Debtor. "Individual" means a natural person and a sole proprietorship, whether or not operating under a trade name. Don't use prefixes (Mr., Mrs., Ms.). Use suffix box only for titles of lineage (Jr., Sr., III) and not for other suffixes or titles (e.g., M.D.). Use married woman's personal name (Mary Smith, not Mrs. John Smith). Enter individual Debtor's family name (surname) in Last Name box, first given name in First Name box, and all additional given names in Middle Name box.
For both entity and individual Debtors: Don't use Debtor's trade name, D/B/A, A/K/A, F/K/A, etc. in place of Debtor's legal name; you may add such other names as additional Debtors if you wish.

1c. An address is always required for the Debtor named in 1a or 1b.

1d. Debtor's social security or tax identification number is required in some states. Enter social security number of a sole proprietor, not tax identification number of the sole proprietorship.

1e,f,g. "Additional information re entity Debtor" is optional. It helps searchers to distinguish this Debtor from others with the same or a similar name. Type of entity and state of organization can be determined from Debtor's current filed charter documents. Organizational I.D. number, if any, is assigned by the agency where the charter document was filed; this is different from taxpayer I.D. number; this should be entered preceded by the 2-character U.S. Postal identification of state of organization (e.g., CA12345, for a California corporation whose organizational I.D. number is 12345).

Note: If Debtor is a transmitting utility as defined in applicable Commercial Code, attach Addendum (Form UCC1Ad) and check box Ad8.

2. If an additional Debtor is included, complete item 2, determined and formatted per Instruction 1. To include further additional Debtors, or one or more additional Secured Parties, attach either Addendum (Form UCC1Ad) or other additional page(s), using correct name format. Follow Instruction 1 for determining and formatting additional names.

3. Enter information, determined and formatted per Instruction 1. If there is more than one Secured Party, see Instruction 2. If there has been a total assignment of the Secured Party's interest prior to filing this form, you may provide either assignor Secured Party's or assignee's name and address in item 3.

4. Use item 4 to indicate the types or describe the items of collateral. If space in item 4 is insufficient, put the entire collateral description or continuation of the collateral description on either Addendum (Form UCC1Ad) or other attached additional page(s).

5, 6. All Debtors must sign. Under certain circumstances, Secured Party may sign instead of Debtor; if applicable, check box in item 5 and provide Secured Party's signature in item 6, and under certain circumstances, in some states, you must also provide additional data; use Addendum (Form UCC1Ad) or attachment to provide such additional data.

7. If filing in the state of Florida you must check one of the two boxes in item 7 to comply with documentary stamp tax requirements.

8. If the collateral consists of or includes fixtures, timber, minerals, and/or mineral-related accounts, check the box in item 8 and complete the required information on Addendum (Form UCC1Ad). If the collateral consists of or includes crops, consult applicable law of state where this Financing Statement is to be filed and complete Ad3b, and Ad4 if required, on Addendum (Form UCC1Ad) and, if required, check box in item 8.

9. Check box 9 to request Search Certificate(s) on all or some of the Debtors named in this Financing Statement. The Certificate will list all Financing Statements on file against the designated Debtor currently effective on the date of the Certificate, including this Financing Statement. There is an additional fee for each Certificate. This item is optional. If you have checked box 9, file copy 3 (Search Request Copy) of this form together with copies 1 and 2. Not all states will honor a search request made via this form; some states require a separate request form.

Instructions re Optional Items A-D

A. To assist filing officers who might wish to communicate with filer, filer may provide information in item A. This item is optional.

B. If filer has an account with filing officer or is authorized to pay fees by means of a card (credit or debit) and wishes to use such means of payment, check the appropriate box and enter filer's account number in item B, or, in the alternative, filer may present this information by a cover letter.

C. Complete item C if you want acknowledgment copy returned and you have presented simultaneously a carbon or other copy of this form for use as an acknowledgment copy.

D. If filer desires to use titles of lessee and lessor, or consignee and consignor, instead of Debtor and Secured Party, check the appropriate box in item D. This item is optional. If this is not a UCC security interest filing (e.g., a tax lien, judgment lien, etc.), check the appropriate box in item D, complete items 1-9 as applicable and attach any other items required under other law.

UCC-3 RELEASE

UNIFORM COMMERCIAL CODE	STATEMENT OF CHANGE	FORM UCC-3 (REV.1993)

This Statement of Change is presented to a filing officer pursuant to the Uniform Commercial Code:

1. Debtor (Last Name First if an individual)		1a. Date of Birth or FEI#
1b. Mailing Address	1c. City, State	1d. Zip Code

2. Additional Debtor or Trade Name (Last Name First if an individual)		2a. Date of Birth or FEI#
2b. Mailing Address	2c. City, State	2d. Zip Code

3. Secured Party (Last Name First if an individual)		
3a. Mailing Address	3b. City, State	3c. Zip Code

4. Additional Secured Party (Last Name First if an individual)		
4a. Mailing Address	4b. City, State	4c. Zip Code

5. This Statement refers to original Financing Statement bearing file number: _____ filed on _____

6. A. ☐ Continuation -   The original Financing Statement between the Debtor and Secured Party bearing the file number shown above is continued.

    B. ☐ Release -   The Secured Party releases the collateral described in Block 7 below from the Financing Statement bearing the file number shown above. RELEASE DOES NOT TERMINATE LIEN AGAINST A DEBTOR.

    C. ☐ Full Assignment -   All of the Secured Party's rights under the Financing Statement have been assigned to the assignee whose name and address is shown in Block 7 below.

    D. ☐ Partial Assignment -   Some of Secured Party's rights under the Financing Statement have been assigned to the assignee whose name and address in shown in Block 7. A description of the collateral subject to the assignment is also shown in Block 7.

    E. ☐ Amendment -   The Financing Statement bearing the file number shown above is amended as set forth in Block 7. (See instructions for signature requirements)

    F. ☐ Termination -   The Secured Party no longer claims an interest under the Financing Statement bearing the file number shown above.

    G. ☐ Other -

7. Description of collateral released or assigned, Assignee name and address, or amendment. Use additional sheet(s) if necessary.

This space for use of Filing Officer

8. Signature(s) of Debtor(s): (only if amendment - see instructions)

9. Signature(s) of Secured party (ies):

10. Number of Additional Sheets Presented

11. Return Copy to:
Name

Address

Address

City, State, Zip

STANDARD FORM - FORM UCC-3

REAL ESTATE SALES CONTRACT

Date:_____, 20____

PARTIES:_____ as

"Buyer" of_____ Phone:_____

and_____ as "Seller"

of _____ Phone:_____

hereby agree that the Buyer shall buy and the Seller shall sell real property described below under the following terms and conditions:

Street Address:_____

Legal Description:

1. PURCHASE PRICE: The full purchase price shall be $_____ payable as follows:

   a) Deposit held in escrow by _____ $_____

   b) New mortgage* to be obtained by Buyer _____

   _____ $_____

   c) Subject to [ ] , or assumption of [ ] mortgage* to _____

   _____ with interest rate of _____%, payable $_____

   per month, having an approximate balance of . . . .$_____

   d) Mortgage* and Note to be held by seller at ___% interest payable

   _____ for _____ years in the amount of . . . .$_____

   e) Other _____

   _____ $_____

   f) Balance to close (U.S. cash, certified or cashier's check)

   subject to adjustments and prorations, plus closing costs . . . .$_____

   Total . . . .$_____

            *or deed of trust

1. FINANCING: Contingent upon Buyer obtaining a firm commitment for a mortgage loan for a minimum of $_____ at a maximum interest rate of _____% for a term of at least ____years. Buyer agrees to make application for and use reasonable diligence to obtain said loan.

2. EXISTING MORTGAGES: Seller represents to Buyer that the existing mortgage on the property is held by _____ and bears interest at _____% per annum with monthly payments of $_____ principal and interest plus $_____ for escrow. Said loan is fully assumable under the following terms: _____.

3. CLOSING DATE & PLACE: Closing shall be on _____, 20_____ at the office of the attorney or title agent selected by Seller.

4. ACCEPTANCE: If this contract is not executed by both parties on or before _____, 20_____ it shall be void and Buyer's deposit returned.

5. PERSONAL PROPERTY: This sale includes all personal property listed on Schedule A. The parties agree that the portion of the purchase price attributable to these items is $_____.

6. TITLE EVIDENCE: Seller shall purchase and deliver to Buyer at or before closing a title insurance policy, or if it is the prevailing custom in the locality, an abstract of title.

7. TITLE DEFECTS: In the event title is found defective, Seller shall have 60 days within which to remove such defects. If Seller is unable to cure them within such time, Buyer may cancel this contract and have all earnest money refunded or may allow Seller additional time to cure. Seller agrees to use diligent effort to correct the defects including the bringing of necessary suits.

8. PRORATIONS: Real and personal property taxes shall be prorated based upon the most recent available information. If closing occurs at a date when the current year's millage is not fixed, and the current year's assessment is available, taxes will be prorated based upon such assessment and the prior year's millage. If current year's assessment is not available, then taxes will be prorated on the prior year's tax; provided, however, that if there are improvements on the property completed by January 1st of the year of closing, which were not in existence on January 1st of the prior year, then taxes shall be prorated based upon the prior year's millage and at an equitable assessment to be agreed upon between the parties, failing which, request will be made to the County Property Appraiser for an informal assessment. Any tax proration based upon an estimate may, at the request of either party, be subsequently readjusted upon receipt of the tax bill. Prepaid rents and other tenant deposits shall be prorated to the date of closing.

9. EXPENSES: The parties herein shall each pay half of the costs and fees for closing costs, documentary stamps and transfer and recording fees.

10. SPECIAL ASSESSMENTS: Certified, confirmed and ratified special assessment liens as of date of closing (and not as of closing date) are to be paid by Seller. Pending liens as of date of closing shall be assumed by Buyer.

11. LIEN AFFIDAVIT: Seller shall, as to both the real and personal property being sold hereunder, furnish to Buyer at time of closing an affidavit attesting to the absence, unless

otherwise provided for herein, of any financing statements, claims of lien or potential lienors known to Seller, and further attesting that there have been no improvements to the property for 90 days immediately preceding the date of closing. If the property has been improved within said time Seller shall deliver releases or waivers of all mechanic's liens, executed by general contractors, subcontractors, suppliers and materialmen, in addition to Seller's affidavit, setting forth the names of all such parties and further reciting that in fact all bills for work to the property which could serve as a basis for a mechanic's lien have been paid or will be paid at closing.

12. CONTINGENCIES: Contingent upon satisfactory inspection of the premises by a licensed contractor.

13. TERMITES: Within 30 days of closing the premises shall be inspected by a certified pest control operator acceptable to Buyer and the cost of said inspection shall be paid equally by Buyer and Seller. In the event infestation by wood destroying organisms is indicated, either party may cancel this contract or Seller may treat the premises at his expense if acceptable to Buyer.

14. PLUMBING AND ELECTRICAL: Major appliances, heating, cooling, electrical and plumbing systems to be in working order as of 6 days prior to closing. Buyer may inspect said items and shall report in writing to seller such items as found not to be in working condition. Unless Buyer reports failures by said date he shall be deemed to have waived Seller's warranty as to failures not reported. Valid reported failures shall be corrected at Seller's cost. Seller agrees to provide access for inspection upon reasonable notice.

15. RESTRICTIONS & EASEMENTS: Property is subject to easements, covenants and restrictions of record provided they do not affect Buyer's intended use of the property.

16. CONDOMINIUMS - 1: If this property is a condominium, sale is contingent upon Buyer or his attorney approving the Declaration of Condominium and all Amendments thereto and any rules and regulations promulgated thereunder within 15 days of receipt from Seller.

17. CONDOMINIUMS - 2: If this property is a condominium, Seller shall convey all rights therein including common elements such as parking spaces and cabanas, if any. This contract is contingent upon the approval by the association or developer, if required, and the parties shall equally pay all costs of approval and transfer. Any assessments shall be prorated as of closing.

18. ZONING & ORDINANCES: Property is subject to governmental zoning and ordinances. VIOLATIONS: Seller represents that he has received no notice of violation on the property of any building, health or other governmental codes or ordinances.

19. INGRESS & EGRESS: Seller warrants that there is ingress and egress to the property which is insurable by a title insurance underwriter.

20. POSSESSION: Seller shall deliver exclusive possession of the premises to Buyer at closing subject only to leases assigned to Buyer.

21. RISK OF LOSS: If the improvements are damaged by fire or other casualty prior to closing, and the cost of restoring same does not exceed 3% of the assessed valuation of the improvements so damaged, Buyer shall have the option of either taking the property as is together with either the 3% or any insurance proceeds available by virtue of such loss or damage, or of cancelling this contract and receiving return of deposits made hereunder.

22. DEFAULT: If the Buyer fails to perform under this contract within the time specified, the deposit(s) paid by the Buyer may be retained by the Seller as liquidated damages, consideration for the execution of this contract and full settlement of any claims, whereupon all parties shall be relieved of all obligations under this contract. If, for any reason other than failure of Seller to render his title marketable after diligent effort, Seller fails, neglects, or refuses to perform under this contract, Buyer may proceed at law or in equity to enforce his rights under this contract.

23. ARBITRATION: In the event of any dispute under this contract the parties agree to binding arbitration under the rules of the American Arbitration Association.

24. CONVEYANCE: Conveyance shall be by Warranty Deed subject only to matters excepted in this contract. Personal property shall, at the request of Buyer be conveyed by an absolute Bill of Sale with warranty of title subject only to such liens as provided herein.

25. SEVERABILITY: In the event any clause in this contract is held to be unenforceable, or against public policy, such holding shall not affect the validity of the remainder of the contract unless it materially alters the terms hereof.

26. OTHER AGREEMENTS: No prior or present agreements or representations shall be binding upon the parties unless incorporated into this contract. No modification or change in this contract shall be binding unless in writing and signed by the party to be bound thereby.

Having read the foregoing, the undersigned hereby ratify, approve and confirm the same as our agreement.

Witnesses: Sellers:

_____   _____

_____   _____

                                              Buyers:

_____   _____

_____   _____

Disclosure of Information on Lead-Based Paint and/or Lead-Based Paint Hazards

Lead Warning Statement

Housing built before 1978 may contain lead-based paint. Lead from paint, paint chips, and dust can pose health hazards if not managed properly. Lead exposure is especially harmful to young children and pregnant women. Before renting pre-1978 housing, lessors must disclose the presence of known lead-based paint and/or lead-based paint hazards in the dwelling. Lessees must also receive a federally approved pamphlet on lead poisoning prevention.

Lessor's Disclosure

(a) Presence of lead-based paint and/or lead-based paint hazards (Check (i) or (ii) below):

(i)_____ Known lead-based paint and/or lead-based paint hazards are present in the housing (explain).

_____

(ii)_____ Lessor has no knowledge of lead-based paint and/or lead-based paint hazards in the housing.

(b) Records and reports available to the lessor (Check (i) or (ii) below):

(i)_____ Lessor has provided the lessee with all available records and reports pertaining to lead-based paint and/or lead-based paint hazards in the housing (list documents below).

_____

(ii)_____ Lessor has no reports or records pertaining to lead-based paint and/or lead-based paint hazards in the housing.

Lessee's Acknowledgment (initial)

(c)_____ Lessee has received copies of all information listed above.

(d)_____ Lessee has received the pamphlet Protect Your Family from Lead in Your Home.

Agent's Acknowledgment (initial)

(e)_____ Agent has informed the lessor of the lessor's obligations under 42 U.S.C. 4852d and is aware of his/her responsibility to ensure compliance.

Certification of Accuracy

The following parties have reviewed the information above and certify, to the best of their knowledge, that the information they have provided is true and accurate.

_____   _____   _____   _____
Lessor   Date   Lessor   Date

_____   _____   _____   _____
Lessee   Date   Lessee   Date

_____   _____   _____   _____
Agent   Date   Agent   Date

WARRANTY DEED

This Warranty Deed, executed on _____, 20_____, between
_____, Grantor, of _____
_____ and
_____, Grantee, of _____
_____.

The Grantor, for and in consideration of the sum of $ _____ and other good and valuable consideration paid by the Grantee, the receipt whereof is hereby acknowledged, does hereby grant, bargain, sell, convey and warrant to the Grantee forever, all the following described real estate, located at _____:

To have and to hold the same in fee simple forever, together with all the buildings, improvements and appurtenances thereto belonging.

And the Grantor hereby covenants with said Grantee that the Grantor is lawfully seized of said land in fee simple; that the Grantor has good right and lawful authority to sell and convey said land; that the Grantor hereby fully warrants the title to said land and will defend the same against the lawful claims of all persons whosoever; and that said land is free of all encumbrances, except _____.

Signed, sealed and delivered:

_____
Grantor

_____
Grantor

_____

_____

STATE OF _____)
COUNTY OF _____)

On _____, 20____, before me personally appeared _____, who is personally known to me or who provided _____ as identification, and signed the above document in my presence.

_____
Notary Public
My Commission expires:

QUITCLAIM DEED

This Quitclaim Deed, executed on _____, 20____ , between
_____, Grantor, of _____
_____ and
_____, Grantee, of _____
_____.

    The Grantor, for and in consideration of the sum of $ _____ and other good and valuable consideration paid by the Grantee, the receipt whereof is hereby acknowledged, does hereby remise, release and quitclaim unto the Grantee forever, all the right, title and interest which the Grantor has in and to the following described real estate, located at
_____:

    To have and to hold the same together with all buildings, improvements and appurtenances thereto belonging.

Signed, sealed and delivered in presence of:

_____   _____

Witness   Grantor

_____

Witness

STATE OF _____)
COUNTY OF _____)

    On _____, 20____, before me personally appeared
_____, who is personally known to me or who provided
_____ as identification, and signed the above document in my presence.

_____

Notary Public
My Commission expires:

Assignment of Mortgage

For value received, _____,
the holder(s) of that certain mortgage dated _____, 20_____, executed
by _____,
and recorded at _____
_____
_____, hereby assigns and transfers to
_____
_____ all of the undersigned's right title and interest in said
mortgage.

IN WITNESS WHEREOF, the undersigned has executed this assignment of mortgage
on the _____ day of _____, 20_____.

Witnessed by:

_____

_____

                                                     _____

                                                     _____

STATE OF   )
COUNTY OF   )

The foregoing instrument was acknowledged before me this _____ day of
_____, 20_____, by _____, who is personally
known to me or who has produced _____ as
identification.

_____
Signature

_____
(Typed Name of Acknowledger)
NOTARY PUBLIC
Commission Number:_____
My Commission Expires:

form 63

SATISFACTION OF MORTGAGE

     For value received, _____,
the holder(s) of that certain mortgage dated _____, 20____, executed by
_____,
and recorded at _____
_____,
hereby acknowledge(s) full payment, satisfaction and discharge of said mortgage.

     IN WITNESS WHEREOF, the undersigned has executed this satisfaction of mortgage
on the _____ day of _____, 20_____.

Witnessed by:

_____

_____

                                    _____

                                      _____

STATE OF   )
COUNTY OF   )

     I certify that _____ ,who ❑ is personally
known to me to be the person whose name is subscribed to the foregoing instrument ❑
produced _____ as identification, personally
appeared before me on _____, 20_____, and acknowledged the execution of the foregoing instrument.

_____

Notary Public, State of

My commission expires:

200

OPTION AGREEMENT

This Option to Purchase is granted on _____, 20____ , by
_____, Optionor, whose post office address is
_____ to
_____, Optionee, whose post office address is
_____ .
The Optionor is the owner of the following described real estate, situated at
_____ :

1. PURPOSE OF AGREEMENT. The Optionor wishes to grant to the Optionee an Option to Purchase the Property. The Optionee wishes to buy from Optionor an Option to Purchase the Property.

2. GRANT OF OPTION. The Optionor, in consideration of the payment of the sum of _____ Dollars ($ _____), the receipt of which is hereby acknowledged, grants to the Optionee the exclusive Option to Purchase the Property.

3. OPTION PERIOD. The option period will be from the date of this Agreement until, if not exercised, its expiration on _____, 20____ .

4. EXERCISE OF OPTION. This Option may be exercised at any time during the option period and prior to its expiration. The Optionee must give written notice of exercise of the Option to the Optionor. If the Option is exercised, the consideration will be applied to the purchase price of the property.

5. FAILURE TO EXERCISE OPTION. If the option is not exercised, the Optionor will retain the consideration.

6. CONTRACT OF SALE/TERMS OF PURCHASE. Attached to this Option Agreement is a completed Contract of Sale. If the Optionee gives the Optionor written notice of exercise of the Option, the parties agree to enter into this Contract of Sale.

7. GOVERNING LAW.   This agreement shall be governed by the laws of _____ .

8. BINDING EFFECT. This Agreement shall be binding upon the parties and upon their successors.

9. ENTIRE AGREEMENT. This instrument, including any attachments, constitutes the entire Agreement of the parties. This Agreement may not be modified except in writing signed by both parties.

_____
Signature of Optionor
_____Printed Name of Optionor

_____
Signature of Optionee
_____Printed Name of Optionee

EXERCISE OF OPTION

Date:

To:

Dear _____ :

    I, as Optionee of the Option Agreement made by you as Optionor dated _____, 20____ for the purchase of property located in _____ , hereby exercise the Option to purchase.

    Enclosed you will find two copies of the Contract of Sale signed by me. Please sign and return one copy of the Contract of Sale to me.

Sincerely,

_____
Signature

RENTAL APPLICATION

Name_____ Date of Birth _____

Name_____ Date of Birth _____

Soc. Sec. Nos._____

Drivers' License Nos._____

Children & Ages_____

Present Landlord_____ Phone_____

Address _____ How Long?_____

Previous Landlord_____ Phone_____

Address_____

Second Previous Landlord_____ Phone_____

Address_____

Nearest Relative_____ Phone_____

Address_____

Employer_____ Phone_____

Address_____

Second Applicant's Employer_____Phone_____

Address_____

Pets_____

Other persons who will stay at premises for more than one week_____

_____

Bank Name_____Acct. #_____

Bank Name_____Acct. #_____

Have you ever been evicted?_____

Have you ever been in litigation with a landlord?_____

The undersigned hereby attest that the above information is true.

_____

_____

HOUSE LEASE - SET TERM

LANDLORD:_____   TENANT:_____

_____   _____

PROPERTY:_____

IN CONSIDERATION of the mutual covenants and agreements herein contained, Landlord hereby leases to Tenant and Tenant hereby leases from Landlord the above-described property together with any personal property listed on "Schedule A" attached hereto, under the following terms and conditions:

1. TERM. This lease shall be for a term of _____ beginning _____, 20_____ and ending _____, 20_____.

2. RENT. The rent shall be $_____ per _____ and shall be due on or before the _____ day of each _____. In the event the full amount of rent is not received on the due date, a late charge of $_____ shall be due. In the event a check bounces or an eviction notice must be posted, Tenant agrees to pay a $15.00 charge.

3. PAYMENT. Payment must be received by Landlord on or before the due date at the following address: _____ or such place as designated by Landlord in writing. Tenant understands that this may require early mailing. In the event a check bounces, Landlord may require cash or certified funds.

4. DEFAULT. In the event Tenant defaults under any term of this lease, Landlord may recover possession as provided by law and seek monetary damages.

5. SECURITY. Tenant shall pay Landlord the sum of $_____ as the last month's rent under this lease, plus $_____ as security deposit. In the event Tenant terminates the lease prior to its expiration date, said amounts are non-refundable as a charge for Landlord's trouble in securing a new tenant, but Landlord reserves the right to seek additional damages if they exceed the above amounts.

6. UTILITIES. Tenant agrees to pay all utility charges on the property except: _____ _____.

7. MAINTENANCE. Tenant has examined the property, acknowledges it to be in good repair and in consideration of the reduced rent, Tenant agrees to be responsible for and to promptly complete all maintenance to the premises.

8. LOCKS. If Tenant adds or changes locks on the premises, Landlord shall be given copies of the keys. Landlord shall at all times have keys for access to the premises in case of emergencies.

9. ASSIGNMENT. Tenant may not assign this lease or sublet any part of the premises without Landlord's written consent, which consent shall be at Landlord's sole discretion.

10. USE. Tenant agrees to use the premises for residential purposes only and not for any illegal purpose or any purpose which will increase the rate of insurance. Tenant further agrees not to violate any zoning laws or subdivision restrictions or to engage in any activity which would injure the premises or constitute a nuisance to the neighbors or Landlord.

11. LAWN. Tenant shall be responsible for maintaining the lawn and shrubbery on the premises at Tenant's expense and for any damages caused by his neglect or abuse thereof.

12. LIABILITY. Tenant agrees to hold Landlord harmless from any and all claims for damages occurring on the premises, and to be solely responsible for insuring Tenant's own possessions on the premises.

13. ACCESS. Landlord reserves the right to enter the premises for the purposes of inspection, repair, or showing to prospective tenants or purchasers.

14. PETS. No pets shall be allowed on the premises except: _____ and there shall be a $_____ non-refundable pet deposit. Landlord reserves the right to revoke consent if pet becomes a nuisance.

15. OCCUPANCY. The premises shall not be occupied by more than _____ persons.

16. TENANT'S APPLIANCES. Tenant agrees not to use any heaters, fixtures or appliances drawing excessive current without the written consent of the Landlord.

17. PARKING. Tenant agrees that no parking is allowed on the premises except:_____ _____. Campers, trailers, boats, recreational vehicles or inoperable vehicles shall not be stored on the premises without the written consent of the Landlord.

18. FURNISHINGS. Any articles provided to Tenant and listed on attached schedule are to be returned in good condition at the termination of this lease.

19. ALTERATIONS AND IMPROVEMENTS. Tenant shall make no alterations or improvements to the premises (including paint) without the written consent of the Landlord and any such alterations or improvements shall become the property of the Landlord unless otherwise agreed in writing.

20. ENTIRE AGREEMENT. This lease constitutes the entire agreement between the parties and may not be modified except in writing signed by both parties.

21. HARASSMENT. Tenant shall not do any acts to intentionally harass the Landlord or other tenants.

22. ATTORNEY'S FEES. In the event it becomes necessary to enforce this Agreement through the services of an attorney, Tenant shall be required to pay Landlord's attorney's fees.

23. SEVERABILITY. In the event any section of this Agreement shall be held to be invalid, all remaining provisions shall remain in full force and effect.

24. RECORDING. This lease shall not be recorded in any public records.

25. WAIVER. Any failure by Landlord to exercise any rights under this agreement shall not constitute a waiver of Landlord's rights.

26. ABANDONMENT. In the event Tenant abandons the property prior to the expiration of this lease, Landlord may relet the premises and hold Tenant liable for any costs, lost rent or damage to the premises. Landlord may dispose of any property abandoned by Tenant.

27. SUBORDINATION. Tenant's interest in the premises shall be subordinate to any encumbrances now or hereafter placed on the premises, to any advances made under such encumbrances, and to any extensions or renewals thereof. Tenant agrees to sign any documents indicating such subordination which may be required by lenders.

28. SURRENDER OF PREMISES. At the expiration of the term of this lease, Tenant shall immediately surrender the premises in as good condition as at the start of this lease. The Tenant shall turn over to Landlord all keys to the premises, including keys made by Tenant or Tenant's agents.

29. HOLDOVER BY TENANT. If Tenant fails to deliver possession of the premises to Landlord at the expiration of this lease, the tenancy shall still be governed by this lease on a month-to-month basis. If such holdover is without the consent of the Landlord, Tenant shall be liable for double the monthly rent for each month or fraction thereof.

30. DAMAGE TO PREMISES. In the event the premises are damaged or destroyed by fire or other casualty or are declared uninhabitable by a governmental authority, Landlord may terminate this lease or may repair the premises.

31. PEST CONTROL. Tenant agrees to be responsible for pest control and extermination services on the premises, and to keep the premises clean and sanitary to avoid such problems. Tenant shall notify Landlord immediately of any evidence of termites. Landlord shall not be responsible to provide living arrangements for Tenant in the event the premises must be vacated for termite or other pest control treatment.

32. LIENS. The estate of Landlord shall not be subject to any liens for improvements contracted by Tenant.

33. WATERBEDS. In the event Tenant uses a flotation type bedding device on the premises, Tenant shall maintain an insurance policy of at least $_____ to cover damages from such device and shall list Landlord as a named insured on said policy.

34. MISCELLANEOUS PROVISIONS. _____

_____.

WITNESS the hands and seals of the parties hereto as of this _____ day of _____, 20_____.

LANDLORD: TENANT:

_____   _____

_____   _____

HOUSE LEASE · MONTH-TO-MONTH

LANDLORD:_____   TENANT:_____

_____   _____
_____

PROPERTY:_____

IN CONSIDERATION of the mutual covenants and agreements herein contained, Landlord hereby leases to Tenant and Tenant hereby leases from Landlord the above-described property together with any personal property listed on "Schedule A" attached hereto, under the following terms and conditions:

1. TERM. This rental agreement shall be for a month-to-month tenancy which may be cancelled by either party upon giving notice to the other party at least 30 days prior to the end of the month.

2. RENT. The rent shall be $_____ per _____ and shall be due on or before the _____ day of each _____. In the event the full amount of rent is not received on the due date, a late charge of $_____ shall be due. In the event a check bounces or an eviction notice must be posted, Tenant agrees to pay a $15.00 charge.

3. PAYMENT. Payment must be received by Landlord on or before the due date at the following address: _____ or such place as designated by Landlord in writing. Tenant understands that this may require early mailing. In the event a check bounces, Landlord may require cash or certified funds.

4. DEFAULT. In the event Tenant defaults under any term of this lease, Landlord may recover possession as provided by law and seek monetary damages.

5. SECURITY. Tenant shall pay Landlord the sum of $_____ as the last month's rent under this lease, plus $_____ as security deposit. In the event Tenant terminates the lease prior to its expiration date, said amounts are non-refundable as a charge for Landlord's trouble in securing a new tenant, but Landlord reserves the right to seek additional damages if they exceed the above amounts.

6. UTILITIES. Tenant agrees to pay all utility charges on the property except: _____ _____.

7. MAINTENANCE. Tenant has examined the property, acknowledges it to be in good repair and in consideration of the reduced rent, Tenant agrees to be responsible for and to promptly complete all maintenance to the premises.

8. LOCKS. If Tenant adds or changes locks on the premises, Landlord shall be given copies of the keys. Landlord shall at all times have keys for access to the premises in case of emergencies.

9. ASSIGNMENT. Tenant may not assign this lease or sublet any part of the premises without Landlord's written consent, which consent shall be at Landlord's sole discretion.

10. USE. Tenant agrees to use the premises for residential purposes only and not for any illegal purpose or any purpose which will increase the rate of insurance. Tenant further agrees not to violate any zoning laws or subdivision restrictions or to engage in any activity which would injure the premises or constitute a nuisance to the neighbors or Landlord.

11. LAWN. Tenant shall be responsible for maintaining the lawn and shrubbery on the premises at Tenant's expense and for any damages caused by his neglect or abuse thereof.

12. LIABILITY. Tenant agrees to hold Landlord harmless from any and all claims for damages occurring on the premises, and to be solely responsible for insuring Tenant's own possessions on the premises.

13. ACCESS. Landlord reserves the right to enter the premises for the purposes of inspection, repair, or showing to prospective tenants or purchasers.

14. PETS. No pets shall be allowed on the premises except: _____ and there shall be a $_____ non-refundable pet deposit. Landlord reserves the right to revoke consent if pet becomes a nuisance.

15. OCCUPANCY. The premises shall not be occupied by more than _____ persons.

16. TENANT'S APPLIANCES. Tenant agrees not to use any heaters, fixtures or appliances drawing excessive current without the written consent of the Landlord.

17. PARKING. Tenant agrees that no parking is allowed on the premises except:_____ _____. Campers, trailers, boats, recreational vehicles or inoperable vehicles shall not be stored on the premises without the written consent of the Landlord.

18. FURNISHINGS. Any articles provided to Tenant and listed on attached schedule are to be returned in good condition at the termination of this lease.

19. ALTERATIONS AND IMPROVEMENTS. Tenant shall make no alterations or improvements to the premises (including paint) without the written consent of the Landlord and any such alterations or improvements shall become the property of the Landlord unless otherwise agreed in writing.

20. ENTIRE AGREEMENT. This lease constitutes the entire agreement between the parties and may not be modified except in writing signed by both parties.

21. HARASSMENT. Tenant shall not do any acts to intentionally harass the Landlord or other tenants.

22. ATTORNEY'S FEES. In the event it becomes necessary to enforce this Agreement through the services of an attorney, Tenant shall be required to pay Landlord's attorney's fees.

23. SEVERABILITY. In the event any section of this Agreement shall be held to be invalid, all remaining provisions shall remain in full force and effect.

24. RECORDING. This lease shall not be recorded in any public records.

25. WAIVER. Any failure by Landlord to exercise any rights under this agreement shall not constitute a waiver of Landlord's rights.

26. ABANDONMENT. In the event Tenant abandons the property prior to the expiration of this lease, Landlord may relet the premises and hold Tenant liable for any costs, lost rent or damage to the premises. Landlord may dispose of any property abandoned by Tenant.

27. SUBORDINATION. Tenant's interest in the premises shall be subordinate to any encumbrances now or hereafter placed on the premises, to any advances made under such encumbrances, and to any extensions or renewals thereof. Tenant agrees to sign any documents indicating such subordination which may be required by lenders.

28. SURRENDER OF PREMISES. At the expiration of the term of this lease, Tenant shall immediately surrender the premises in as good condition as at the start of this lease. The Tenant shall turn over to Landlord all keys to the premises, including keys made by Tenant or Tenant's agents.

29. HOLDOVER BY TENANT. If Tenant fails to deliver possession of the premises to Landlord at the expiration of this lease, the tenancy shall still be governed by this lease on a month-to-month basis. If such holdover is without the consent of the Landlord, Tenant shall be liable for double the monthly rent for each month or fraction thereof.

30. DAMAGE TO PREMISES. In the event the premises are damaged or destroyed by fire or other casualty or are declared uninhabitable by a governmental authority, Landlord may terminate this lease or may repair the premises.

31. PEST CONTROL. Tenant agrees to be responsible for pest control and extermination services on the premises, and to keep the premises clean and sanitary to avoid such problems. Tenant shall notify Landlord immediately of any evidence of termites. Landlord shall not be responsible to provide living arrangements for Tenant in the event the premises must be vacated for termite or other pest control treatment.

32. LIENS. The estate of Landlord shall not be subject to any liens for improvements contracted by Tenant.

33. WATERBEDS. In the event Tenant uses a flotation type bedding device on the premises, Tenant shall maintain an insurance policy of at least $_____ to cover damages from such device and shall list Landlord as a named insured on said policy.

34. MISCELLANEOUS PROVISIONS. _____

_____.

WITNESS the hands and seals of the parties hereto as of this _____ day of _____, 20_____.

LANDLORD: TENANT:

_____   _____

_____   _____

APARTMENT RENTAL AGREEMENT - SET TERM

LANDLORD:_____   TENANT:_____

_____   _____

PROPERTY:_____

IN CONSIDERATION of the mutual covenants and agreements herein contained, Landlord hereby leases to Tenant and Tenant hereby leases from Landlord the above-described property together with any personal property listed on "Schedule A" attached hereto, under the following terms and conditions:

     1. TERM. This lease shall be for a term of _____ beginning _____, 20____ and ending _____, 20____.

     2. RENT. The rent shall be $_____ per _____ and shall be due on or before the _____ day of each _____. In the event the full amount of rent is not received on the due date, a late charge of $_____ shall be due. In the event a check bounces or an eviction notice must be posted, Tenant agrees to pay a $15.00 charge.

     3. PAYMENT. Payment must be received by Landlord on or before the due date at the following address: _____ or such place as designated by Landlord in writing. Tenant understands that this may require early mailing. In the event a check bounces, Landlord may require cash or certified funds.

     4. DEFAULT. In the event Tenant defaults under any term of this lease, Landlord may recover possession as provided by law and seek monetary damages.

     5. SECURITY. Tenant shall pay Landlord the sum of $_____ as security for the performance of this lease. Said amount shall not be used as rent.

     6. UTILITIES. Tenant agrees to pay all utility charges on the property except: _____ _____.

     7. MAINTENANCE. Tenant has examined the property, acknowledges it to be in good repair and agrees to inform Landlord promptly of any maintenance problems. Tenant agrees to keep the premises in clean and sanitary condition. In the event damage has been done by Tenant or Tenant's guests, either intentionally or negligently, Tenant shall pay for such repairs within ten days.

     8. LOCKS. If Tenant adds or changes locks on the premises, Landlord shall be given copies of the keys. Landlord shall at all times have keys for access to the premises in case of emergencies.

     9. ASSIGNMENT. Tenant may not assign this lease or sublet any part of the premises without Landlord's written consent, which consent shall be at Landlord's sole discretion.

     10. USE. Tenant agrees to use the premises for residential purposes only and not for any illegal purpose or any purpose which will increase the rate of insurance. Tenant further agrees not to violate any zoning laws or subdivision restrictions or to engage in any activity which would injure the premises or constitute a nuisance to the neighbors or Landlord.

     11. CONDOMINIUM. In the event the premises are a condominium unit, Tenant agrees to abide by all applicable rules and regulations. Maintenance and recreation fees are to be paid by _____. This lease is subject to the approval of the condominium association and Tenant agrees to pay any fee necessary for such approval.

     12. LIABILITY. Tenant agrees to hold Landlord harmless from any and all claims for damages occurring on the premises, and to be solely responsible for insuring Tenant's own possessions on the premises.

     13. ACCESS. Landlord reserves the right to enter the premises for the purposes of inspection, repair, or showing to prospective tenants or purchasers.

     14. PETS. No pets shall be allowed on the premises except: _____ and there shall be a $_____ non-refundable pet deposit. Landlord reserves the right to revoke consent if pet becomes a nuisance.

     15. OCCUPANCY. The premises shall not be occupied by more than _____ persons.

     16. TENANT'S APPLIANCES. Tenant agrees not to use any heaters, fixtures or appliances drawing excessive current without the written consent of the Landlord.

17. PARKING. Tenant agrees that no parking is allowed on the premises except:_____
_____. Campers, trailers, boats, recreational vehicles or inoperable vehicles shall not be stored on the premises without the written consent of the Landlord.

18. FURNISHINGS. Any articles provided to Tenant and listed on attached schedule are to be returned in good condition at the termination of this lease.

19. ALTERATIONS AND IMPROVEMENTS. Tenant shall make no alterations or improvements to the premises (including paint) without the written consent of the Landlord and any such alterations or improvements shall become the property of the Landlord unless otherwise agreed to in writing.

20. ENTIRE AGREEMENT. This lease constitutes the entire agreement between the parties and may not be modified except in writing signed by both parties.

21. HARASSMENT. Tenant shall not do any acts to intentionally harass the Landlord or other tenants.

22. ATTORNEY'S FEES. In the event it becomes necessary to enforce this Agreement through the services of an attorney, Tenant shall be required to pay Landlord's attorney's fees.

23. SEVERABILITY. In the event any section of this Agreement shall be held to be invalid, all remaining provisions shall remain in full force and effect.

24. RECORDING. This lease shall not be recorded in any public records.

25. WAIVER. Any failure by Landlord to exercise any rights under this agreement shall not constitute a waiver of Landlord's rights.

26. ABANDONMENT. In the event Tenant abandons the property prior to the expiration of this lease, Landlord may relet the premises and hold Tenant liable for any costs, lost rent or damage to the premises. Landlord may dispose of any property abandoned by Tenant.

27. SUBORDINATION. Tenant's interest in the premises shall be subordinate to any encumbrances now or hereafter placed on the premises, to any advances made under such encumbrances, and to any extensions or renewals thereof. Tenant agrees to sign any documents indicating such subordination which may be required by lenders.

28. SURRENDER OF PREMISES. At the expiration of the term of this lease, Tenant shall immediately surrender the premises in as good condition as at the start of this lease. The Tenant shall turn over to Landlord all keys to the premises, including keys made by Tenant or Tenant's agents.

29. HOLDOVER BY TENANT. If Tenant fails to deliver possession of the premises to Landlord at the expiration of this lease, the tenancy shall still be governed by this lease on a month-to-month basis. If such holdover is without the consent of the Landlord, Tenant shall be liable for double the monthly rent for each month or fraction thereof.

30. DAMAGE TO PREMISES. In the event the premises are damaged or destroyed by fire or other casualty or are declared uninhabitable by a governmental authority, Landlord may terminate this lease or may repair the premises.

31. LIENS. The estate of Landlord shall not be subject to any liens for improvements contracted by Tenant.

32. WATERBEDS. In the event Tenant uses a flotation type bedding device on the premises, Tenant shall maintain an insurance policy of at least $_____ to cover damages from such device and shall list Landlord as a named insured on said policy.

33. MISCELLANEOUS PROVISIONS. _____
_____.

WITNESS the hands and seals of the parties hereto as of this _____ day of _____, 20____.

LANDLORD: TENANT:

_____   _____

_____   _____

APARTMENT RENTAL AGREEMENT - MONTH-TO-MONTH

LANDLORD:_____   TENANT:_____

_____   _____

PROPERTY:_____

IN CONSIDERATION of the mutual covenants and agreements herein contained, Landlord hereby leases to Tenant and Tenant hereby leases from Landlord the above-described property together with any personal property listed on "Schedule A" attached hereto, under the following terms and conditions:

1. TERM. This rental agreement shall be for a month-to-month tenancy which may be cancelled by either party upon giving notice to the other party at least 30 days prior to the end of the month.

2. RENT. The rent shall be $_____ per _____ and shall be due on or before the _____ day of each _____. In the event the full amount of rent is not received on the due date, a late charge of $_____ shall be due. In the event a check bounces or an eviction notice must be posted, Tenant agrees to pay a $15.00 charge.

3. PAYMENT. Payment must be received by Landlord on or before the due date at the following address: _____ or such place as designated by Landlord in writing. Tenant understands that this may require early mailing. In the event a check bounces, Landlord may require cash or certified funds.

4. DEFAULT. In the event Tenant defaults under any term of this lease, Landlord may recover possession as provided by law and seek monetary damages.

5. SECURITY. Tenant shall pay Landlord the sum of $_____ as security for the performance of this lease. Said amount shall not be used as rent.

6. UTILITIES. Tenant agrees to pay all utility charges on the property except: _____ _____.

7. MAINTENANCE. Tenant has examined the property, acknowledges it to be in good repair and agrees to inform Landlord promptly of any maintenance problems. Tenant agrees to keep the premises in clean and sanitary condition. In the event damage has been done by Tenant or Tenant's guests, either intentionally or negligently, Tenant shall pay for such repairs within ten days.

8. LOCKS. If Tenant adds or changes locks on the premises, Landlord shall be given copies of the keys. Landlord shall at all times have keys for access to the premises in case of emergencies.

9. ASSIGNMENT. Tenant may not assign this lease or sublet any part of the premises without Landlord's written consent, which consent shall be at Landlord's sole discretion.

10. USE. Tenant agrees to use the premises for residential purposes only and not for any illegal purpose or any purpose which will increase the rate of insurance. Tenant further agrees not to violate any zoning laws or subdivision restrictions or to engage in any activity which would injure the premises or constitute a nuisance to the neighbors or Landlord.

11. CONDOMINIUM. In the event the premises are a condominium unit, Tenant agrees to abide by all applicable rules and regulations. Maintenance and recreation fees are to be paid by _____. This lease is subject to the approval of the condominium association and Tenant agrees to pay any fee necessary for such approval.

12. LIABILITY. Tenant agrees to hold Landlord harmless from any and all claims for damages occurring on the premises, and to be solely responsible for insuring Tenant's own possessions on the premises.

13. ACCESS. Landlord reserves the right to enter the premises for the purposes of inspection, repair, or showing to prospective tenants or purchasers.

14. PETS. No pets shall be allowed on the premises except: _____ and there shall be a $_____ non-refundable pet deposit. Landlord reserves the right to revoke consent if pet becomes a nuisance.

15. OCCUPANCY. The premises shall not be occupied by more than _____ persons.

16. TENANT'S APPLIANCES. Tenant agrees not to use any heaters, fixtures or appliances drawing excessive current without the written consent of the Landlord.

17. PARKING. Tenant agrees that no parking is allowed on the premises except:_____
_____. Campers, trailers, boats, recreational vehicles or inoperable vehicles shall not be stored on the premises without the written consent of the Landlord.

18. FURNISHINGS. Any articles provided to Tenant and listed on attached schedule are to be returned in good condition at the termination of this lease.

19. ALTERATIONS AND IMPROVEMENTS. Tenant shall make no alterations or improvements to the premises (including paint) without the written consent of the Landlord and any such alterations or improvements shall become the property of the Landlord unless otherwise agreed to in writing.

20. ENTIRE AGREEMENT. This lease constitutes the entire agreement between the parties and may not be modified except in writing signed by both parties.

21. HARASSMENT. Tenant shall not do any acts to intentionally harass the Landlord or other tenants.

22. ATTORNEY'S FEES. In the event it becomes necessary to enforce this Agreement through the services of an attorney, Tenant shall be required to pay Landlord's attorney's fees.

23. SEVERABILITY. In the event any section of this Agreement shall be held to be invalid, all remaining provisions shall remain in full force and effect.

24. RECORDING. This lease shall not be recorded in any public records.

25. WAIVER. Any failure by Landlord to exercise any rights under this agreement shall not constitute a waiver of Landlord's rights.

26. ABANDONMENT. In the event Tenant abandons the property prior to the expiration of this lease, Landlord may relet the premises and hold Tenant liable for any costs, lost rent or damage to the premises. Landlord may dispose of any property abandoned by Tenant.

27. SUBORDINATION. Tenant's interest in the premises shall be subordinate to any encumbrances now or hereafter placed on the premises, to any advances made under such encumbrances, and to any extensions or renewals thereof. Tenant agrees to sign any documents indicating such subordination which may be required by lenders.

28. SURRENDER OF PREMISES. At the expiration of the term of this lease, Tenant shall immediately surrender the premises in as good condition as at the start of this lease. The Tenant shall turn over to Landlord all keys to the premises, including keys made by Tenant or Tenant's agents.

29. HOLDOVER BY TENANT. If Tenant fails to deliver possession of the premises to Landlord at the expiration of this lease, the tenancy shall still be governed by this lease on a month-to-month basis. If such holdover is without the consent of the Landlord, Tenant shall be liable for double the monthly rent for each month or fraction thereof.

30. DAMAGE TO PREMISES. In the event the premises are damaged or destroyed by fire or other casualty or are declared uninhabitable by a governmental authority, Landlord may terminate this lease or may repair the premises.

31. LIENS. The estate of Landlord shall not be subject to any liens for improvements contracted by Tenant.

32. WATERBEDS. In the event Tenant uses a flotation type bedding device on the premises, Tenant shall maintain an insurance policy of at least $_____ to cover damages from such device and shall list Landlord as a named insured on said policy.

33. MISCELLANEOUS PROVISIONS. _____
_____.

WITNESS the hands and seals of the parties hereto as of this _____ day of _____, 20_____.

LANDLORD: TENANT:

_____   _____

_____   _____

AMENDMENT TO LEASE AGREEMENT

For valuable consideration, the receipt and sufficiency of which is hereby acknowledged by each of the parties, this agreement amends a lease agreement (the "Lease") between _____ (the "Landlord") and _____ (the "Tenant") dated _____, relating to property located at _____ _____.

This agreement is hereby incorporated into the Lease.

Except as changed by this amendment, the Lease shall continue in effect according to its terms. The amendments herein shall be effective on the date this document is executed by both parties.

Executed on _____, 20____.

Landlord: Tenant:

_____   _____

_____   _____

LEASE ASSIGNMENT

This Lease Assignment is entered into by and among _____ (the "Assignor"), _____ (the "Assignee"), and _____ (the "Landlord").
For valuable consideration, it is agreed by the parties as follows:

1. The Landlord and the Assignor have entered into a lease agreement (the "Lease") dated _____, concerning the premises described as:

2. The Assignor hereby assigns and transfers to the Assignee all of Assignor's rights and delegates all of Assignor's duties under the Lease effective _____ (the "Effective Date").

3. The Assignee hereby accepts such assignment of rights and delegation of duties and agrees to pay all rents promptly when due and perform all of Assignor's obligations under the Lease accruing on and after the Effective Date. The Assignee further agrees to indemnify and hold the Assignor harmless from any breach of Assignee's duties hereunder.

4. ❑ The Assignor agrees to transfer possession of the leased premises to the Assignee on the Effective Date. All rents and obligations of the Assignor under the Lease accruing before the Effective Date shall have been paid or discharged.

   ❑ The Landlord hereby assents to the assignment of the Lease hereunder and as of the Effective Date hereby releases and discharges the Assignor from all duties and obligations under the Lease accruing after the Effective Date.

   ❑ The Landlord hereby assents to this lease assignment provided that the Landlord's assent shall not discharge the Assignor of any obligations under the Lease in the event of breach by the Assignee. The Landlord will give notice to the Assignor of any breach by the Assignee. If the Assignor pays all accrued rents and cures any other default of the Assignee, the Assignor may enforce the terms of the Lease and this Assignment against the Assignee, in the name of the Landlord, if necessary.

5. There shall be no further assignment of the Lease without the written consent of the Landlord.

6. This agreement shall be binding upon and inure to the benefit of the parties, their successors, assigns and personal representatives.

This assignment was executed under seal on _____.

Assignor: Assignee:

_____   _____

_____   _____

Landlord:

_____

_____

LANDLORD'S CONSENT TO SUBLEASE

FOR VALUABLE CONSIDERATION, the undersigned (the "Landlord") hereby consents to the sublease of all or part of the premises located at _____ _____ which is the subject of a lease agreement between Landlord and _____ (the "Tenant"), pursuant to an Agreement to Sublease dated _____, 20_____, between the Tenant and _____ as Subtenant dated _____, 20_____.

This consent was signed by the Landlord on _____, 20_____.

Landlord:

_____

Roommate Agreement

The undersigned, intending to share a dwelling unit located at _____ _____, in consideration of the mutual promises contained in this agreement, agree as follows:

1. They shall share the unit as follows: _____ _____ _____ _____

2. Rent shall be paid as follows: _____ _____

3. Each party shall be responsible for his/her own long distance and toll charges on the telephone bill(s) regardless of whose name the bill is in.

4. The other utilities and fees shall be paid as follows: _____ _____ _____

5. No party is obligated to pay another party's share of the rent or other bills, but in the event one party finds it necessary to pay a bill for another party to stop eviction or termination of service, the party paying shall have the right to reimbursement in full plus a $_____ charge. In the event the nonpaying party fails to reimburse such amounts, the paying party shall be entitled to interest at the highest legal rate, attorneys' fees, and court costs if legal action is necessary.

6. The parties also agree:

Smoking _____

Overnight guests _____

7. The parties agree to respect each other's privacy, to keep the shared areas reasonably clean, not to make unreasonable noise during normal sleeping hours, not to leave food where it would invite infestation, and to be courteous and considerate of the other's needs. They agree that if their guests do not follow these rules, such guests shall not be permitted in the unit. They further agree not to do anything which violates the lease and could cause eviction.

8. The parties further agree as follows: _____ _____ _____

_____

_____

form 75

NOTICE TO LANDLORD TO MAKE REPAIRS

To Landlord:

From Tenant:

Re rental premises:

This is notice that the above-referenced rental premises are in need of repairs as follows:

Unless these are made by you we shall enforce our legal remedies under state law which may include, but not be limited to, making the repairs and deducting the cost from rent, or terminating the rental agreement.

_____

Tenant

216

WAIVER AND ASSUMPTION OF RISK

I, _____,
hereby voluntarily sign this Waiver and Assumption of Risk in favor of
_____ (the "Owner"),
fully waiving and releasing the Owner from any and all claims for personal injury, property damage, or death that may result from my use of the Owner property, or from my participation in the following activities ("activities"):

I sign this Waiver and Assumption of Risk in consideration of the opportunity to use the Owner property, or to participate in activities as described above.

I acknowledge and understand that there are dangers and risks associated with the activities described above, which have been fully explained to me. I fully assume the dangers and risks, and agree to use my best judgment in engaging in those activities and to follow the safety instructions provided.

I am a competent adult, aged _____, and I freely and voluntarily assume the risks associated with the activities described above.

Dated:_____

Witness:_____   _____

                                            Name:_____
                                            Address:_____
                                            _____
                                            Telephone:_____

In case of emergency, please contact:

             Name:_____
             Address:_____
             _____
             Telephone:_____
             Relationship:_____

DECLARATION OF HOMESTEAD

I, _____, hereby declare:

    1. I declare as homestead the premises located in _____
_____, more particularly
described as follows:

        _____
        _____
        _____
        _____

    2. I am the homestead owner of the above declared homestead.

    3. I own the following interest in the above declared homestead:

        _____

    4. The above declared homestead is
      __   my principal dwelling
      __   the principal dwelling of my spouse and
    I am currently residing on that declared homestead.
      My spouse is _____.

Dated _____

_____

State of _____)
County of _____)

    On   _____,   20____,   before   me   personally   appeared
_____, who are personally known to me or who provided
_____ as identification, and
signed the above document in my presence.

_____
Notary Public
My Commission expires:

APPLICATION FOR EMPLOYMENT

We consider applicants for all positions without regard to race, color, religion, sex, national origin, age, marital or veteran status, the presence of a non-job-related medical condition or handicap, or any other legally protected status. Proof of citizenship or immigration status will be required upon employment.

(PLEASE TYPE OR PRINT)

Position Applied For   Date of Application

Last Name	First Name	Middle Name or Initial

Is there any other information regarding your name that will be needed to check work or school records? ❏ Yes ❏ No

Address   *Number Street*   *City*   *State*   *Zip Code*

Telephone Number(s) [indicate home or work]	Social Security Number

Date Available:_____   Are you available: ❏ Full Time   ❏ Part Time   ❏ Weekends

Are you 18 years of age or older?   ❏ Yes   ❏ No

Have you been convicted of a felony within the past 7 years?   ❏ Yes   ❏ No

Conviction will not necessarily disqualify an applicant from employment.

If Yes, attach explanation.

Can you produce documents proving you are authorized to work in the United States? ❏ Yes   ❏ No

Education

	High School	Undergraduate	Graduate
School Name & Location			
Years Completed	1 2 3 4	1 2 3 4	1 2 3 4
Diploma / Degree			
Course of Study			

State any additional information you feel may be helpful to us in considering your application (such as any specialized training; skills; apprenticeships; honors received; professional, trade, business or civic organizations or activities; job-related military training or experience; foreign language abilities; etc.)

_____

_____

_____

_____

Employment Experience

Start with your present or last job. Include any job-related military service assignments and voluntary activities. You may exclude organizations which indicate race, color, religion, gender, national origin, handicap, or other protected status.

1.	Employer Name & Address	Dates Employed	Job Title/Duties
		Hourly Rate/Salary	
	May we contact this employer? ❑ Yes ❑ No	Hours Per Week	
	Employer Phone		
	Supervisor		
	Reason for Leaving		

2.	Employer Name & Address	Dates Employed	Job Title/Duties
		Hourly Rate/Salary	
	Employer Phone	Hours Per Week	
	Supervisor		
	Reason for Leaving		

3.	Employer Name & Address	Dates Employed	Job Title/Duties
		Hourly Rate/Salary	
	Employer Phone	Hours Per Week	
	Supervisor		
	Reason for Leaving		

References: Name   Occupation   Address   Phone #   Relationship   Years known

1. _____
2. _____
3. _____

If you need additional space, continue on a separate sheet of paper.

Applicant's Statement

I certify that the information given on this application is true and complete to the best of my knowledge. I authorize investigation of all statements contained in this application, and understand that false or misleading information given in my application or interview(s) may result in discharge.

I understand and acknowledge that, unless otherwise defined by applicable law, any employment relationship with this organization is "at will," which means that I may resign at any time and the employer may discharge me at any time with or without cause. I further understand that this "at will" employment relationship may not be changed orally, by any written document, or by conduct, unless such change is specifically acknowledged in writing by an authorized executive of this organization.

_____   _____
Signature of Applicant   Date

AUTHORIZATION TO RELEASE EMPLOYMENT INFORMATION

To:

The undersigned applicant hereby authorizes you to release records of his/her dates of employment, job title, salary and reason for leaving your company and to:

_____

_____

_____

_____

Applicant's signature

VERIFICATION OF EDUCATION

To:

The undersigned applicant hereby authorizes you to release records verifying his/her education at your institution to:

_____

_____

_____

_____

Applicant's signature

VERIFICATION OF LICENSURE

To:

The undersigned applicant hereby authorizes you to verify that he/she is licensed as a
_____ that such license has been valid since _____ and is
still valid.

_____

_____

_____

_____

Applicant's signature

EMPLOYMENT ELIGIBILITY VERIFICATION (I-9)

U.S. Department of Justice
Immigration and Naturalization Service

OMB No. 1115-0136

Employment Eligibility Verification

INSTRUCTIONS
PLEASE READ ALL INSTRUCTIONS CAREFULLY BEFORE COMPLETING THIS FORM.

Anti-Discrimination Notice. It is illegal to discriminate against any individual (other than an alien not authorized to work in the U.S.) in hiring, discharging, or recruiting or referring for a fee because of that individual's national origin or citizenship status. It is illegal to discriminate against work eligible individuals. Employers **CANNOT** specify which document(s) they will accept from an employee. The refusal to hire an individual because of a future expiration date may also constitute illegal discrimination.

Section 1 - Employee. All employees, citizens and noncitizens, hired after November 6, 1986, must complete Section 1 of this form at the time of hire, which is the actual beginning of employment. **The employer is responsible for ensuring that Section 1 is timely and properly completed.**

Preparer/Translator Certification. The Preparer/Translator Certification must be completed if Section 1 is prepared by a person other than the employee. A preparer/translator may be used only when the employee is unable to complete Section 1 on his/her own. However, the employee must still sign Section 1.

Section 2 - Employer. For the purpose of completing this form, the term "employer" includes those recruiters and referrers for a fee who are agricultural associations, agricultural employers or farm labor contractors.

Employers must complete Section 2 by examining evidence of identity and employment eligibility within three (3) business days of the date employment begins. If employees are authorized to work, but are unable to present the required document(s) within three business days, they must present a receipt for the application of the document(s) within three business days and the actual document(s) within ninety (90) days. However, if employers hire individuals for a duration of less than three business days, Section 2 must be completed at the time employment begins. Employers must record: 1) document title; 2) issuing authority; 3) document number, 4) expiration date, if any; and 5) the date employment begins. Employers must sign and date the certification. Employees must present original documents. Employers may, but are not required to, photocopy the document(s) presented. These photocopies may only be used for the verification process and must be retained with the I-9. **However, employers are still responsible for completing the I-9.**

Section 3 - Updating and Reverification. Employers must complete Section 3 when updating and/or reverifying the I-9. Employers must reverify employment eligibility of their employees on or before the expiration date recorded in Section 1. Employers **CANNOT** specify which document(s) they will accept from an employee.

- If an employee's name has changed at the time this form is being updated/ reverified, complete Block A.

- If an employee is rehired within three (3) years of the date this form was originally completed and the employee is still eligible to be employed on the same basis as previously indicated on this form (updating), complete Block B and the signature block.

- If an employee is rehired within three (3) years of the date this form was originally completed and the employee's work authorization has expired **or** if a current employee's work authorization is about to expire (reverification), complete Block B and:
  - examine any document that reflects that the employee is authorized to work in the U.S. (see List A **or** C),
  - record the document title, document number and expiration date (if any) in Block C, and complete the signature block.

Photocopying and Retaining Form I-9. A blank I-9 may be reproduced, provided both sides are copied. The Instructions must be available to all employees completing this form. Employers must retain completed I-9s for three (3) years after the date of hire or one (1) year after the date employment ends, whichever is later.

For more detailed information, you may refer to the INS Handbook for Employers, (Form M-274). You may obtain the handbook at your local INS office.

Privacy Act Notice. The authority for collecting this information is the Immigration Reform and Control Act of 1986, Pub. L. 99-603 (8 USC 1324a).

This information is for employers to verify the eligibility of individuals for employment to preclude the unlawful hiring, or recruiting or referring for a fee, of aliens who are not authorized to work in the United States.

This information will be used by employers as a record of their basis for determining eligibility of an employee to work in the United States. The form will be kept by the employer and made available for inspection by officials of the U.S. Immigration and Naturalization Service, the Department of Labor and the Office of Special Counsel for Immigration Related Unfair Employment Practices.

Submission of the information required in this form is voluntary. However, an individual may not begin employment unless this form is completed, since employers are subject to civil or criminal penalties if they do not comply with the Immigration Reform and Control Act of 1986.

Reporting Burden. We try to create forms and instructions that are accurate, can be easily understood and which impose the least possible burden on you to provide us with information. Often this is difficult because some immigration laws are very complex. Accordingly, the reporting burden for this collection of information is computed as follows: 1) learning about this form, 5 minutes; 2) completing the form, 5 minutes; and 3) assembling and filing (recordkeeping) the form, 5 minutes, for an average of 15 minutes per response. If you have comments regarding the accuracy of this burden estimate, or suggestions for making this form simpler, you can write to the Immigration and Naturalization Service, HQPDI, 425 I Street, N.W., Room 4307r, Washington, DC 20536. OMB No. 1115-0136.

EMPLOYERS MUST RETAIN COMPLETED FORM I-9
PLEASE DO NOT MAIL COMPLETED FORM I-9 TO INS

Form I-9 (Rev. 11-21-91)N

OMB No. 1115-0136

Employment Eligibility Verification

Please read instructions carefully before completing this form. The instructions must be available during completion of this form. ANTI-DISCRIMINATION NOTICE: It is illegal to discriminate against work eligible individuals. Employers CANNOT specify which document(s) they will accept from an employee. The refusal to hire an individual because of a future expiration date may also constitute illegal discrimination.

Section 1. Employee Information and Verification. To be completed and signed by employee at the time employment begins.

Print Name: Last	First	Middle Initial	Maiden Name

Address (Street Name and Number)	Apt. #	Date of Birth (month/day/year)

City	State	Zip Code	Social Security #

I am aware that federal law provides for imprisonment and/or fines for false statements or use of false documents in connection with the completion of this form.	I attest, under penalty of perjury, that I am (check one of the following): ☐ A citizen or national of the United States ☐ A Lawful Permanent Resident (Alien # A_____) ☐ An alien authorized to work until __/__/__ (Alien # or Admission #) _____

Employee's Signature	Date (month/day/year)

Preparer and/or Translator Certification. *(To be completed and signed if Section 1 is prepared by a person other than the employee.) I attest, under penalty of perjury, that I have assisted in the completion of this form and that to the best of my knowledge the information is true and correct.*

Preparer's/Translator's Signature	Print Name

Address (Street Name and Number, City, State, Zip Code)	Date (month/day/year)

Section 2. Employer Review and Verification. To be completed and signed by employer. Examine one document from List A OR examine one document from List B and one from List C, as listed on the reverse of this form, and record the title, number and expiration date, if any, of the document(s)

List A	OR	List B	AND	List C
Document title: _____		_____		_____
Issuing authority: _____		_____		_____
Document #: _____		_____		_____
Expiration Date (if any): __/__/__		__/__/__		__/__/__
Document #: _____				
Expiration Date (if any): __/__/__				

CERTIFICATION - I attest, under penalty of perjury, that I have examined the document(s) presented by the above-named employee, that the above-listed document(s) appear to be genuine and to relate to the employee named, that the employee began employment on *(month/day/year)* __/__/__ **and that to the best of my knowledge the employee is eligible to work in the United States. (State employment agencies may omit the date the employee began employment.)**

Signature of Employer or Authorized Representative	Print Name	Title

Business or Organization Name	Address (Street Name and Number, City, State, Zip Code)	Date (month/day/year)

Section 3. Updating and Reverification. To be completed and signed by employer.

A. New Name (if applicable)	B. Date of rehire (month/day/year) (if applicable)

C. If employee's previous grant of work authorization has expired, provide the information below for the document that establishes current employment eligibility.

Document Title:_____ Document #:_____ Expiration Date (if any): __/__/__

I attest, under penalty of perjury, that to the best of my knowledge, this employee is eligible to work in the United States, and if the employee presented document(s), the document(s) I have examined appear to be genuine and to relate to the individual.

Signature of Employer or Authorized Representative	Date (month/day/year)

Form I-9 (Rev. 11-21-91)N Page 2

LISTS OF ACCEPTABLE DOCUMENTS

LIST A		LIST B		LIST C
Documents that Establish Both Identity and Employment Eligibility	**OR**	**Documents that Establish Identity**	**AND**	**Documents that Establish Employment Eligibility**

LIST A — Documents that Establish Both Identity and Employment Eligibility

1. U.S. Passport (unexpired or expired)

2. Certificate of U.S. Citizenship (INS Form N-560 or N-561)

3. Certificate of Naturalization (INS Form N-550 or N-570)

4. Unexpired foreign passport, with I-551 stamp or attached INS Form I-94 indicating unexpired employment authorization

5. Alien Registration Receipt Card with photograph (INS Form I-151 or I-551)

6. Unexpired Temporary Card (INS Form I-688)

7. Unexpired Employment Authorization Card (INS Form I-688A)

8. Unexpired Reentry Permit (INS Form I-327)

9. Unexpired Refugee Travel Document (INS Form I-571)

10. Unexpired Employment Authorization Document issued by the INS which contains a photograph (INS Form I-688B)

LIST B — Documents that Establish Identity

1. Driver's license or ID card issued by a state or outlying possession of the United States provided it contains a photograph or information such as name, date of birth, sex, height, eye color and address

2. ID card issued by federal, state or local government agencies or entities, provided it contains a photograph or information such as name, date of birth, sex, height, eye color and address

3. School ID card with a photograph

4. Voter's registration card

5. U.S. Military card or draft record

6. Military dependent's ID card

7. U.S. Coast Guard Merchant Mariner Card

8. Native American tribal document

9. Driver's license issued by a Canadian government authority

For persons under age 18 who are unable to present a document listed above:

10. School record or report card

11. Clinic, doctor or hospital record

12. Day-care or nursery school record

LIST C — Documents that Establish Employment Eligibility

1. U.S. social security card issued by the Social Security Administration (other than a card stating it is not valid for employment)

2. Certification of Birth Abroad issued by the Department of State (Form FS-545 or Form DS-1350)

3. Original or certified copy of a birth certificate issued by a state, county, municipal authority or outlying possession of the United States bearing an official seal

4. Native American tribal document

5. U.S. Citizen ID Card (INS Form I-197)

6. ID Card for use of Resident Citizen in the United States (INS Form I-179)

7. Unexpired employment authorization document issued by the INS (other then those listed under List A)

Illustrations of many of these documents appear in Part 8 of the Handbook for Employers (M-274)

APPLICATION FOR EMPLOYER IDENTIFICATION NUMBER (SS-4)

Form **SS-4** (Rev. April 2000) Department of the Treasury Internal Revenue Service	**Application for Employer Identification Number** (For use by employers, corporations, partnerships, trusts, estates, churches, government agencies, certain individuals, and others. See instructions.) ▶ **Keep a copy for your records.**	EIN OMB No. 1545-0003

(Please type or print clearly.)

1 Name of applicant (legal name) (see instructions)

2 Trade name of business (if different from name on line 1)	**3** Executor, trustee, "care of" name

4a Mailing address (street address) (room, apt., or suite no.)	**5a** Business address (if different from address on lines 4a and 4b)

4b City, state, and ZIP code	**5b** City, state, and ZIP code

6 County and state where principal business is located

7 Name of principal officer, general partner, grantor, owner, or trustor—SSN or ITIN may be required (see instructions) ▶ _____

8a Type of entity (Check only one box.) (see instructions)

Caution: If applicant is a limited liability company, see the instructions for line 8a.

- ☐ Sole proprietor (SSN) _____
- ☐ Partnership   ☐ Personal service corp.
- ☐ REMIC   ☐ National Guard
- ☐ State/local government   ☐ Farmers' cooperative
- ☐ Church or church-controlled organization
- ☐ Other nonprofit organization (specify) ▶ _____
- ☐ Other (specify) ▶
- ☐ Estate (SSN of decedent) _____
- ☐ Plan administrator (SSN) _____
- ☐ Other corporation (specify) ▶ _____
- ☐ Trust
- ☐ Federal government/military
- (enter GEN if applicable) _____

8b If a corporation, name the state or foreign country (if applicable) where incorporated

State	Foreign country

9 Reason for applying (Check only one box.) (see instructions)
- ☐ Started new business (specify type) ▶ _____
- ☐ Hired employees (Check the box and see line 12.)
- ☐ Created a pension plan (specify type) ▶
- ☐ Banking purpose (specify purpose) ▶ _____
- ☐ Changed type of organization (specify new type) ▶ _____
- ☐ Purchased going business
- ☐ Created a trust (specify type) ▶ _____
- ☐ Other (specify) ▶

10 Date business started or acquired (month, day, year) (see instructions)	**11** Closing month of accounting year (see instructions)

12 First date wages or annuities were paid or will be paid (month, day, year). **Note:** *If applicant is a withholding agent, enter date income will first be paid to nonresident alien. (month, day, year)* . . . . ▶

13 Highest number of employees expected in the next 12 months. **Note:** *If the applicant does not expect to have any employees during the period, enter -0-. (see instructions)* . . . . . ▶

Nonagricultural	Agricultural	Household

14 Principal activity (see instructions) ▶

15 Is the principal business activity manufacturing? . . . . ☐ Yes   ☐ No
If "Yes," principal product and raw material used ▶

16 To whom are most of the products or services sold? Please check one box.   ☐ Business (wholesale)
☐ Public (retail)   ☐ Other (specify) ▶   ☐ N/A

17a Has the applicant ever applied for an employer identification number for this or any other business? . . . . ☐ Yes   ☐ No
Note: *If "Yes," please complete lines 17b and 17c.*

17b If you checked "Yes" on line 17a, give applicant's legal name and trade name shown on prior application, if different from line 1 or 2 above.
Legal name ▶   Trade name ▶

17c Approximate date when and city and state where the application was filed. Enter previous employer identification number if known.

Approximate date when filed (mo., day, year)	City and state where filed	Previous EIN

Under penalties of perjury, I declare that I have examined this application, and to the best of my knowledge and belief, it is true, correct, and complete.	Business telephone number (include area code) ( )
	Fax telephone number (include area code) ( )
Name and title (Please type or print clearly.) ▶	

Signature ▶	Date ▶

Note: *Do not write below this line. For official use only.*

Please leave blank ▶	Geo.	Ind.	Class	Size	Reason for applying

For Privacy Act and Paperwork Reduction Act Notice, see page 4.   Cat. No. 16055N   Form **SS-4** (Rev. 4-2000)

General Instructions

Section references are to the Internal Revenue Code unless otherwise noted.

Purpose of Form

Use Form SS-4 to apply for an employer identification number (EIN). An EIN is a nine-digit number (for example, 12-3456789) assigned to sole proprietors, corporations, partnerships, estates, trusts, and other entities for tax filing and reporting purposes. The information you provide on this form will establish your business tax account.

Caution: *An EIN is for use in connection with your business activities only. Do **not** use your EIN in place of your social security number (SSN).*

Who Must File

You must file this form if you have not been assigned an EIN before and:

• You pay wages to one or more employees including household employees.

• You are required to have an EIN to use on any return, statement, or other document, even if you are not an employer.

• You are a withholding agent required to withhold taxes on income, other than wages, paid to a nonresident alien (individual, corporation, partnership, etc.). A withholding agent may be an agent, broker, fiduciary, manager, tenant, or spouse, and is required to file **Form 1042,** Annual Withholding Tax Return for U.S. Source Income of Foreign Persons.

• You file **Schedule C,** Profit or Loss From Business, **Schedule C-EZ,** Net Profit From Business, or **Schedule F,** Profit or Loss From Farming, of **Form 1040,** U.S. Individual Income Tax Return, **and** have a Keogh plan or are required to file excise, employment, or alcohol, tobacco, or firearms returns.

The following must use EINs even if they do not have any employees:

• State and local agencies who serve as tax reporting agents for public assistance recipients, under Rev. Proc. 80-4, 1980-1 C.B. 581, should obtain a separate EIN for this reporting. See **Household employer** on page 3.

• Trusts, except the following:

1. Certain grantor-owned trusts. (See the **Instructions for Form 1041,** U.S. Income Tax Return for Estates and Trusts.)

2. Individual retirement arrangement (IRA) trusts, unless the trust has to file **Form 990-T,** Exempt Organization Business Income Tax Return. (See the **Instructions for Form 990-T.**)

• Estates

• Partnerships

• REMICs (real estate mortgage investment conduits) (See the **Instructions for Form 1066,** U.S. Real Estate Mortgage Investment Conduit (REMIC) Income Tax Return.)

• Corporations

• Nonprofit organizations (churches, clubs, etc.)

• Farmers' cooperatives

• Plan administrators (A plan administrator is the person or group of persons specified as the administrator by the instrument under which the plan is operated.)

When To Apply for a New EIN

New Business. If you become the new owner of an existing business, **do not** use the EIN of the former owner. **If you already have an EIN, use that number.** If you do not have an EIN, apply for one on this form. If you become the "owner" of a corporation by acquiring its stock, use the corporation's EIN.

Changes in Organization or Ownership. If you already have an EIN, you may need to get a new one if either the organization or ownership of your business changes. If you incorporate a sole proprietorship or form a partnership, you must get a new EIN. However, **do not** apply for a new EIN if:

• You change only the name of your business,

• You elected on **Form 8832,** Entity Classification Election, to change the way the entity is taxed, or

• A partnership terminates because at least 50% of the total interests in partnership capital and profits were sold or exchanged within a 12-month period. (See Regulations section 301.6109-1(d)(2)(iii).) The EIN for the terminated partnership should continue to be used.

Note: *If you are electing to be an "S corporation," be sure you file **Form 2553,** Election by a Small Business Corporation.*

File Only One Form SS-4. File only one Form SS-4, regardless of the number of businesses operated or trade names under which a business operates. However, each corporation in an affiliated group must file a separate application.

EIN Applied for, But Not Received. If you do not have an EIN by the time a return is due, write "Applied for" and the date you applied in the space shown for the number. **Do not** show your social security number (SSN) as an EIN on returns.

If you do not have an EIN by the time a tax deposit is due, send your payment to the Internal Revenue Service Center for your filing area. (See **Where To Apply** below.) Make your check or money order payable to "United States Treasury" and show your name (as shown on Form SS-4), address, type of tax, period covered, and date you applied for an EIN. Send an explanation with the deposit.

For more information about EINs, see **Pub. 583,** Starting a Business and Keeping Records, and **Pub. 1635,** Understanding Your EIN.

How To Apply

You can apply for an EIN either by mail or by telephone. You can get an EIN immediately by calling the Tele-TIN number for the service center for your state, or you can send the completed Form SS-4 directly to the service center to receive your EIN by mail.

Application by Tele-TIN. Under the Tele-TIN program, you can receive your EIN by telephone and use it immediately to file a return or make a payment. To receive an EIN by telephone, complete Form SS-4, then call the Tele-TIN number listed for your state under **Where To Apply.** The person making the call must be authorized to sign the form. (See **Signature** on page 4.)

An IRS representative will use the information from the Form SS-4 to establish your account and assign you an EIN. Write the number you are given on the upper right corner of the form and sign and date it.

*Mail or fax (facsimile) the signed Form SS-4 **within 24 hours** to the Tele-TIN Unit at the service center address for your state.* The IRS representative will give you the fax number. The fax numbers are also listed in Pub. 1635.

Taxpayer representatives can receive their client's EIN by telephone if they first send a fax of a completed **Form 2848,** Power of Attorney and Declaration of Representative, or **Form 8821,** Tax Information Authorization, to the Tele-TIN unit. The Form 2848 or Form 8821 will be used solely to release the EIN to the representative authorized on the form.

Application by Mail. Complete Form SS-4 at least 4 to 5 weeks before you will need an EIN. Sign and date the application and mail it to the service center address for your state. You will receive your EIN in the mail in approximately 4 weeks.

Where To Apply

The Tele-TIN numbers listed below will involve a long-distance charge to callers outside of the local calling area and can be used only to apply for an EIN. **The numbers may change without notice.** Call 1-800-829-1040 to verify a number or to ask about the status of an application by mail.

If your principal business, office or agency, or legal residence in the case of an individual, is located in:	Call the Tele-TIN number shown or file with the Internal Revenue Service Center at:
Florida, Georgia, South Carolina	Attn: Entity Control Atlanta, GA 39901 770-455-2360
New Jersey, New York (New York City and counties of Nassau, Rockland, Suffolk, and Westchester)	Attn: Entity Control Holtsville, NY 00501 516-447-4955
New York (all other counties), Connecticut, Maine, Massachusetts, New Hampshire, Rhode Island, Vermont	Attn: Entity Control Andover, MA 05501 978-474-9717
Illinois, Iowa, Minnesota, Missouri, Wisconsin	Attn: Entity Control Stop 6800 2306 E. Bannister Rd. Kansas City, MO 64999 816-926-5999
Delaware, District of Columbia, Maryland, Pennsylvania, Virginia	Attn: Entity Control Philadelphia, PA 19255 215-516-6999
Indiana, Kentucky, Michigan, Ohio, West Virginia	Attn: Entity Control Cincinnati, OH 45999 859-292-5467

Kansas, New Mexico, Oklahoma, Texas	Attn: Entity Control Austin, TX 73301 512-460-7843
Alaska, Arizona, California (counties of Alpine, Amador, Butte, Calaveras, Colusa, Contra Costa, Del Norte, El Dorado, Glenn, Humboldt, Lake, Lassen, Marin, Mendocino, Modoc, Napa, Nevada, Placer, Plumas, Sacramento, San Joaquin, Shasta, Sierra, Siskiyou, Solano, Sonoma, Sutter, Tehama, Trinity, Yolo, and Yuba), Colorado, Idaho, Montana, Nebraska, Nevada, North Dakota, Oregon, South Dakota, Utah, Washington, Wyoming	Attn: Entity Control Mail Stop 6271 P.O. Box 9941 Ogden, UT 84201 801-620-7645
California (all other counties), Hawaii	Attn: Entity Control Fresno, CA 93888 559-452-4010
Alabama, Arkansas, Louisiana, Mississippi, North Carolina, Tennessee	Attn: Entity Control Memphis, TN 37501 901-546-3920
If you have no legal residence, principal place of business, or principal office or agency in any state	Attn: Entity Control Philadelphia, PA 19255 215-516-6999

Specific Instructions

The instructions that follow are for those items that are not self-explanatory. Enter N/A (nonapplicable) on the lines that do not apply.

Line 1. Enter the legal name of the entity applying for the EIN exactly as it appears on the social security card, charter, or other applicable legal document.

Individuals. Enter your first name, middle initial, and last name. If you are a sole proprietor, enter your individual name, not your business name. Enter your business name on line 2. Do not use abbreviations or nicknames on line 1.

Trusts. Enter the name of the trust.

Estate of a decedent. Enter the name of the estate.

Partnerships. Enter the legal name of the partnership as it appears in the partnership agreement. **Do not** list the names of the partners on line 1. See the specific instructions for line 7.

Corporations. Enter the corporate name as it appears in the corporation charter or other legal document creating it.

Plan administrators. Enter the name of the plan administrator. A plan administrator who already has an EIN should use that number.

Line 2. Enter the trade name of the business if different from the legal name. The trade name is the "doing business as" name.

Note: *Use the full legal name on line 1 on all tax returns filed for the entity. However, if you enter a trade name on line 2 and choose to use the trade name instead of the legal name, enter the trade name on all returns you file. To prevent processing delays and errors, **always** use either the legal name only or the trade name only on all tax returns.*

Line 3. Trusts enter the name of the trustee. Estates enter the name of the executor, administrator, or other fiduciary. If the entity applying has a designated person to receive tax information, enter that person's name as the "care of" person. Print or type the first name, middle initial, and last name.

Line 7. Enter the first name, middle initial, last name, and SSN of a principal officer if the business is a corporation; of a general partner if a partnership; of the owner of a single member entity that is disregarded as an entity separate from its owner; or of a grantor, owner, or trustor if a trust. If the person in question is an alien individual with a previously assigned individual taxpayer identification number (ITIN), enter the ITIN in the space provided, instead of an SSN. You are not required to enter an SSN or ITIN if the reason you are applying for an EIN is to make an entity classification election (see Regulations section 301.7701-1 through 301.7701-3), and you are a nonresident alien with no effectively connected income from sources within the United States.

Line 8a. Check the box that best describes the type of entity applying for the EIN. If you are an alien individual with an ITIN previously assigned to you, enter the ITIN in place of a requested SSN.

Caution: *This is not an election for a tax classification of an entity. See "Limited liability company (LLC)" below.*

If not specifically mentioned, check the "Other" box, enter the type of entity and the type of return that will be filed (for example, common trust fund, Form 1065). Do not enter N/A. If you are an alien individual applying for an EIN, see the **Line 7** instructions above.

Sole proprietor. Check this box if you file Schedule C, C-EZ, or F (Form 1040) and have a qualified plan, or are required to file excise, employment, or alcohol, tobacco, or firearms returns, or are a payer of gambling winnings. Enter your SSN (or ITIN) in the space provided. If you are a nonresident alien with are a nonresident alien with no effectively

connected income from sources within the United States, you do not need to enter an SSN or ITIN.

REMIC. Check this box if the entity has elected to be treated as a real estate mortgage investment conduit (REMIC). See the Instructions for Form 1066 for more information.

Other nonprofit organization. Check this box if the nonprofit organization is other than a church or church-controlled organization and specify the type of nonprofit organization (for example, an educational organization).

If the organization also seeks tax-exempt status, you must file either **Package 1023,** Application for Recognition of Exemption, or **Package 1024,** Application for Recognition of Exemption Under Section 501(a). Get **Pub. 557,** Tax Exempt Status for Your Organization, for more information.

Group exemption number (GEN). If the organization is covered by a group exemption letter, enter the four-digit GEN. (Do not confuse the GEN with the nine-digit EIN.) If you do not know the GEN, contact the parent organization. Get Pub. 557 for more information about group exemption numbers.

Withholding agent. If you are a withholding agent required to file Form 1042, check the "Other" box and enter "Withholding agent."

Personal service corporation. Check this box if the entity is a personal service corporation. An entity is a personal service corporation for a tax year only if:

● The principal activity of the entity during the testing period (prior tax year) for the tax year is the performance of personal services substantially by employee-owners, and

● The employee-owners own at least 10% of the fair market value of the outstanding stock in the entity on the last day of the testing period.

Personal services include performance of services in such fields as health, law, accounting, or consulting. For more information about personal service corporations, see the **Instructions for Forms 1120 and 1120-A,** and **Pub. 542,** Corporations.

Limited liability company (LLC). See the definition of limited liability company in the **Instructions for Form 1065,** U.S. Partnership Return of Income. An LLC with two or more members can be a partnership or an association taxable as a corporation. An LLC with a single owner can be an association taxable as a corporation or an entity disregarded as an entity separate from its owner. See Form 8832 for more details.

Note: *A domestic LLC with at least two members that does not file Form 8832 is classified as a partnership for Federal income tax purposes.*

● If the entity is classified as a partnership for Federal income tax purposes, check the "partnership" box.

● If the entity is classified as a corporation for Federal income tax purposes, check the "Other corporation" box and write "limited liability co." in the space provided.

● If the entity is disregarded as an entity separate from its owner, check the "Other" box and write in "disregarded entity" in the space provided.

Plan administrator. If the plan administrator is an individual, enter the plan administrator's SSN in the space provided.

Other corporation. This box is for any corporation other than a personal service corporation. If you check this box, enter the type of corporation (such as insurance company) in the space provided.

Household employer. If you are an individual, check the "Other" box and enter "Household employer" and your SSN. If you are a state or local agency serving as a tax reporting agent for public assistance recipients who become household employers, check the "Other" box and enter "Household employer agent." If you are a trust that qualifies as a household employer, you do not need a separate EIN for reporting tax information relating to household employees; use the EIN of the trust.

QSub. For a qualified subchapter S subsidiary (QSub) check the "Other" box and specify "QSub."

Line 9. Check only **one** box. Do not enter N/A.

Started new business. Check this box if you are starting a new business that requires an EIN. If you check this box, enter the type of business being started. **Do not** apply if you already have an EIN and are only adding another place of business.

Hired employees. Check this box if the existing business is requesting an EIN because it has hired or is hiring employees and is therefore required to file employment tax returns. **Do not** apply if you already have an EIN and are only hiring employees. For information on the applicable employment taxes for family members, see **Circular E,** Employer's Tax Guide (Publication 15).

Created a pension plan. Check this box if you have created a pension plan and need an EIN for reporting purposes. Also, enter the type of plan.

Note: *Check this box if you are applying for a trust EIN when a new pension plan is established.*

Banking purpose. Check this box if you are requesting an EIN for banking purposes only, and enter the banking purpose (for example, a bowling league for depositing dues or an investment club for dividend and interest reporting).

Changed type of organization. Check this box if the business is changing its type of organization, for example, if the business was a sole proprietorship and has been incorporated or has become a partnership. If you check this box, specify in the space provided the type of change made, for example, "from sole proprietorship to partnership."

Purchased going business. Check this box if you purchased an existing business. **Do not** use the former owner's EIN. **Do not** apply for a new EIN if you already have one. Use your own EIN.

Created a trust. Check this box if you created a trust, and enter the type of trust created. For example, indicate if the trust is a nonexempt charitable trust or a split-interest trust.

Note: *Do not check this box if you are applying for a trust EIN when a new pension plan is established. Check "Created a pension plan."*

Exception. Do **not** file this form for certain grantor-type trusts. The trustee does not need an EIN for the trust if the trustee furnishes the name and TIN of the grantor/owner and the address of the trust to all payors. See the Instructions for Form 1041 for more information.

Other (specify). Check this box if you are requesting an EIN for any other reason, and enter the reason.

Line 10. If you are starting a new business, enter the starting date of the business. If the business you acquired is already operating, enter the date you acquired the business. Trusts should enter the date the trust was legally created. Estates should enter the date of death of the decedent whose name appears on line 1 or the date when the estate was legally funded.

Line 11. Enter the last month of your accounting year or tax year. An accounting or tax year is usually 12 consecutive months, either a calendar year or a fiscal year (including a period of 52 or 53 weeks). A calendar year is 12 consecutive months ending on December 31. A fiscal year is either 12 consecutive months ending on the last day of any month other than December or a 52-53 week year. For more information on accounting periods, see **Pub. 538,** Accounting Periods and Methods.

Individuals. Your tax year generally will be a calendar year.

Partnerships. Partnerships generally must adopt one of the following tax years:
- The tax year of the majority of its partners,
- The tax year common to all of its principal partners,
- The tax year that results in the least aggregate deferral of income, or
- In certain cases, some other tax year.

See the Instructions for Form 1065 for more information.

REMIC. REMICs must have a calendar year as their tax year.

Personal service corporations. A personal service corporation generally must adopt a calendar year unless:
- It can establish a business purpose for having a different tax year, or
- It elects under section 444 to have a tax year other than a calendar year.

Trusts. Generally, a trust must adopt a calendar year except for the following:
- Tax-exempt trusts,
- Charitable trusts, and
- Grantor-owned trusts.

Line 12. If the business has or will have employees, enter the date on which the business began or will begin to pay wages. If the business does not plan to have employees, enter N/A.

Withholding agent. Enter the date you began or will begin to pay income to a nonresident alien. This also applies to individuals who are required to file Form 1042 to report alimony paid to a nonresident alien.

Line 13. For a definition of agricultural labor (farmwork), see **Circular A,** Agricultural Employer's Tax Guide (Publication 51).

Line 14. Generally, enter the exact type of business being operated (for example, advertising agency, farm, food or beverage establishment, labor union, real estate agency, steam laundry, rental of coin-operated vending machine, or investment club). Also state if the business will involve the sale or distribution of alcoholic beverages.

Governmental. Enter the type of organization (state, county, school district, municipality, etc.).

Nonprofit organization (other than governmental). Enter whether organized for religious, educational, or humane purposes, and the principal activity (for example, religious organization—hospital, charitable).

Mining and quarrying. Specify the process and the principal product (for example, mining bituminous coal, contract drilling for oil, or quarrying dimension stone).

Contract construction. Specify whether general contracting or special trade contracting. Also, show the type of work normally performed (for example, general contractor for residential buildings or electrical subcontractor).

Food or beverage establishments. Specify the type of establishment and state whether you employ workers who receive tips (for example, lounge—yes).

Trade. Specify the type of sales and the principal line of goods sold (for example, wholesale dairy products, manufacturer's representative for mining machinery, or retail hardware).

Manufacturing. Specify the type of establishment operated (for example, sawmill or vegetable cannery).

Signature. The application must be signed by (a) the individual, if the applicant is an individual, (b) the president, vice president, or other principal officer, if the applicant is a corporation, (c) a responsible and duly authorized member or officer having knowledge of its affairs, if the applicant is a partnership or other unincorporated organization, or (d) the fiduciary, if the applicant is a trust or an estate.

How To Get Forms and Publications

Phone. You can order forms, instructions, and publications by phone 24 hours a day, 7 days a week. Just call 1-800-TAX-FORM (1-800-829-3676). You should receive your order or notification of its status within 10 workdays.

Personal computer. With your personal computer and modem, you can get the forms and information you need using IRS's Internet Web Site at **www.irs.gov** or File Transfer Protocol at **ftp.irs.gov.**

CD-ROM. For small businesses, return preparers, or others who may frequently need tax forms or publications, a CD-ROM containing over 2,000 tax products (including many prior year forms) can be purchased from the National Technical Information Service (NTIS).

To order Pub. 1796, Federal Tax Products on CD-ROM, call **1-877-CDFORMS** (1-877-233-6767) toll free or connect to **www.irs.gov/cdorders**

Privacy Act and Paperwork Reduction Act Notice. We ask for the information on this form to carry out the Internal Revenue laws of the United States. We need it to comply with section 6109 and the regulations thereunder which generally require the inclusion of an employer identification number (EIN) on certain returns, statements, or other documents filed with the Internal Revenue Service. Information on this form may be used to determine which Federal tax returns you are required to file and to provide you with related forms and publications. We disclose this form to the Social Security Administration for their use in determining compliance with applicable laws. We will be unable to issue an EIN to you unless you provide all of the requested information which applies to your entity.

You are not required to provide the information requested on a form that is subject to the Paperwork Reduction Act unless the form displays a valid OMB control number. Books or records relating to a form or its instructions must be retained as long as their contents may become material in the administration of any Internal Revenue law. Generally, tax returns/return information are confidential, as required by section 6103.

The time needed to complete and file this form will vary depending on individual circumstances. The estimated average time is:

Recordkeeping	7 min.
Learning about the law or the form	22 min.
Preparing the form	46 min.
Copying, assembling, and sending the form to the IRS . .	20 min.

If you have comments concerning the accuracy of these time estimates or suggestions for making this form simpler, we would be happy to hear from you. You can write to the Tax Forms Committee, Western Area Distribution Center, Rancho Cordova, CA 95743-0001. **Do not** send the form to this address. Instead, see **Where To Apply** on page 2.

EMPLOYEE'S WITHHOLDING ALLOWANCE CERTIFICATE (W-4)

Form W-4 (2001)

Purpose. Complete Form W-4 so your employer can withhold the correct Federal income tax from your pay. Because your tax situation may change, you may want to refigure your withholding each year.

Exemption from withholding. If you are exempt, complete only lines 1, 2, 3, 4, and 7, and sign the form to validate it. Your exemption for 2001 expires February 18, 2002.

Note: *You cannot claim exemption from withholding if (1) your income exceeds $750 and includes more than $250 of unearned income (e.g., interest and dividends) and (2) another person can claim you as a dependent on their tax return.*

Basic instructions. If you are not exempt, complete the **Personal Allowances Worksheet** below. The worksheets on page 2 adjust your withholding allowances based on itemized deductions, certain credits, adjustments to

income, or two-earner/two-job situations. Complete all worksheets that apply. They will help you figure the number of withholding allowances you are entitled to claim. **However, you may claim fewer (or zero) allowances.**

Head of household. Generally, you may claim head of household filing status on your tax return only if you are unmarried and pay more than 50% of the costs of keeping up a home for yourself and your dependent(s) or other qualifying individuals. See line E below.

Tax credits. You can take projected tax credits into account in figuring your allowable number of withholding allowances. Credits for child or dependent care expenses and the child tax credit may be claimed using the **Personal Allowances Worksheet** below. See **Pub. 919,** How Do I Adjust My Tax Withholding? for information on converting your other credits into withholding allowances.

Nonwage income. If you have a large amount of nonwage income, such as interest or dividends,

consider making estimated tax payments using **Form 1040-ES,** Estimated Tax for Individuals. Otherwise, you may owe additional tax.

Two earners/two jobs. If you have a working spouse or more than one job, figure the total number of allowances you are entitled to claim on all jobs using worksheets from only one Form W-4. Your withholding usually will be most accurate when all allowances are claimed on the Form W-4 for the highest paying job and zero allowances are claimed on the others.

Check your withholding. After your Form W-4 takes effect, use Pub. 919 to see how the dollar amount you are having withheld compares to your projected total tax for 2001. Get Pub. 919 especially if you used the **Two-Earner/Two-Job Worksheet** on page 2 and your earnings exceed $150,000 (Single) or $200,000 (Married).

Recent name change? If your name on line 1 differs from that shown on your social security card, call 1-800-772-1213 for a new social security card.

Personal Allowances Worksheet (Keep for your records.)

A Enter "1" for **yourself** if no one else can claim you as a dependent . . . . **A** _____

B Enter "1" if:
- You are single and have only one job; or
- You are married, have only one job, and your spouse does not work; or
- Your wages from a second job or your spouse's wages (or the total of both) are $1,000 or less.

. . B _____

C Enter "1" for your **spouse.** But, you may choose to enter -0- if you are married and have either a working spouse or more than one job. (Entering -0- may help you avoid having too little tax withheld.) . . . . **C** _____

D Enter number of **dependents** (other than your spouse or yourself) you will claim on your tax return . . . . **D** _____

E Enter "1" if you will file as **head of household** on your tax return (see conditions under **Head of household** above) . **E** _____

F Enter "1" if you have at least $1,500 of **child or dependent care expenses** for which you plan to claim a credit . . **F** _____

(**Note:** *Do not include child support payments. See* **Pub. 503,** *Child and Dependent Care Expenses, for details.*)

G **Child Tax Credit** (including additional child tax credit):
- If your total income will be between $18,000 and $50,000 ($23,000 and $63,000 if married), enter "1" for each eligible child.
- If your total income will be between $50,000 and $80,000 ($63,000 and $115,000 if married), enter "1" if you have two eligible children, enter "2" if you have three or four eligible children, or enter "3" if you have five or more eligible children. **G** _____

H Add lines A through G and enter total here. (**Note:** *This may be different from the number of exemptions you claim on your tax return.*) ▶ **H** _____

For accuracy, complete all worksheets that apply.
- If you plan to **itemize or claim adjustments to income** and want to reduce your withholding, see the **Deductions and Adjustments Worksheet** on page 2.
- If you are **single,** have **more than one job** and your combined earnings from all jobs exceed $35,000, **or** if you are **married** and have a **working spouse or more than one job** and the combined earnings from all jobs exceed $60,000, see the **Two-Earner/Two-Job Worksheet** on page 2 to avoid having too little tax withheld.
- If **neither** of the above situations applies, **stop here** and enter the number from line H on line 5 of Form W-4 below.

- - - - - - - - - - **Cut here and give Form W-4 to your employer. Keep the top part for your records.** - - - - - - - - - -

Form W-4
Department of the Treasury
Internal Revenue Service

Employee's Withholding Allowance Certificate

▶ **For Privacy Act and Paperwork Reduction Act Notice, see page 2.**

OMB No. 1545-0010

2001

1 Type or print your first name and middle initial | Last name | **2** Your social security number

3 ☐ Single ☐ Married ☐ Married, but withhold at higher Single rate.
Home address (number and street or rural route)
Note: *If married, but legally separated, or spouse is a nonresident alien, check the Single box.*

City or town, state, and ZIP code | **4** If your last name differs from that on your social security card, check here. You must call 1-800-772-1213 for a new card. ▶ ☐

5 Total number of allowances you are claiming (from line H above **or** from the applicable worksheet on page 2) | **5** _____

6 Additional amount, if any, you want withheld from each paycheck . . . . | **6** $ _____

7 I claim exemption from withholding for 2001, and I certify that I meet **both** of the following conditions for exemption:
- Last year I had a right to a refund of **all** Federal income tax withheld because I had **no** tax liability **and**
- This year I expect a refund of **all** Federal income tax withheld because I expect to have **no** tax liability.
If you meet both conditions, write "Exempt" here . . . . ▶ **7** _____

Under penalties of perjury, I certify that I am entitled to the number of withholding allowances claimed on this certificate, or I am entitled to claim exempt status.

Employee's signature
(Form is not valid unless you sign it.) ▶ | **Date** ▶

8 Employer's name and address (Employer: Complete lines 8 and 10 only if sending to the IRS.) | **9** Office code (optional) | **10** Employer identification number

Cat. No. 10220Q

Deductions and Adjustments Worksheet

Note: *Use this worksheet only if you plan to itemize deductions, claim certain credits, or claim adjustments to income on your 2001 tax return.*

1	Enter an estimate of your 2001 itemized deductions. These include qualifying home mortgage interest, charitable contributions, state and local taxes, medical expenses in excess of 7.5% of your income, and miscellaneous deductions. (For 2001, you may have to reduce your itemized deductions if your income is over $132,950 ($66,475 if married filing separately). See **Worksheet 3** in Pub. 919 for details.) . . .	1	$
2	Enter: { $7,600 if married filing jointly or qualifying widow(er) / $6,650 if head of household / $4,550 if single / $3,800 if married filing separately }	2	$
3	**Subtract** line 2 from line 1. If line 2 is greater than line 1, enter -0-	3	$
4	Enter an estimate of your 2001 adjustments to income, including alimony, deductible IRA contributions, and student loan interest	4	$
5	**Add** lines 3 and 4 and enter the total (Include any amount for credits from **Worksheet 7** in Pub. 919.) .	5	$
6	Enter an estimate of your 2001 nonwage income (such as dividends or interest)	6	$
7	**Subtract** line 6 from line 5. Enter the result, but not less than -0-	7	$
8	**Divide** the amount on line 7 by $3,000 and enter the result here. Drop any fraction . . .	8	
9	Enter the number from the **Personal Allowances Worksheet,** line H, page 1	9	
10	**Add** lines 8 and 9 and enter the total here. If you plan to use the **Two-Earner/Two-Job Worksheet,** also enter this total on line 1 below. Otherwise, **stop here** and enter this total on Form W-4, line 5, page 1 .	10	

Two-Earner/Two-Job Worksheet

Note: *Use this worksheet only if the instructions under line H on page 1 direct you here.*

1	Enter the number from line H, page 1 (or from line 10 above if you used the **Deductions and Adjustments Worksheet**)	1	
2	Find the number in **Table 1** below that applies to the **lowest** paying job and enter it here	2	
3	If line 1 is **more than or equal to** line 2, subtract line 2 from line 1. Enter the result here (if zero, enter -0-) and on Form W-4, line 5, page 1. **Do not** use the rest of this worksheet	3	

Note: *If line 1 is **less than** line 2, enter -0- on Form W-4, line 5, page 1. Complete lines 4–9 below to calculate the additional withholding amount necessary to avoid a year end tax bill.*

4	Enter the number from line 2 of this worksheet 4		
5	Enter the number from line 1 of this worksheet 5		
6	**Subtract** line 5 from line 4	6	
7	Find the amount in **Table 2** below that applies to the **highest** paying job and enter it here	7	$
8	**Multiply** line 7 by line 6 and enter the result here. This is the additional annual withholding needed . .	8	$
9	Divide line 8 by the number of pay periods remaining in 2001. For example, divide by 26 if you are paid every two weeks and you complete this form in December 2000. Enter the result here and on Form W-4, line 6, page 1. This is the additional amount to be withheld from each paycheck	9	$

Table 1: Two-Earner/Two-Job Worksheet

Married Filing Jointly				All Others			
If wages from **LOWEST** paying job are—	Enter on line 2 above	If wages from **LOWEST** paying job are—	Enter on line 2 above	If wages from **LOWEST** paying job are—	Enter on line 2 above	If wages from **LOWEST** paying job are—	Enter on line 2 above
$0 - $4,000	0	42,001 - 47,000	8	$0 - $6,000	0	65,001 - 80,000	8
4,001 - 8,000	1	47,001 - 55,000	9	6,001 - 12,000	1	80,001 - 105,000	9
8,001 - 14,000	2	55,001 - 65,000	10	12,001 - 17,000	2	105,001 and over	10
14,001 - 19,000	3	65,001 - 70,000	11	17,001 - 22,000	3		
19,001 - 25,000	4	70,001 - 90,000	12	22,001 - 28,000	4		
25,001 - 32,000	5	90,001 - 105,000	13	28,001 - 40,000	5		
32,001 - 38,000	6	105,001 - 115,000	14	40,001 - 50,000	6		
38,001 - 42,000	7	115,001 and over	15	50,001 - 65,000	7		

Table 2: Two-Earner/Two-Job Worksheet

Married Filing Jointly		All Others	
If wages from **HIGHEST** paying job are—	Enter on line 7 above	If wages from **HIGHEST** paying job are—	Enter on line 7 above
$0 - $50,000	$440	$0 - $30,000	$440
50,001 - 100,000	800	30,001 - 60,000	800
100,001 - 130,000	900	60,001 - 120,000	900
130,001 - 250,000	1,000	120,001 - 270,000	1,000
250,001 and over	1,100	270,001 and over	1,100

HOUSEHOLD HELP AGREEMENT

This agreement is between _____(the employer) and _____ (the employee) as follows:

1. Employee is being hired to provide household help including but not limited to the following:
    ❏ Child care   ❏ Interior cleaning   ❏ Food preparation

    ❏ Gardening   ❏ Exterior cleaning   ❏ Laundry

    ❏ Shopping   ❏ Transportation

2. The employment is agreed by both parties to be "at will" meaning it can be terminated by either party at any time. Employee represents that no verbal promises to the contrary have been made.

3. The first ____ days of employment shall be probationary for both sides. If the employee's work is not satisfactory, or the employee is not satisfied with the job, the employment shall end at the end of this period.

4. The employee's hours may be adjusted from time to time. Initially the employee's hours shall be: _____. Employee shall be entitled to the following breaks and holidays: _____

_____

_____

_____

Employee _____ be paid for holidays.

5. The employee's initial compensation shall be as follows: _____

_____.

6. The employee shall not have the power to bind the employer in any contracts.

7. Employee agrees not to divulge any information of a personal nature about the employer or employer's family to anyone and not to publish any such information in any manner.

8. Employee agrees not to drink alcohol or take any illegal drugs during working hours and not to smoke in employer's home or vehicles.

9. Employee shall not permit anyone to come onto employer's property without employer's express consent.

10. Employee agrees at all times to perform his/her duties to the best of his/her ability. Employee will not perform work for anyone else while on duty for employer.

11. If employee notices any dangerous condition on the property of employer employee agrees to immediately bring it to the attention of the employer.

12. This agreement shall be governed by the laws of the state of _____.

13. This agreement constitutes the entire agreement between the parties. No representations or promises have been made.

14. The company and employee agree that any disputes between them will be submitted to binding arbitration, rather than taken to court, and the costs of said arbitration shall be decided by the arbitrator. Each party specifically waives the right to take such disputes to court.

15. The parties agree to the following additional terms: ❑ None

Dated: _____

Employee: Employer:

_____   _____

DETERMINATION OF EMPLOYEE WORK STATUS (SS-8)

Form SS-8

(Rev. June 1997)

Department of the Treasury
Internal Revenue Service

Determination of Employee Work Status for Purposes of Federal Employment Taxes and Income Tax Withholding

OMB No. 1545-0004

Paperwork Reduction Act Notice

We ask for the information on this form to carry out the Internal Revenue laws of the United States. You are required to give us the information. We need it to ensure that you are complying with these laws and to allow us to figure and collect the right amount of tax.

You are not required to provide the information requested on a form that is subject to the Paperwork Reduction Act unless the form displays a valid OMB control number. Books or records relating to a form or its instructions must be retained as long as their contents may become material in the administration of any Internal Revenue law. Generally, tax returns and return information are confidential, as required by Code section 6103.

The time needed to complete and file this form will vary depending on individual circumstances. The estimated average time is: **Recordkeeping,** 34 hr., 55 min.; **Learning about the law or the form,** 12 min.; and **Preparing and sending the form to the IRS,** 46 min. If you have comments concerning the accuracy of these time estimates or suggestions for making this form simpler, we would be happy to hear from you. You can write to the Tax Forms Committee, Western Area Distribution Center, Rancho Cordova, CA 95743-0001. **DO NOT** send the tax form to this address. Instead, see **General Information** for where to file.

Purpose

Employers and workers file Form SS-8 to get a determination as to whether a worker is an employee for purposes of Federal employment taxes and income tax withholding.

General Information

Complete this form carefully. If the firm is completing the form, complete it for **ONE** individual who is representative of the class of workers whose status is in question. If you want a written determination for more than one class of workers, complete a separate Form SS-8 for one worker

from each class whose status is typical of that class. A written determination for any worker will apply to other workers of the same class if the facts are not materially different from those of the worker whose status was ruled upon.

Caution: Form SS-8 is not a claim for refund of social security and Medicare taxes or Federal income tax withholding. Also, a determination that an individual is an employee does not necessarily reduce any current or prior tax liability. A worker must file his or her income tax return even if a determination has not been made by the due date of the return.

Where to file.—In the list below, find the state where your legal residence, principal place of business, office, or agency is located. Send Form SS-8 to the address listed for your location.

Location:	Send to:
Alaska, Arizona, Arkansas, California, Colorado, Hawaii, Idaho, Illinois, Iowa, Kansas, Minnesota, Missouri, Montana, Nebraska, Nevada, New Mexico, North Dakota, Oklahoma, Oregon, South Dakota, Texas, Utah, Washington, Wisconsin, Wyoming	Internal Revenue Service SS-8 Determinations P.O. Box 1231, Stop 4106 AUSC Austin, TX 78767
Alabama, Connecticut, Delaware, District of Columbia, Florida, Georgia, Indiana, Kentucky, Louisiana, Maine, Maryland, Massachusetts, Michigan, Mississippi, New Hampshire, New Jersey, New York, North Carolina, Ohio, Pennsylvania, Rhode Island, South Carolina, Tennessee, Vermont, Virginia, West Virginia, All other locations not listed	Internal Revenue Service SS-8 Determinations Two Lakemont Road Newport, VT 05855-1555
American Samoa, Guam, Puerto Rico, U.S. Virgin Islands	Internal Revenue Service Mercantile Plaza 2 Avenue Ponce de Leon San Juan, Puerto Rico 00918

Name of firm (or person) for whom the worker performed services	Name of worker
Address of firm (include street address, apt. or suite no., city, state, and ZIP code)	Address of worker (include street address, apt. or suite no., city, state, and ZIP code)

Trade name	Telephone number (include area code) ( )	Worker's social security number

Telephone number (include area code) ( )	Firm's employer identification number	

Check type of firm for which the work relationship is in question:

☐ Individual ☐ Partnership ☐ Corporation ☐ Other (specify) ▶ ....

Important Information Needed To Process Your Request

This form is being completed by: ☐ Firm ☐ Worker

If this form is being completed by the worker, the IRS **must** have your permission to disclose your name to the firm.

Do you object to disclosing your name and the information on this form to the firm? . . . . ☐ Yes ☐ No

If you answer "Yes," the IRS cannot act on your request. **Do not complete the rest of this form unless the IRS asks for it.**

Under section 6110 of the Internal Revenue Code, the information on this form and related file documents will be open to the public if any ruling or determination is made. However, names, addresses, and taxpayer identification numbers will be removed before the information is made public.

Is there any other information you want removed? . . . . ☐ Yes ☐ No

If you check "Yes," we cannot process your request unless you submit a copy of this form and copies of all supporting documents showing, in brackets, the information you want removed. Attach a separate statement showing which specific exemption of section 6110(c) applies to each bracketed part.

Cat. No. 16106T

Form **SS-8** (Rev. 6-97)

*This form is designed to cover many work activities, so some of the questions may not apply to you. **You must answer ALL items or mark them "Unknown" or "Does not apply."** If you need more space, attach another sheet.*

Total number of workers in this class. (Attach names and addresses. If more than 10 workers, list only 10.) ▶ _____

This information is about services performed by the worker from _____ to _____
(month, day, year)   (month, day, year)

Is the worker still performing services for the firm? . . . . ☐ Yes ☐ No

● If "No," what was the date of termination? ▶ _____
(month, day, year)

1a Describe the firm's business ....
  b Describe the work done by the worker ....
  ....

2a If the work is done under a written agreement between the firm and the worker, attach a copy.
  b If the agreement is not in writing, describe the terms and conditions of the work arrangement ....
  ....
  c If the actual working arrangement differs in any way from the agreement, explain the differences and why they occur ......
  ....

3a Is the worker given training by the firm? . . . . ☐ Yes ☐ No
  ● If "Yes," what kind? ....
  ● How often? ....
  b Is the worker given instructions in the way the work is to be done (exclusive of actual training in 3a)? . ☐ Yes ☐ No
  ● If "Yes," give specific examples ....
  c Attach samples of any written instructions or procedures.
  d Does the firm have the right to change the methods used by the worker or direct that person on how to
  do the work? . . . . ☐ Yes ☐ No
  ● Explain your answer ....
  ....
  e Does the operation of the firm's business require that the worker be supervised or controlled in the
  performance of the service? . . . . ☐ Yes ☐ No
  ● Explain your answer ....
  ....

4a The firm engages the worker:
  ☐ To perform and complete a particular job only
  ☐ To work at a job for an indefinite period of time
  ☐ Other (explain) ....
  b Is the worker required to follow a routine or a schedule established by the firm? . . . . ☐ Yes ☐ No
  ● If "Yes," what is the routine or schedule? ....
  ....
  c Does the worker report to the firm or its representative?. . . . . ☐ Yes ☐ No
  ● If "Yes," how often? ....
  ● For what purpose? ....
  ● In what manner (in person, in writing, by telephone, etc.)? ....
  ● Attach copies of any report forms used in reporting to the firm.
  d Does the worker furnish a time record to the firm? . . . . ☐ Yes ☐ No
  ● If "Yes," attach copies of time records.
5a State the kind and value of tools, equipment, supplies, and materials furnished by:
  ● The firm ....
  ....
  ● The worker ....
  ....
  b What expenses are incurred by the worker in the performance of services for the firm? ....
  ....
  c Does the firm reimburse the worker for any expenses? . . . . ☐ Yes ☐ No
  ● If "Yes," specify the reimbursed expenses ....

6a Will the worker perform the services personally? . . . . ☐ Yes ☐ No

b Does the worker have helpers? . . . . ☐ Yes ☐ No

  ● If "Yes," who hires the helpers? ☐ Firm ☐ Worker

  ● If the helpers are hired by the worker, is the firm's approval necessary? . . . . ☐ Yes ☐ No

  ● Who pays the helpers? ☐ Firm ☐ Worker

  ● If the worker pays the helpers, does the firm repay the worker? . . . . ☐ Yes ☐ No

  ● Are social security and Medicare taxes and Federal income tax withheld from the helpers' pay? . . ☐ Yes ☐ No

  ● If "Yes," who reports and pays these taxes? ☐ Firm ☐ Worker

  ● Who reports the helpers' earnings to the Internal Revenue Service? ☐ Firm ☐ Worker

  ● What services do the helpers perform? ....

7 At what location are the services performed? ☐ Firm's ☐ Worker's ☐ Other (specify) ....

8a Type of pay worker receives:

  ☐ Salary ☐ Commission ☐ Hourly wage   ☐ Piecework ☐ Lump sum   ☐ Other (specify) ....

b Does the firm guarantee a minimum amount of pay to the worker? . . . . ☐ Yes ☐ No

c Does the firm allow the worker a drawing account or advances against pay? . . . . ☐ Yes ☐ No

  ● If "Yes," is the worker paid such advances on a regular basis? . . . . ☐ Yes ☐ No

d How does the worker repay such advances? ....

9a Is the worker eligible for a pension, bonus, paid vacations, sick pay, etc.? . . . . ☐ Yes ☐ No

  ● If "Yes," specify ....

b Does the firm carry worker's compensation insurance on the worker? . . . . ☐ Yes ☐ No

c Does the firm withhold social security and Medicare taxes from amounts paid the worker? . . . . . ☐ Yes ☐ No

d Does the firm withhold Federal income tax from amounts paid the worker? . . . . ☐ Yes ☐ No

e How does the firm report the worker's earnings to the Internal Revenue Service?

  ☐ Form W-2 ☐ Form 1099-MISC   ☐ Does not report ☐ Other (specify) ....

  ● Attach a copy.

f Does the firm bond the worker? . . . . ☐ Yes ☐ No

10a Approximately how many hours a day does the worker perform services for the firm? ....

b Does the firm set hours of work for the worker? . . . . ☐ Yes ☐ No

  ● If "Yes," what are the worker's set hours? _____ a.m./p.m. to _____ a.m./p.m. (Circle whether a.m. or p.m.)

c Does the worker perform similar services for others? . . . . ☐ Yes ☐ No ☐ Unknown

  ● If "Yes," are these services performed on a daily basis for other firms? . . . . . . ☐ Yes ☐ No ☐ Unknown

  ● Percentage of time spent in performing these services for:

   This firm .... % Other firms .... %   ☐ Unknown

  ● Does the firm have priority on the worker's time? . . . . ☐ Yes ☐ No

  ● If "No," explain ....

d Is the worker prohibited from competing with the firm either while performing services or during any later
period? . . . . ☐ Yes ☐ No

11a Can the firm discharge the worker at any time without incurring a liability? . . . . ☐ Yes ☐ No

  ● If "No," explain ....

b Can the worker terminate the services at any time without incurring a liability? . . . . ☐ Yes ☐ No

  ● If "No," explain ....

12a Does the worker perform services for the firm under:

  ☐ The firm's business name ☐ The worker's own business name   ☐ Other (specify) ....

b Does the worker advertise or maintain a business listing in the telephone directory, a trade
journal, etc.? . . . . ☐ Yes ☐ No ☐ Unknown

  ● If "Yes," specify ....

c Does the worker represent himself or herself to the public as being in business to perform
the same or similar services? . . . . ☐ Yes ☐ No ☐ Unknown

  ● If "Yes," how? ....

d Does the worker have his or her own shop or office? . . . . ☐ Yes ☐ No ☐ Unknown

  ● If "Yes," where? ....

e Does the firm represent the worker as an employee of the firm to its customers? . . . . ☐ Yes ☐ No

  ● If "No," how is the worker represented? ....

f How did the firm learn of the worker's services? ....

13 Is a license necessary for the work? . . . . ☐ Yes ☐ No ☐ Unknown

  ● If "Yes," what kind of license is required? ....

  ● Who issues the license? ....

  ● Who pays the license fee?

237

14 Does the worker have a financial investment in a business related to the services
performed?. . . . . ☐ Yes   ☐ No   ☐ Unknown
   ● If "Yes," specify and give amount of the investment ....

15 Can the worker incur a loss in the performance of the service for the firm? . . . . ☐ Yes   ☐ No
   ● If "Yes," how? ....

16a Has any other government agency ruled on the status of the firm's workers? . . . . ☐ Yes   ☐ No
   ● If "Yes," attach a copy of the ruling.

  b Is the same issue being considered by any IRS office in connection with the audit of the worker's tax
return or the firm's tax return, or has it been considered recently? . . . . ☐ Yes   ☐ No
   ● If "Yes," for which year(s)? ....

17 Does the worker assemble or process a product at home or away from the firm's place of business? ☐ Yes   ☐ No
   ● If "Yes," who furnishes materials or goods used by the worker? ☐ Firm   ☐ Worker   ☐ Other
   ● Is the worker furnished a pattern or given instructions to follow in making the product? . . . . . ☐ Yes   ☐ No
   ● Is the worker required to return the finished product to the firm or to someone designated by the firm? ☐ Yes ☐ No
18 Attach a detailed explanation of any other reason why you believe the worker is an employee or an independent contractor.

Answer items 19a through o only if the worker is a salesperson or provides a service directly to customers.

19a Are leads to prospective customers furnished by the firm?. . . . . ☐ Yes   ☐ No   ☐ Does not apply
  b Is the worker required to pursue or report on leads? . . . . ☐ Yes   ☐ No   ☐ Does not apply
  c Is the worker required to adhere to prices, terms, and conditions of sale established by the firm? . . ☐ Yes ☐ No
  d Are orders submitted to and subject to approval by the firm? . . . . ☐ Yes ☐ No
  e Is the worker expected to attend sales meetings? . . . . ☐ Yes ☐ No
   ● If "Yes," is the worker subject to any kind of penalty for failing to attend? . . . . ☐ Yes ☐ No
  f Does the firm assign a specific territory to the worker? . . . . ☐ Yes ☐ No
  g Whom does the customer pay?   ☐ Firm   ☐ Worker
   ● If worker, does the worker remit the total amount to the firm? . . . . ☐ Yes ☐ No
  h Does the worker sell a consumer product in a home or establishment other than a permanent retail
establishment? . . . . ☐ Yes ☐ No
  i List the products and/or services distributed by the worker, such as meat, vegetables, fruit, bakery products, beverages (other
than milk), or laundry or dry cleaning services. If more than one type of product and/or service is distributed, specify the
principal one ....
  j Did the firm or another person assign the route or territory and a list of customers to the worker? . . ☐ Yes ☐ No
   ● If "Yes," enter the name and job title of the person who made the assignment ....
  k Did the worker pay the firm or person for the privilege of serving customers on the route or in the territory? ☐ Yes ☐ No
   ● If "Yes," how much did the worker pay (not including any amount paid for a truck or racks, etc.)? $ ....
   ● What factors were considered in determining the value of the route or territory? ....
  l How are new customers obtained by the worker? Explain fully, showing whether the new customers called the firm for service,
were solicited by the worker, or both ....
  m Does the worker sell life insurance? . . . . ☐ Yes ☐ No
   ● If "Yes," is the selling of life insurance or annuity contracts for the firm the worker's entire business
activity? . . . . ☐ Yes ☐ No
   ● If "No," list the other business activities and the amount of time spent on them ....
  n Does the worker sell other types of insurance for the firm? . . . . ☐ Yes ☐ No
   ● If "Yes," state the percentage of the worker's total working time spent in selling other types of insurance.............. %
   ● At the time the contract was entered into between the firm and the worker, was it their intention that the worker sell life
insurance for the firm: ☐ on a full-time basis   ☐ on a part-time basis
   ● State the manner in which the intention was expressed ....
  o Is the worker a traveling or city salesperson? . . . . ☐ Yes ☐ No
   ● If "Yes," from whom does the worker principally solicit orders for the firm? ....
   ● If the worker solicits orders from wholesalers, retailers, contractors, or operators of hotels, restaurants, or other similar
establishments, specify the percentage of the worker's time spent in the solicitation .... %
   ● Is the merchandise purchased by the customers for resale or for use in their business operations? If used by the customers
in their business operations, describe the merchandise and state whether it is equipment installed on their premises or a
consumable supply

Signature ▶   Title ▶   Date ▶

✹

INDEPENDENT CONTRACTOR AGREEMENT

This indemnification agreement is entered into by and between _____
_____ (the "Company") and
_____ (the "Contractor"). It is agreed
by the parties as follows:

1. The Contractor shall supply all of the labor and materials to perform the following work for the Company as an independent contractor:

❏ The attached plans and specifications are to be followed and are hereby made a part of this Agreement.

2. The Contractor agrees to the following completion dates for portions of the work and final completion of the work:

<u>Description of Work</u>   <u>Completion Date</u>

3. The Contractor shall perform the work in a workman-like manner, according to standard industry practices, unless other standards or requirements are set forth in any attached plans and specifications.

4. The Company shall pay the Contractor the sum of $_____, in full payment for the work as set forth in this Agreement, to be paid as follows:

5. Any additional work or services shall be agreed to in writing, signed by both parties.

6. The Contractor shall obtain and maintain any licenses or permits necessary for the work to be performed. The Contractor shall obtain and maintain any required insurance, including but not limited to workers' compensation insurance, to cover the Contractor's employees and agents.

7. The Contractor shall be responsible for the payment of any sub-contractors and shall obtain lien releases from sub-contractors as may be necessary. The Contractor agrees to indemnify and hold harmless the Company from any claims or liability arising out of the work performed by the Contractor under this Agreement.

8. Time is of the essence of this Agreement.

9. This instrument, including any attached exhibits and addenda, constitutes the entire agreement of the parties. No representations or promises have been made except those that are set out in this agreement. This agreement may not be modified except in writing signed by all the parties.

10. This agreement shall be governed by the laws of _____.

11. If any part of this agreement is adjudged invalid, illegal, or unenforceable, the remaining parts shall not be affected and shall remain in full force and effect.

12. This agreement shall be binding upon the parties, and upon their heirs, executors, personal representatives, administrators, and assigns. No person shall have a right or cause of action arising out of or resulting from this agreement except those who are parties to it and their successors in interest.

13. This instrument, including any attached exhibits and addenda, constitutes the entire agreement of the parties. No representations or promises have been made except those that are set out in this agreement. This agreement may not be modified except in writing signed by all the parties.

IN WITNESS WHEREOF the parties have signed this agreement under seal on _____.

Company: Contractor:

_____   _____

_____   _____

MODIFICATION OF INDEPENDENT CONTRACTOR AGREEMENT

For valuable consideration, the receipt and sufficiency of which is acknowledged by each of the parties, this agreement amends an Independent Contractor Agreement dated _____, 20___, between _____ and _____ , relating to _____.

This amendment is hereby incorporated into the Contract.

Except as changed by this amendment, the Independent Contractor Agreement shall continue in effect according to its terms. The amendments herein shall be effective on the date this document is executed by all parties.

IN WITNESS WHEREOF the parties have signed this agreement under seal on _____.

_____   _____

_____   _____

TERMINATION OF INDEPENDENT CONTRACTOR AGREEMENT

For valuable consideration, the receipt and sufficiency of which is acknowledged by each of the parties to that certain Independent Contractor Agreement dated _____, 20____, between _____ and _____ , relating to _____ hereby agree that said Independent Contractor Agreement shall be terminated by mutual agreement and that each party releases the other from any and all claims thereunder.

IN WITNESS WHEREOF the parties have signed this termination under seal on _____, 20____.

_____   _____

_____   _____

AFFIDAVIT

The undersigned, being first duly sworn, deposes and says:

This affidavit was executed by me on _____, 20_____.

_____

STATE OF   )
COUNTY OF   )

    I certify that _____ ,who ❑ is personally known to me to be the person whose name is subscribed to the foregoing instrument ❑ produced _____ as identification, personally appeared before me on _____, and ❑ acknowledged the execution of the foregoing instrument ❑ acknowledged that (s)he is (Assistant) Secretary of _____ _____and that by authority duly given and as the act of the corporation, the foregoing instrument was signed in its name by its (Vice) President, sealed with its corporate seal and attested by him/her as its (Assistant) Secretary.

_____
Notary Public, State of

My commission expires:

General Release

In exchange for the sum of $10.00 and other valuable consideration, the receipt and sufficiency of which is hereby acknowledged, the undersigned corporation hereby forever releases, discharges and acquits _____,
and [its/his/her] successors, assigns, heirs and personal representatives, from any and all claims, actions, suits, agreements or liabilities in favor of or owed to the undersigned, existing at any time up to the date of this release.

IN WITNESS WHEREOF, the undersigned has executed this release under seal on
_____.

_____

SPECIFIC RELEASE

In exchange for the sum of $10.00 and other valuable consideration, the receipt and sufficiency of which is hereby acknowledged, the undersigned hereby forever releases, discharges and acquits _____, and [its/his/her] successors, assigns, heirs and personal representatives, from any and all claims, actions, suits, agreements or liabilities arising out of or related to:

IN WITNESS WHEREOF, the undersigned has executed this release under seal on _____.

_____

Mutual Release

In exchange for the sum of $10.00 and other valuable consideration, the receipt and sufficiency of which is hereby acknowledged, the undersigned hereby forever release, discharge and acquit each other, and their successors, assigns, heirs and personal representatives, from any and all claims, actions, suits, agreements or liabilities arising out of or related to:

IN WITNESS WHEREOF, the undersigned have executed this release under seal on

_____.

_____   _____

_____   _____

ARBITRATION AGREEMENT

This Arbitration Agreement is made this _____ day of _____, 20_____, by and between _____ and _____, who agree as follows:

1. The parties agree that any controversy, claim or dispute arising out of or related to:

shall be submitted to arbitration. Such arbitration shall take place at _____
_____
or at such other place as may be agreed upon by the parties.

2. The parties shall attempt to agree on one arbitrator. If they are unable to so agree, then each party shall appoint one arbitrator and those appointed shall appoint a third arbitrator.

3. The expenses of arbitration shall be divided equally by the parties.

4. The arbitrators shall conclusively decide all issues of law and fact related to the arbitrated dispute. Judgment upon an award rendered by the arbitrator may be entered in any court having jurisdiction.

5. The prevailing party ❑ shall ❑ shall not be entitled to reasonable attorneys' fees.

_____   _____

_____   _____

MEDIATION AGREEMENT

This Mediation Agreement is made this _____ day of _____, 20_____, by and between _____ and _____, who agree as follows:

    1. The parties agree that any controversy, claim or dispute arising out of or related to:

shall be submitted to mediation. Such mediation shall take place at _____ _____ or at such other place as may be agreed upon by the parties.

    2. The parties have agreed to use _____ as mediator.

    3. The expenses of mediation shall be divided equally by the parties.

_____   _____

_____   _____

COVENANT NOT TO SUE

This agreement is made by and between _____
_____ (the "Covenantor"), for [itself/himself/herself]
and for its heirs, legal representatives and assigns, and _____
_____ (the "Covenantee").

1. In exchange for the Covenantor's covenant herein, the Covenantee
_____
_____
_____
_____.

2. In exchange for the consideration stated in paragraph 1 above, the receipt and sufficiency of which is hereby acknowledged by the Covenantor, the Covenantor covenants with
the Covenantee never to institute any suit or action at law or in equity against the
Covenantee by reason of any claim the Covenantor now has or may hereafter acquire related
to: _____
_____.

This agreement was executed by the parties under seal on _____, 20____.

Covenantor: Covenantee:

_____   _____

_____   _____

REQUEST FOR INFORMATION UNDER
FREEDOM OF INFORMATION ACT

To:

Under the Freedom of Information Act, I request any and all information you have regarding the following:

In the event that the cost for such information exceeds $_____, please advise me in advance of what material will be included and what the cost will be

Thank you,

_____

INDEX

Your #1 Source for Real World Legal Information...

SPHINX® PUBLISHING
A Division of Sourcebooks, Inc.®

- Written by lawyers
- Simple English explanation of the law
- Forms and instructions included

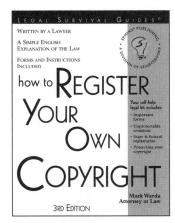

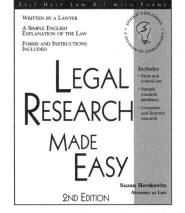

HOW TO REGISTER YOUR OWN COPYRIGHT, 3RD ED.

Protect your original creative works by applying for a U.S. copyright! This book explains what types of work are protected, from computer programs to the visual arts. It also explains the benefits of protection and more! With forms and instructions.

224 pages; $21.95;
ISBN 1-57248-124-2

LEGAL RESEARCH MADE EASY, 2ND ED.

Simplify the process of doing your own legal research in law libraries and on computers. This book explains how to research statutes, case law, databases, law reports and more Learn how to access your state's statutes on the Internet. Save yourself enormous amounts of time and money.

128 pages; $14.95;
ISBN 1-57071-400-2

THE MOST VALUABLE BUSINESS LEGAL FORMS YOU'LL EVER NEED, 2ND ED.

Using the right legal forms can add to your profits and help you avoid legal problems. This book provides businesses with the many and varied legal forms they will need. They are so simple and standard, you will wonder why anyone would pay a lawyer to fill them out!

140 pages; $19.95;
ISBN 1-57071-345-6

See the following order form for books written specifically for California, Florida, Georgia, Illinois, Massachusetts, Michigan, Minnesota, New York, North Carolina, Pennsylvania, Ohio, and Texas!

What our customers say about our books:

"It couldn't be more clear for the lay person." —R.D.

"I want you to know I really appreciate your book. It has saved me a lot of time and money." —L.T.

"Your real estate contracts book has saved me nearly $12,000.00 in closing costs over the past year." —A.B.

"...many of the legal questions that I have had over the years were answered clearly and concisely through your plain English interpretation of the law." —C.E.H.

"If there weren't people out there like you I'd be lost. You have the best books of this type out there." —S.B.

"...your forms and directions are easy to follow." —C.V.M.

Sphinx Publishing's Legal Survival Guides
are directly available from the Sourcebooks, Inc., or from your local bookstores.
For credit card orders call 1–800–43–BRIGHT, write P.O. Box 4410, Naperville, IL 60567-4410,
or fax 630-961-2168

SPHINX® PUBLISHING'S NATIONAL TITLES

Valid in All 50 States

LEGAL SURVIVAL IN BUSINESS

How to Form a Limited Liability Company	$19.95
How to Form Your Own Corporation (3E)	$19.95
How to Form Your Own Partnership	$19.95
How to Register Your Own Copyright (3E)	$19.95
How to Register Your Own Trademark (3E)	$19.95
Most Valuable Business Legal Forms You'll Ever Need (2E)	$19.95
Most Valuable Corporate Forms You'll Ever Need (2E)	$24.95
Software Law (with diskette)	$29.95

LEGAL SURVIVAL IN COURT

Crime Victim's Guide to Justice	$19.95
Debtors' Rights (3E)	$12.95
Grandparents' Rights (2E)	$19.95
Help Your Lawyer Win Your Case (2E)	$12.95
Jurors' Rights (2E)	$9.95
Legal Research Made Easy (2E)	$14.95
Winning Your Personal Injury Claim	$19.95

LEGAL SURVIVAL IN REAL ESTATE

How to Buy a Condominium or Townhome	$16.95
How to Negotiate Real Estate Contracts (3E)	$16.95
How to Negotiate Real Estate Leases (3E)	$16.95

LEGAL SURVIVAL IN PERSONAL AFFAIRS

Guia de Inmigracion a Estados Unidos (2E)	$19.95
How to File Your Own Bankruptcy (4E)	$19.95
How to File Your Own Divorce (4E)	$19.95
How to Make Your Own Will (2E)	$12.95
How to Write Your Own Living Will (2E)	$12.95
How to Write Your Own Premarital Agreement (2E)	$19.95
How to Win Your Unemployment Compensation Claim	$19.95
Living Trusts and Simple Ways to Avoid Probate (2E)	$19.95
Most Valuable Personal Legal Forms You Will Ever Need	$19.95
Neighbor v. Neighbor (2E)	$12.95
The Nanny and Domestic Help Legal Kit	$19.95
The Power of Attorney Handbook (3E)	$19.95
Quick Divorce Book	$19.95
Social Security Benefits Handbook (2E)	$14.95
Unmarried Parents' Rights	$19.95
U.S.A. Immigration Guide (3E)	$19.95
Your Right to Child Custody, Visitation and Support	$19.95

Legal Survival Guides are directly available from Sourcebooks, Inc., or from your local bookstores.
Prices are subject to change without notice.

For credit card orders call 1–800–43–BRIGHT, write P.O. Box 4410, Naperville, IL 60567-4410
or fax 630-961-2168

SPHINX® PUBLISHING ORDER FORM

BILL TO:		SHIP TO:	
Phone #	Terms	F.O.B. Chicago, IL	Ship Date

Charge my: ☐ VISA ☐ MasterCard ☐ American Express

☐ **Money Order or Personal Check**

Credit Card Number Expiration Date

Qty	ISBN	Title	Retail	Ext.
		SPHINX PUBLISHING NATIONAL TITLES		
	1-57071-166-6	Crime Victim's Guide to Justice	$19.95	
	1-57071-342-1	Debtors' Rights (3E)	$12.95	
	1-57248-082-3	Grandparents' Rights (2E)	$19.95	
	1-57248-087-4	Guia de Inmigracion a Estados Unidos (2E)	$19.95	
	1-57248-103-X	Help Your Lawyer Win Your Case (2E)	$12.95	
	1-57071-164-X	How to Buy a Condominium or Townhome	$16.95	
	1-57071-223-9	How to File Your Own Bankruptcy (4E)	$19.95	
	1-57248-132-3	How to File Your Own Divorce (4E)	$19.95	
	1-57248-100-5	How to Form a DE Corporation from Any State	$19.95	
	1-57248-083-1	How to Form a Limited Liability Company	$19.95	
	1-57248-101-3	How to Form a NV Corporation from Any State	$19.95	
	1-57248-099-8	How to Form a Nonprofit Corporation	$24.95	
	1-57248-133-1	How to Form Your Own Corporation (3E)	$19.95	
	1-57071-343-X	How to Form Your Own Partnership	$19.95	
	1-57248-119-6	How to Make Your Own Will (2E)	$12.95	
	1-57071-331-6	How to Negotiate Real Estate Contracts (3E)	$16.95	
	1-57071-332-4	How to Negotiate Real Estate Leases (3E)	$16.95	
	1-57248-124-2	How to Register Your Own Copyright (3E)	$19.95	
	1-57248-104-8	How to Register Your Own Trademark (3E)	$19.95	
	1-57071-349-9	How to Win Your Unemployment Compensation Claim	$19.95	
	1-57248-118-8	How to Write Your Own Living Will (2E)	$12.95	
	1-57071-344-8	How to Write Your Own Premarital Agreement (2E)	$19.95	
	1-57071-333-2	Jurors' Rights (2E)	$9.95	
	1-57071-400-2	Legal Research Made Easy (2E)	$14.95	
	1-57071-336-7	Living Trusts and Simple Ways to Avoid Probate (2E)	$19.95	
	1-57071-345-6	Most Valuable Bus. Legal Forms You'll Ever Need (2E)	$19.95	

Qty	ISBN	Title	Retail	Ext.
	1-57071-346-4	Most Valuable Corporate Forms You'll Ever Need (2E)	$24.95	
	1-57248-130-7	Most Valuable Personal Legal Forms You'll Ever Need	$19.95	
	1-57248-098-X	The Nanny and Domestic Help Legal Kit	$19.95	
	1-57248-089-0	Neighbor v. Neighbor (2E)	$14.95	
	1-57071-348-0	The Power of Attorney Handbook (3E)	$19.95	
	1-57248-131-5	Quick Divorce Boook	$19.95	
	1-57071-337-5	Social Security Benefits Handbook (2E)	$14.95	
	1-57071-163-1	Software Law (w/diskette)	$29.95	
	1-57071-399-5	Unmarried Parents' Rights	$19.95	
	1-57071-354-5	U.S.A. Immigration Guide (3E)	$19.95	
	1-57071-165-8	Winning Your Personal Injury Claim	$19.95	
	1-57248-097-1	Your Right to Child Custody, Visitation and Support	$19.95	
		CALIFORNIA TITLES		
	1-57071-360-X	CA Power of Attorney Handbook	$12.95	
	1-57248-126-9	How to File for Divorce in CA (2E)	$19.95	
	1-57071-356-1	How to Make a CA Will	$12.95	
	1-57071-358-8	How to Win in Small Claims Court in CA	$14.95	
	1-57071-359-6	Landlords' Rights and Duties in CA	$19.95	
		FLORIDA TITLES		
	1-57071-363-4	Florida Power of Attorney Handbook (2E)	$12.95	
	1-57248-093-9	How to File for Divorce in FL (6E)	$24.95	
	1-57071-380-4	How to Form a Corporation in FL (4E)	$19.95	
	1-57248-086-6	How to Form a Limited Liability Co. in FL	$19.95	
	1-57071-401-0	How to Form a Partnership in FL	$19.95	
	1-57248-113-7	How to Make a FL Will (6E)	$12.95	
	1-57248-088-2	How to Modify Your FL Divorce Judgment (4E)	$22.95	
		Form Continued on Following Page SUBTOTAL		

To order, call Sourcebooks at 1-800-43-BRIGHT or FAX (630)961-2168 (Bookstores, libraries, wholesalers—please call for discount)

Prices are subject to change without notice.

SPHINX® PUBLISHING ORDER FORM

Qty	ISBN	Title	Retail	Ext.
___	1-57248-081-5	How to Start a Business in FL (5E)	$16.95	___
___	1-57071-362-6	How to Win in Small Claims Court in FL (6E)	$14.95	___
___	1-57248-123-4	Landlords' Rights and Duties in FL (8E)	$19.95	___
		GEORGIA TITLES		
___	1-57071-376-6	How to File for Divorce in GA (3E)	$19.95	___
___	1-57248-075-0	How to Make a GA Will (3E)	$12.95	___
___	1-57248-076-9	How to Start a Business in Georgia	$16.95	___
		ILLINOIS TITLES		
___	1-57071-405-3	How to File for Divorce in IL (2E)	$19.95	___
___	1-57071-415-0	How to Make an IL Will (2E)	$12.95	___
___	1-57071-416-9	How to Start a Business in IL (2E)	$16.95	___
___	1-57248-078-5	Landlords' Rights & Duties in IL	$19.95	___
		MASSACHUSETTS TITLES		
___	1-57071-329-4	How to File for Divorce in MA (2E)	$19.95	___
___	1-57248-115-3	How to Form a Corporation in MA	$19.95	___
___	1-57248-108-0	How to Make a MA Will (2E)	$12.95	___
___	1-57248-106-4	How to Start a Business in MA (2E)	$16.95	___
___	1-57248-107-2	Landlords' Rights and Duties in MA (2E)	$19.95	___
		MICHIGAN TITLES		
___	1-57071-409-6	How to File for Divorce in MI (2E)	$19.95	___
___	1-57248-077-7	How to Make a MI Will (2E)	$12.95	___
___	1-57071-407-X	How to Start a Business in MI (2E)	$16.95	___
		NEW YORK TITLES		
___	1-57071-184-4	How to File for Divorce in NY	$24.95	___
___	1-57248-105-6	How to Form a Corporation in NY	$19.95	___
___	1-57248-095-5	How to Make a NY Will (2E)	$12.95	___
___	1-57071-185-2	How to Start a Business in NY	$16.95	___
___	1-57071-187-9	How to Win in Small Claims Court in NY	$14.95	___
___	1-57071-186-0	Landlords' Rights and Duties in NY	$19.95	___

Qty	ISBN	Title	Retail	Ext.
___	1-57248-188-7	New York Power of Attorney Handbook	$19.95	___
___	1-57248-122-6	Tenants' Rights in NY	$19..95	___
		NORTH CAROLINA TITLES		
___	1-57071-326-X	How to File for Divorce in NC (2E)	$19.95	___
___	1-57248-129-3	How to Make a NC Will (3E)	$12.95	___
___	1-57248-096-3	How to Start a Business in NC (2E)	$16.95	___
___	1-57248-091-2	Landlords' Rights & Duties in NC	$19.95	___
		OHIO TITLES		
___	1-57248-102-1	How to File for Divorce in OH	$19.95	___
		PENNSYLVANIA TITLES		
___	1-57248-127-7	How to File for Divorce in PA (2E)	$19.95	___
___	1-57248-094-7	How to Make a PA Will (2E)	$12.95	___
___	1-57248-112-9	How to Start a Business in PA (2E)	$16.95	___
___	1-57071-179-8	Landlords' Rights and Duties in PA	$19.95	___
		TEXAS TITLES		
___	1-57071-330-8	How to File for Divorce in TX (2E)	$19.95	___
___	1-57248-114-5	How to Form a Corporation in TX (2E)	$19.95	___
___	1-57071-417-7	How to Make a TX Will (2E)	$12.95	___
___	1-57071-418-5	How to Probate an Estate in TX (2E)	$19.95	___
___	1-57071-365-0	How to Start a Business in TX (2E)	$16.95	___
___	1-57248-111-0	How to Win in Small Claims Court in TX (2E)	$14.95	___
___	1-57248-110-2	Landlords' Rights and Duties in TX (2E)	$19.95	___

SUBTOTAL THIS PAGE ___

SUBTOTAL PREVIOUS PAGE ___

Illinois residents add 6.75% sales tax

Florida residents add 6% state sales tax plus applicable discretionary surtax ___

Shipping— $4.00 for 1st book, $1.00 each additional ___

TOTAL ___

To order, call Sourcebooks at 1-800-43-BRIGHT or FAX (630)961-2168 (Bookstores, libraries, wholesalers—please call for discount)
Prices are subject to change without notice.